If you are a Christian therapist, psychologist, social worker, past⌐
a must-read volume. Both those who serve and those ⌐
than ever, and in *A Counselor's Guide to Chri*⌐
and John Trent offer practical exercises, adap
highly recommend this resource on the importa   ⌐ness.

—JAMIE ATEN, PhD   ⌐ctor, Humanitarian
⌐aster Institute, Wheaton College

A Counselor's Guide to Christian Mindfulness by Regina Chow Trammel and John Trent
is an excellent resource that equips Christian counselors and practitioners to incorporate
the rich practice of Christian mindfulness in their work and in their lives. It delves into
theory and research behind mindfulness, but at the same time, it is practical, providing
basic steps, exercises, scripts, and illustrations about when and where and how to apply
Christian mindfulness. It is grounded in both the social sciences as well as Scripture, and
includes a wealth of biblical references both in the text and for further study. The book
focuses on the benefits of mindfulness for one's clients, but it also reinforces how mindfulness helps counselors connect more effectively with Christ and grow in their faith. I
commend Drs. Trammel and Trent for their clear and effective integration of Christian
faith and clinical practice in this important new book.

—RICK CHAMIEC-CASE, PhD, MSW, MAR, director, North
American Association of Christians in Social Work

Regina Trammel and John Trent apply mindfulness in a distinctively Christian way that
avoids the pitfalls of secular mindfulness when working with Christian clients. This book
contains many practical strategies that will be very useful to Christian therapists. Highly
recommended!

—FERNANDO GARZON, PsyD, assistant dean, professor, School
of Psychology and Counseling, Regent University

The ability to stay present in our everyday lives is quickly becoming a lost discipline.
Too often we default to functioning on autopilot, failing to pay attention to, or worse,
be intentional about, what influences our daily decisions. Mindfulness practices have
traditionally served to draw our attention to the here and now, recognizing how our bodies, emotions, relationships, and environments all play a significant role in how we react
to and engage in the world around us. This book incorporates the powerful discipline

of mindfulness from the critical and foundational perspective of biblical truth and practice. A must for any counselor who sees the importance of incorporating spiritual disciplines into mental health care, *A Counselor's Guide to Christian Mindfulness* provides invaluable tools for promoting wholistic transformation through the therapeutic process.

—DEBORAH GORTON, PhD, Gary D. Chapman Chair
of Marriage, Family Ministry, and Counseling, CMHC
program director, Moody Theological Seminary

Having experienced my share of anxiety and depression over the decades, I have learned much of considerable help from extrabiblical sources as long as they did not contradict the authoritative inerrant Word of God and seemed wise and sensible. Among the help I received was psychological teaching about mindfulness. While the secular approach was helpful, it was also limited, sometimes misleading, and required care to apply. For years, I have longed for Christian thinkers to write a book on the biblical basis of and distinctively Christian approach to mindfulness. With this book, my prayers have been answered. This is the only book of its kind and should be central reading to all who want to grow spiritually and emotionally in a healthy and Christian way.

—J. P. MORELAND, PhD, Distinguished Professor of Philosophy,
Talbot School of Theology, Biola University; author, *Finding Quiet*

Drs. Regina Chow Trammel and John Trent have written the definitive book on Christian-based mindfulness. It is a must-read primer for counselors on faith-based mindfulness. Read this book and learn from the best.

—JENNIFER SHEPARD PAYNE, PhD, LCSW, associate professor,
Department of Social Work, School of Behavioral and Applied
Sciences, Azusa Pacific University; founder, POOF (Culturally
Tailored Acceptance and Commitment Therapy)

In the work of therapy, there is nothing more important than paying attention to the presence of Love. *A Counselor's Guide to Christian Mindfulness* offers much-needed resources to remain so anchored in the presence of the God who loves us that we cannot help but extend that presence to our clients.

—K. J. RAMSEY, licensed professional counselor; author, *This
Too Shall Last: Finding Grace When Suffering Lingers*

A rich and timely contribution to the growing body of Christian literature exploring mindfulness and contemplation. At times, evangelicals can feel alone in the mental health field. From time to time, you discover a wise and mature guide who knows the landscape and can provide helpful insights and instruction. Trammel and Trent are such guides, skilled clinicians with depth in understanding both the contemplative and mindfulness literature. *A Counselor's Guide to Christian Mindfulness* is immensely readable with great examples and practical exercises and demonstrations. References are provided to accommodate scholars and students, but it does not read like a technical manual or heady philosophy text. I highly recommend this book for both the classroom and for practicing clinicians.

—JUSTIN SMITH, PsyD, director of counseling program and professor
of professional and pastoral counseling, Phoenix Seminary

A Counselor's Guide to Christian Mindfulness by Regina Chow Trammel and John Trent is a clearly and simply written book with helpful and practical Christian mindfulness exercises and therapeutic strategies that are biblically based, covering a comprehensive list of areas of application. Highly recommended to anyone interested in a Christian approach to mindfulness, including therapists, counselors, pastors, and clients.

—SIANG-YANG TAN, PhD, Senior Professor of Clinical Psychology,
Fuller Theological Seminary; senior pastor, First Evangelical Church
Glendale; author, *Counseling and Psychotherapy: A Christian Perspective*

A COUNSELOR'S GUIDE TO
CHRISTIAN MINDFULNESS

A COUNSELOR'S GUIDE TO
CHRISTIAN
MINDFULNESS

Engaging the Mind, Body & Soul in
Biblical Practices & Therapies

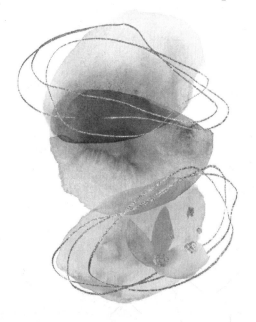

REGINA CHOW TRAMMEL
AND JOHN TRENT

ZONDERVAN
REFLECTIVE

ZONDERVAN REFLECTIVE

A Counselor's Guide to Christian Mindfulness
Copyright © 2021 by Regina Chow Trammel and John Trent

Requests for information should be addressed to:
Zondervan, *3900 Sparks Dr. SE, Grand Rapids, Michigan 49546*

Zondervan titles may be purchased in bulk for educational, business, fundraising, or sales promotional use. For information, please email SpecialMarkets@Zondervan.com.

ISBN 978-0-310-11473-4 (softcover)
ISBN 978-0-310-11475-8 (audio)
ISBN 978-0-310-11474-1 (ebook)

Cover Design: Brand Navigation
Cover Art: © *Naticka / Shutterstock*
Interior Design: Denise Froehlich

Printed in the United States of America

21 22 23 24 25 /LSC/ 10 9 8 7 6 5 4 3 2 1

Contents

Acknowledgments

FROM REGINA

- Thank you first and foremost to my husband, Madison, and my sons, Asher and Kai. Your love and support for me has been instrumental and an inspiration. I wrote this book during a pandemic, while we were all home for months on end. Being in the same house together made the writing of this book all the more special. Our family togetherness was a treasure.

- To my coauthor, Dr. John Trent: your mentorship, your love for God, your gentle collaboration, and skillful writing inspire me. Our zoom calls were a regular treat for me!

- Thank you to my family: Mom and Dad, in-laws, aunts, uncles, and cousins, and my grandmother. I appreciate your support and cheers for me as I began this project. Much of what I write is embedded in the knowledge of who I am as a Chinese American, drawing from cultural knowledge that goes back generations.

- Special thanks to Diana Jamison, Rhiannon De Carlo, Lynn Raine, Amanda Jaggard, and Larry Warner, who checked in with me and supported me throughout the writing of this book. Thank you to my students—former and current—from the Azusa Pacific University Social Work department, who urged me on, who share this joy in and love for the work of therapy. Thanks to all my colleagues, many of whom I also count as friends.

- Thank you to my writing and research mentor, Marsha Fowler, PhD, who helped create a weekly supportive space for writers.

- To K. J. Ramsey and Clarissa Moll—two authors in their own right—who encouraged me to say what needs to be said, to show up, and to do so with the integrity of my message in service to God's kingdom.

From John

- Deepest thanks to Dr. Carol Kershaw, my major professor in my PhD program, who was our model and who challenged us as fledgling counselors to be mindful in therapy and in life.
- To Dr. Bill Retz, who remains the best listener and question asker of any counselor I've ever known.
- To Regina for her incredible faith and commitment to this book and for inviting me along on this journey. From your deep research to powerful writing, God has indeed gifted you to teach, train, and change lives, starting with your own family and now to counselors and counseling students everywhere.

And both of us would like to express our thanks to the Zondervan editorial team: Kyle Rohane, Ryan Pazdur, Brian Phipps, and the marketing team.

Introduction

Capture the Power of the Present Moment

> *I pray that the eyes of your heart may be enlightened
> in order that you may know the hope to which he has
> called you, the riches of his glorious inheritance in his
> holy people, and his incomparably great power for us
> who believe.*
> —EPHESIANS 1:18–19

As counselors, we've seen hurting, haunted, downcast eyes. We've sat with those who feel lost, come alongside those who feel lonely, sought to help those who are heartsick from getting their hopes up only to fall back into discouragement or even despair.

What if we could see people's eyes opened today to a hope that really can lift them higher? To help someone realize that right now, they are chosen and adopted into a priceless inheritance pointing them toward a special future? That even in today's complex, challenging, crushing world, "his incomparably great power" is there for them, able to unleash them to live in abundance because of all he's promised, provided, and done for them?

We all need that kind of knowledge and the vital application of God's real presence in our lives. And in this book, we believe there is a way to capture the power offered "for us who believe" by helping ourselves and others capture the present moment.

I (Regina) am a clinical social worker. And I (John) am a marriage and family therapist. We are both professors, PhD trained and fully on board with training the next generation of those who are intent on making a difference in their world. But the prophet Jeremiah's words ring so true in our day. So many are selling so much that is helping so few: "They dress the wound of my people as though it were not serious. 'Peace, peace,' they say, when there is no peace" (Jer. 6:14).

But Christ followers are called to more. As the psalmist writes, "Deep calls to deep in the roar of your waterfalls; all your waves and breakers have swept over me" (Ps. 42:7).

How do we help those we counsel take the next step toward wholeness and healing, to help them stand close enough to that waterfall that the spray washes over their faces? How do we help them to see that they can quiet and open their hearts to the truth and life in God's living Word, and with Jesus, who is life?

With this book, we welcome you and call you to consider bringing into your life and practice something we believe is fully biblical and profoundly helpful.

Christian mindfulness.

What if we could scroll through the first chapter of Ephesians to help those we counsel in this day, this hour, really see and hold close its amazing promises to his people—that God has indeed blessed us, chosen us, adopted us, redeemed us, forgiven us, lavished on us his grace (giving us what we don't deserve) and mercy (not giving us what we do deserve) through the birth, life, death, resurrection, and amazing love of our Lord, Jesus Christ?

Cultivating a Christian mindfulness practice is a way to reconnect with Christ, who is active, alive, and present and who longs for a deeper relationship with us and the clients we serve.

When We Become Mindful of the God Who Loves Us

In Christian mindfulness, we learn how to pay attention and listen to God again. Above the noise and go-go-go of our lives, we become more awake to what God is doing in our lives, our clients, our communities, and our world. And when we are awakened to what God is doing, our passions are refreshed and we reset our lives accordingly. We can look outside of ourselves more readily to reorient our lives to others. We can listen better. We can access grace, peace, compassion, the gifts of the Holy Spirit (Gal. 5:22–26).

When we become mindful of God in our thoughts and everyday rhythms, our faith expands. We experience God more fully in our minds, hearts, and souls. We rely on his voice to guide us in our work. If we say that we value our time with our families, then we begin to recognize and notice our patterns of inattention. If we commit to acts of service within our communities, then we stay present with the people whom we are partnering with. If we want to grow in love with our loved ones and friends, then we listen to and communicate with them with understanding and nonjudgment. If we want to help bring healing in others' lives, we know how to engage our clients on a sustainable path toward that healing.

Mindfulness, for the Christian, provides space for God's wisdom to abound. We need this wisdom desperately, for we are a desperate people, needy of our Lord. We who do the hard work of helping others—whether as Christian counselors, therapists, social workers, psychologists, pastoral counselors, or lay counselors—cannot ignore our own neediness. We often sacrifice ourselves because we understand the sacrifice Christ made on the cross. However, Christian mindfulness calls us back to ourselves—as God meant us to—so we can be of better service to the One.

Our Purpose and Your Purpose

We've tailored this book to the Christian counselor, therapist, social worker, psychologist, and other healing practitioner who wants to incorporate in their practice mindfulness from a Christian perspective. The skills and practices we discuss in this book are practical, and we have made it easy for you to weave them into your work with clients and for your own self-care.

In addition to sprinkling exercises throughout every chapter, we have also generated scripts that you can use if you need an easy place to begin. Also, we have included a list of references at the end of each chapter for you to peruse at your convenience if you are interested in further studying the topics we discuss. You can be reassured that the practices contained in this book are based in the praxis of Scripture and social science, because both of us are Christian practitioners and scholars in our fields. All of the exercises, practices, and ideas we suggest are informed by evidence, founded on academic research around Christian mindfulness that you can access in academic journals.

We are both mental health practitioners and educators. We love what we do because we, like you, care to bring healing into the lives of those who seek our help. We both teach courses training future counselors and therapists, equipping them with knowledge from research and a Christian worldview. This book is an expression of our shared passion to equip you with what we have learned about mindfulness and what we have practiced in our day-to-day work. We have written this book in the spirit of service, taking the best of academic research on mindfulness and placing it on a Christian foundation to support your work with your clients and counselees.

We wrote this book to fill a gap in resources for Christians in the counseling and healing professions: psychotherapists, social workers, psychologists, counselors, pastors, lay counselors, coaches, spiritual directors, and more. In addition, the mindfulness concepts, practices, and faith-driven explanations are for your self-care so that your work with your clients can be rooted in our Christian faith, explicitly or implicitly. We know that you feel your best and that your work is most excellent when you feel the peace of God while you do the hard work of helping others. Though it is not well studied or taught, the biblical basis of Christian mindfulness is not new. This book will thus not only encourage you in your own faith as a practitioner but also provide a real, effective, and evidence-based intervention to assist in the healing of your clients or counselees.

Book Structure Overview

Christian mindfulness, in general, is no different from other counseling practice skills. Mindfulness has a robust research base, offers a wisdom that develops out of your work with clients, and is fairly easy to learn and apply to specific situations. This book contains all of these elements and thus serves as a thorough resource for you.

We want you to know and understand the theory behind mindfulness and the research base of Christian mindfulness. In part 1, we offer the background knowledge you need to grasp the unique skills of a Christian mindfulness practice and how Christian mindfulness contrasts with other mindfulness-based practices and skills. Part 1 gives you a strong historical and theoretical overview of mindfulness rooted in our Christian faith, in research and in practice.

In part 2 we go over the Christian mindfulness skills necessary for counseling and therapeutic practice. Each chapter begins with a short (fictional) case narrative that relates to the chapter's topic. We then provide the conceptual background to guide you in how to use Christian mindfulness in your work as counselors and therapists with similar clients. What we share in these chapters draws on our training, practice, and teaching and therefore provides real-life applications and practical steps to guide your work with clients or counselees.

Part 2 is written to help move you or your clients through a basic, general Christian mindfulness practice that you can use and modify with your training and skills as professionals. We'll come alongside you to build your Christian mindfulness practice by working through the contemplation exercises in each chapter first. You can then adapt these concepts and skills for your clients or counselees, using the language we provide. These are not scripts, per se, but they offer basic language that you can adapt for your clients to help lead them through their various issues. For instance, the contemplation exercises in part 2 can be helpful in addressing anxiety, stress, and burnout.

Part 3 of this book addresses specific challenges or situations that your clients or counselees face. Each chapter includes exercises that can be applied to specific situations, such as work, health, and relationships. You can use each chapter in part 3 as a stand-alone or have your clients progress through each area, using the exercises in succession so you can address each aspect of what they present to you. We have tried to make each chapter specific enough that you can feel confident that these practices will assist your clients in the issues addressed in each chapter. Contemplation verses, exercises, and questions for reflection are embedded in each of these chapters as well. The general skills we discuss in them can be used with or without Christian language with clients and counselees, especially those who are dealing with an issue from a solution-focused perspective.

Part 4 presents Christian mindfulness scripts that you can easily apply to the theoretical orientation you are most comfortable with. We hope these scripts will offer you the language to help you lead your client through specific applications word for word. You can easily adapt these scripts to a specific purpose in your work.

We conclude the book with a few appendixes that help you debrief with clients a few of these scripts as homework or to supplement your mindfulness-based interventions.

It is important to note that this book is not meant to replace the training, skills, and competence you acquire as a professional in the counseling and therapeutic fields. Rather it is a resource to assist you in building basic skills in Christian mindfulness practice. It is a supplement to the training and skills of mindfulness-based interventions that are already established and used in the professional counseling and therapy fields.

We do hope you will consider practicing these mindfulness skills personally, first, for your own experience, because we are confident that they will transform and support your relationship with our Lord. Also, we believe the first step to good counseling practice in Christian mindfulness is to develop competence. Competence comes when you have applied the practices for yourself before you teach them to others. Then you can be professionally confident in applying Christian mindfulness to your work with clients because you have developed personal competence. We have thus written this book so that it can be a starting point for counselors and therapists who want to infuse Christian mindfulness practice into counseling or therapy.

Contemplation Exercises and Developing Competence

Throughout the book we offer contemplation exercises. We hope that this book will be an experience for you of being poured into—that your cup will refill and overflow when you tap into the source who dwells within you as a Christ follower in your work. We also hope that your clients enjoy these exercises as a form of therapeutic support. Mindfulness in its Christian and biblical forms is rooted in an unending source, a loving source, a healing source. God, our creator, provides the water we all need to quench our thirst for him: "Each one will be like a shelter from the wind and a refuge from the storm, like streams of water in the desert and the shadow of a great rock in a thirsty land" (Isa. 32:2).

PART 1

WHAT IS CHRISTIAN MINDFULNESS?

Mindfulness is easy to comprehend but challenging to implement. Mindfulness has become such a ubiquitous term that many wonder what it actually means. Therefore, how we define mindfulness affects how we practice it.

Pastors often use the word mindful to mean to think about God. Various sermons reference the verse from Psalm 8:4: "What is mankind that you are mindful of them, human beings that you care for them?" In most cases, being mindful is likened to God's careful thought toward his creation. I (Regina) recently heard a podcast about habits in which the hosts mentioned mindfulness as one way to build habits in the new year. They described mindfulness as the opposite of an unconscious autopilot response—building good habits requires some thoughtfulness, but we tend not to think about it. Thus, on a popular level, mindfulness is often defined as a thought-oriented activity. However, we would like to expand the definition and say upfront that mindfulness engages our minds, bodies, and souls. Christian mindfulness is holistic. It allows us to invite God into all aspects of how we were created. What we consider to be the thinking aspect of mindfulness is grounded in the wisdom that comes from our relationship with Christ.

Though there are many definitions of mindfulness, especially in the academic disciplines of medicine, social work, and psychology (where the mindfulness movement first took root in the West), a simple one is "awareness." Christians have been using the term mindfulness to remind us to "remember" or "be aware of." But how many of us actually live our lives mindfully, with an awareness of God, who is active in our lives?

For the Christian who wants to learn how to think and live mindfully, and to guide others to do so, this awareness leads to our ultimate awareness that this life is not our home. We are spiritual beings, a holy people called by a holy God who is as present with us as he was for the Israelites, shining as a pillar of fire by night, who now shines his glory and leads us on the path that is everlasting. His presence makes all the difference for the Christian who practices mindfulness.

In the following chapters of part 1, we hope you will find the background and history of mindfulness grounding for you and your work. In chapter 1, we discuss the different streams of mindfulness and offer a definition of Christian mindfulness. In chapter 2, we show how mindfulness can be used therapeutically and equip you to do so with specifics about why mindfulness is used and some of the research on Christian mindfulness. In chapter 3, we share the gifts that spring from mindfulness practice, gifts that we are certain you will be blessed by because they come from our eternal source.

We hope, as you read this book, you sense the ever-present and unchanging fount of wisdom that comes from God through Christ. May this book equip you and encourage you as you do the hard work of bringing healing to those you serve in the sacred space of the counseling room.

CHAPTER 1

Mindfulness versus Christian Mindfulness

Definition and Historic Roots

When we talk about mindfulness to a person or persons in circles that are largely Christian evangelical, we have observed that there seem to be two lines of thought about it: mindfulness is either too Eastern and therefore should be avoided just like yoga or other Eastern influences, or mindfulness is similar to the contemplative aspect of Christian history. Folks like Father Basil Pennington, Thomas Merton, and Saint Ignatius are often quoted for the latter. What these two differing opinions about mindfulness mean to us—counselors, therapists, and healing professionals—is that there will be clients who may feel wary or skeptical of the practice of it, and there will be clients with some fluency based on their exposure to contemplative thinkers through their books or from spiritual direction courses. However, most folks will say that they like the relaxation or stress relief that mindfulness brings, understanding that mindfulness has been growing in popularity as a response to the general stress and anxiety many people feel.

The popularization of mindfulness is perhaps a symptom of the demands, pressures, and expectations we place on ourselves. We like to be busy. It's part of our Christian Protestant heritage and ethos of faithful work. We look to the ants, so to speak, to be models of our busy lives (Prov. 6:6–8). However, how many of us give in to the demands of our busy lives and miss the nuggets of truths that God has left us along the way to ponder and store up for ourselves spiritually? Truly, we cannot live on bread alone, but we often do little to contemplate the meaning of God in our lives, and therefore often lack a purpose or an awareness of how God is working in us and through us. We are mindless, rather than mindful of God's presence and position in our lives.

When we are practicing mindfulness, we are no longer finding our identity and purpose in productivity. Instead, mindfulness helps us to listen and honor the energy (mental, physical, spiritual) that we expend and helps us clarify toward what kingdom purpose we would like to fashion our lives. For you, we hope that the practice of Christian mindfulness enhances your delight in your faith and gives you tools to be the soothing healer that God called you to be for your people. One way to help you delight in your faith in Christ and the mindfulness-skill-building aspects of that faith is to compare historical Christian teachings with popular notions of mindfulness.

Mindfulness originates in Buddhist tenets, and the modern Western mindfulness movement emphasizes a secular or Buddhist worldview. This makes many Christians wary, and rightly so. However, mindfulness has a rich history in our Christian faith as well. The purpose of this book is to provide practical guidance in the Christian practice of mindfulness that is rooted in a biblical worldview.

Nevertheless, understanding basic Buddhist thought around mindfulness can help us to understand the major differences in worldview, which impacts how we can then think about mindfulness through a scriptural worldview.

The Development of Mindfulness in the Secular World

According to Smith (1991), Buddhism began when a wealthy prince living in sixth-century-BC India named Siddhartha Gautama left his wealthy and privileged life to find answers to basic questions about suffering. He began meditating under a bodhi tree and achieved nirvana, which is the end of suffering, or enlightenment, and also ends the cycle of samsara (the Hindu belief that life is a continuous, karmic cycle of birth, death, and rebirth). The Buddha began his ministry thereafter and taught the Four Noble Truths:

1. All life is suffering.
2. Suffering is caused by our cravings in life—the truth is that there is impermanence in life.
3. Detachment to cravings and seeing that we are one will end suffering.
4. The path of cessation of attachment, which is the eightfold path.

It is in the eightfold path that mindfulness is identified. The purpose of such mindfulness is to lead one into enlightenment.

In the 1970s, Dr. Jon Kabat-Zinn, a researcher and well-known author from Massachusetts, popularized mindfulness in the West. His books are bestsellers because he has made the practice of mindfulness palatable to our Western taste. The practice of mindfulness used in his interventions is a secularized version of Buddhist thought on detachment. His work and research contain a few key elements of mindfulness practice, including:

- intentional observation of one's own thoughts
- use of breath and sitting meditation
- present-moment awareness
- nonjudgment (Kabat-Zinn, 2011)

Kabat-Zinn developed the modern meaning of mindfulness based on his work as a researcher at Massachusetts General Hospital. He defines mindfulness as "the awareness that arises from paying attention on purpose in the present moment nonjudgmentally" (Mindful staff, 2017). Since the 1970s, Kabat-Zinn developed a mindfulness program based on these concepts to address chronic pain in patients at the hospital (Kabat-Zinn, 2011).

He writes, "I like to think of mindfulness as the art of conscious living" (Kabat-Zinn, 1994, p. 6). He eloquently describes the multifaceted cultivation of mindfulness, and ultimately a mindful life, in his bestselling seminal work, *Full Catastrophe Living*. In his book, he guides the reader and describes the process of dropping into awareness, observing our minds by paying attention to our thoughts. He writes that the observation of our minds lets us see how we often function without thinking, without awareness, leading to living as if we are on autopilot. The awareness cultivated through mindfulness, Kabat-Zinn writes, leads back to ourselves. We know ourselves better, we see the resources and resilience contained within. The wisdom, simplicity, and beauty of life, and appreciation for our human experiences generated by mindfulness practice has no origin, or contains an origin rooted in a different worldview.

Because of Kabat-Zinn's influence and his work in teaching mindfulness in the United States, there has been an explosion of research around mindfulness. In the fields of psychology, neurology, medicine, and social work, mindfulness has been effectively used to treat depression, anxiety, trauma, chronic pain, anger, and emotional volatility. The outcomes of mindfulness are well documented: improved cognitive flexibility, better emotional regulation, decreased symptoms of stress and anxiety, decreased symptomatology of trauma, enhanced productivity, and better decision-making skills because of less reactivity.

Beginning in the 1970s, Jack Kornfield and Joseph Goldstein, two major figures in the proliferation of mindfulness, founded insight meditation centers (Gethin, 2011). These centers, whose name reflects the "insight" (or the Hindu term, *vipassana*) emphasized in secular mindfulness, teach key concepts of insight inherent in mindfulness as being in a state of nonjudgment, observing mind and body in the present moment, with the goal of detachment to cravings. According to this line of thought, to be detached is key to finding enlightenment.

Christian Skepticism toward Mindfulness

So why mindfulness? Shouldn't Christians veer away from this New Age, Eastern religious practice?

For one thing, Christ-centered mindfulness is actually part of our Christian heritage. Centering Prayer, taught by figures such as Thomas Keating and M. Basil Pennington, can be considered a spiritual practice that leads to Christian mindfulness. *Lectio Divina*, an ancient form of prayer of reading Scripture slowly and deliberately, is an excellent way to infuse your Christian mindfulness practice with the Word of God. Historical figures in the Christian faith who reference the use of *Lectio Divina* include Basil the Great (329–379 AD), John Cassian (360–435 AD), Gregory the Great (c. 540–640 AD), and Saint Benedict (c. 480–547 AD) (Hall, 2010, p. 145). Though Christians have been skeptical of mindfulness because of its roots outside of Christianity, it is high time to reconnect with these tried and true Christian practices that are based in the Bible's teaching of silence, stillness, and meditation.

Many popular mindfulness teachers take great pains to differentiate a secular version of mindfulness from a Buddhist one. However, their worldview creeps in. Secular mindfulness practitioners reject organized religion but do not differentiate between the Buddhist-lite approach that remains— breath work, cultivation of awareness and understanding (i.e., enlightenment), and goals toward self-fulfillment, replacing religious understanding with enhanced neurological and behavioral capabilities (e.g., resilience, more adaptable brain connectivity, focus, and work productivity).

Though secular mindfulness practitioners are often humanists, their aims, goals, and values remain: strive toward greater human flourishing on your own individual strength, a guru-based community of mindfulness practitioners to teach you, and the object and aim of the practice likened to Maslow's hierarchy of needs—toward a self-fulfillment that reflects the concept of enlightenment.

How Christian Mindfulness Deviates from Secular Mindfulness

There are worldview and theological differences between secular or Buddhist mindfulness and a Christian understanding of human nature and our capacity for change through the work of the Holy Spirit. Let's explore some of these differences before we move forward in our discussion of Christian mindfulness.

The major departure of a Buddhist view of mindfulness from a Christian one is the assumption that human beings are essentially good and have the capacity to strive toward a self-actualized state (nirvana). Christians assume a sinful nature, originating from the first rebellion in the account from Genesis 1. This is an important distinction because as Christian counselors and therapists, we are confronted often by the sinful nature of humanity.

Ultimately, the goals of mindfulness in several main Buddhist traditions are to detach from the world's sufferings and to find the buddha-nature within (Reeves, 2008). We can call forth God's wisdom in our clients' lives but are realistic of the sinful pulls of this world: addictions, disease, mental health problems that wreak havoc in our clients' lives. It is not the call of the Christian to detach from this suffering. We find compassion and salvation in Christ, who was intimately acquainted with human suffering because he became human. The divine nature of God brings us comfort because we know that as humans, we are made in his image, and the world and its sufferings are not what life is meant to be. Therefore, to be mindful means to realize and be provoked by the sufferings our clients understand. We can be incarnational witnesses of Christ's love and forgiveness and his wisdom through a mindful attentiveness to our clients' sufferings. And hopefully by our example of Christian love and his lovingkindness in the counseling or therapy room, we can point them to the presence of God working in their lives, calling them to find his burden light and his yoke easy.

Christian Mindfulness

A Christian understanding of mindfulness includes the active presence of God. Whether through God's Word, through the Holy Spirit, prayer, or even turning our thoughts toward him, we activate our awareness toward God's presence in Christian mindfulness. Therefore, Christian mindfulness includes inviting Christ into one's mind and attention. As counselors and therapists, we know that any time a person seeks our help, their capacity for change will depend on their openness and willingness to remain open.

Part of that openness means that we as counselors are attuned to the present moment. This attunement allows the chatter of our self-preoccupation via judgment or superficial thoughts to submit themselves to the power of the Holy Spirit. We take every thought captive, in service to Christ (2 Cor. 10:5) through the mindfulness tools of awareness and attention to those thoughts. Then, as we are attuned, our clients can be attuned. When they sense the shift in us, we can open up the time we have with them to the presence of God, who is the God of peace, which we know they so badly need. Peace, grace, hope—these are the gifts of Christian mindfulness.

So we offer an alternative take on mindfulness, one that is steeped in ancient Christian practices that our culture has lost. Mindfulness for the Christian should be about paying attention to the present moment with Christ as the center of each moment. Mindfulness is to remain aware of the present and to be both in the world and not of the world at the same time. Here is a definition of Christian mindfulness: *Christian mindfulness is about making time to turn our whole attention to God so that we can hear and abide in his voice above the chatter and stress of our lives.*

Historical Roots of Christian Mindfulness

There are two major historical traditions that we can look to in order to cultivate a Christian mindfulness practice. One is called the via negativa, which is found more often in Eastern Orthodox Christianity and early Christian mysticism of the Catholic traditions and in a written work by an unknown author called the *Cloud of Unknowing* (McLeod, 1986).

This type of Christian belief and mindfulness practice is embedded in apophatic prayer, which emphasizes the mystery of God and is therefore less directed and guided. The awe and mystery of God are emphasized in this type of prayer. An example from the fourteenth century is hesychasm (derived from the Greek word *hesychia*, meaning "quietude" or "tranquility"), found in Eastern Orthodox Christianity. The hesychasts pray the

Jesus Prayer: "Lord Jesus Christ, Son of God, have mercy on me." The thought is that there is power in saying this prayer over and over, bringing awareness to the truth of God's presence and his work of mercy through salvation. The outcome of such awareness of Christ's mercy is that we begin to lose our focus on ourselves and our minds. The focus changes direction toward Jesus, his personhood, his incarnation, his sacrifice, and his mercy. What a relief to get away from thoughts of ourselves only!

The other tradition is rooted in the via positiva, which emphasizes kataphatic prayer and spiritual exercises, which contains more structure and guided direction. Saint Ignatius of Loyola and Thomas Keating are exemplars of this Christian tradition. They both use the merging of breath awareness and guided imagery to quiet the mind and open up mental and spiritual space for Christ.

More overt examples of mindfulness are present in modern monastic traditions with leaders such as Thomas Merton, M. Basil Pennington, and Thomas Keating, who use forms of prayer and meditation employing silence and stillness. The silence and stillness are to induce a present-moment awareness of body, mind, and soul, expanding the moment so that God's presence is felt and accessed. Centering Prayer is one such practice that inhabits the aims and process of such a mindfulness state, as discussed earlier regarding Buddhist mindfulness.

In Centering Prayer, breath and a sacred word are used to "ground" oneself. According to Keating (2008), the goal of Centering Prayer is not to ask God for help but to unite with God, the Holy Spirit, and experience God in a way that is true and unpolluted by selfish desires. The process of this prayer is open, quiet, and nonlinear. The prayer experience leads to entering into God's presence so that one becomes more "fully awake" to God, who is the source, who is "too deep to be grasped in images, in words, or even in clear concepts and … [we] know by unknowing" (Keating, 1992). Thomas Merton refers to this process as prayer of the heart rather than the mind (Bochen, 2004, pp. 58–59). Prayers of the mind are focused on the self/ego and on self-serving interests; prayers of the heart relinquish the idea of self and discern the truths of God's realities instead.

What is most important to know about Christian mindfulness practices such as these is that it is a practice and not a goal-oriented thing one can attain to achieve peace. Mindfulness is more like an approach to life, a mindset or a lifestyle. The various practices—the Jesus Prayer, Centering Prayer, visualizing or breath prayers—aren't the point in and of themselves but are ways to cultivate mindfulness.

Regina's Tea-Drinking Exercise

Here is a practice that I (Regina) often use in the everyday that you can use between your counseling sessions or to help your clients cultivate as stress relief and a reminder of God's grace.

- Begin by warming up a cup of tea and holding the mug of tea in your hands. Feel the sensation of the warmth of the cup, feel the weight of the mug in your hands.
- As you hold the mug, breathe in and out three times to calm and focus your attention to just the mug of tea in your hands. Notice the smell of the tea as you inhale. Take it in, enjoying the aroma. Contemplate the aroma of Christ, God's goodness, God's peace, and nourishment. As you exhale, notice the steam rising from the hot liquid. Use that movement as an expression of the action you are taking—your movement toward God—at each exhalation as you take this time being in God's truth, steeping in Christ's love for you.
- Look at your hands holding the mug and use them as an analogy of God's love surrounding you. If you are that mug, God is your hands. He holds you and keeps you. Breathe in and out.
- Then take a sip, slowly. When you sip, imagine that you are drinking in God's grace and peace. Feel the liquid moving down your throat into your belly. The warmth of God's grace is ingested, his salvation saturates you and quenches your thirst. Concentrate your thoughts on the sipping of the tea and the truths of God's salvation.

References for Chapter 1

Bochen, C. M. (Ed.). (2004). *Thomas Merton: Essential writings.* Orbis.

Gethin, R. (2011). On some definitions of mindfulness. *Contemporary Buddhism, 12*(1), 263–279. https://doi.org/10.1080/14639947.2011.564843

Hall, C. (2010). The theological foundations of *lectio divina*. In J. P. Greenman & G. Kalantzis (Eds.), *Life in the Spirit: Spiritual formation in theological perspective* (pp. 180–197). InterVarsity Press.

Kabat-Zinn, J. (1994). *Wherever you go, there you are: Mindfulness meditation in everyday life.* Hyperion.

Kabat-Zinn, J. (2011). Some reflections on the origins of MBSR, skillful means, and the trouble with maps. *Contemporary Buddhism, 12*(1), 281–306. https://doi.org/10.1080/14639947.2011.564844

Keating, T. (1992). *Open mind, open heart: The contemplative dimension of the gospel.* Amity House.

Keating, T. (2008). *The heart of the world: An introduction to contemplative Christianity.* Crossroad.

McLeod, F. G. (1986). Apophatic or kataphatic prayer. *Spirituality Today, 38,* 41–52. http://www.domcentral.org/library/spir2day/863815mcleod.html

Mindful staff (2017). Jon Kabat-Zinn: Defining mindfulness. What is mindfulness? The founder of Mindfulness-Based Stress Reduction explains. Retrieved from https://www.mindful.org/jon-kabat-zinn-defining-mindfulness/

Reeves, G. (2008). *A contemporary translation of a Buddhist classic.* Wisdom Publishers.

Smith, H. (1991). *The world's religions.* Harper One.

CHAPTER 2

Therapeutic Benefits of Mindfulness

We truly are burden carriers, we counselors, therapists, and healing professionals. We hear stories of suffering, heartbreak, mental health issues, the effects of sin, trauma, separation, injustice. We could go on, but you get the gist. Because of our work, our often high caseloads, especially in settings where we serve and meet the most vulnerable populations, many of us are at risk of experiencing or already have experienced burnout: fatigue, numbness, disengagement. There is much research on the benefits of mindfulness for us healers, us burden carriers. Read on to learn more about some of that research. Also, know this: the benefits of mindfulness are for our clients, but they are also for us, and they point us to the endless, majestic Source, who never burns out on us.

Benefits of Mindfulness

Because mindfulness has become such a prevalent movement in our Western secular and therapeutic culture, it is important to recognize that benefits have been both experienced and documented in academic research, popular psychology, and popular culture.

Mindfulness-based therapies that counselors and therapists use to treat mental health conditions such as depression, anxiety, and trauma are on the cutting edge of cognitive behavioral interventions. There are mindfulness principles that leaders use to develop insight into decision making. For you, the reader, what is most important to learn about mindfulness is that there are myriad benefits in many areas of life: body, mind, spirit, and relationships. For instance, in the body, mindfulness has been shown to maximize neurological connections in the brain that support emotional regulation, which corresponds to decrease in reactivity. This means that when you feel heated—upset, grief, frustration, loss—mindfulness is documented to calm these heated moments and promote neuroplasticity, which means that your brain is making new connections that strengthen the ability to self-regulate emotions.

When we, and our clients, become more mindful of God in our thoughts, and even every day, our faith is built up. We experience God's healing touch more fully in our minds, hearts, and souls. His voice can help our clients set appropriate boundaries in relationships. If we say that we value our time with our families, then we begin to recognize and notice our patterns of inattention. If we commit to acts of service within our communities, then we stay present with the people whom we are partnering with. If we want to grow in love with our loved ones and friends, then we listen and communicate with them with understanding and nonjudgment. Mindfulness practice helps foster the things in life we most appreciate. We become better stewards of our time and attention, with the understanding that our time is a resource, our focused attention something not to be wasted, because God is in those places and spaces.

If you are a Christian counselor, therapist, or other healing practitioner, then you know that mindfulness has not been taught in the professional fields with any kind of Christian integration. I (Regina) recently published an article on research I conducted in which I asked Christian counselors, psychologists, and social workers who used mindfulness-based therapies in their practices a set of questions to explore their comfort as well as meaning making when using mindfulness in therapy. Many of these practitioners reported feeling a sense of God in the room, who directed or even illuminated clinical issues of concern to their clients after a period of mindfulness. What was most familiar to these practitioners was the idea of

God's presence being in the therapeutic space. What was less familiar was how to incorporate Christian mindfulness practices into that work with their clients. The more familiar and more experienced practitioners felt more comfortable integrating the two: Christian faith with mindfulness practice. However, none received formal Christian mindfulness training. They had to be resourceful and rely on their therapeutic or clinical wits to do so. Hence our writing this book, so that you can assist your clients who struggle with anxiety, stress, and other mental health issues for which mindfulness has been proven to be useful.

For clients struggling with worry and anxiety, mindfulness practice allows one to detach from ruminative thoughts that are destructive to brain, psyche, and soul. Christian mindfulness provides a healing touch, for the present moment helping anyone who practices it to begin to distance themselves from their thoughts rather than feeling sucked in by them. Understanding the difference between our negative thought patterns and allowing God to enter our mindset lets his power redirect our thoughts to the hope and future he promises. We find resilience in our suffering, and perhaps relief from our mental pain.

In our relationships at home, at work, and in our church communities, Christian mindfulness practice provides a pathway toward peace. That does not mean we must avoid conflict. Rather, peace is a reflection of what is to come in heaven in our relationships with God. Mindfulness practice applied to how our clients interact in relationships is a means of cultivating patterns of communication and a generous mindset that allows them to forgive and foster resolution, rather than ignoring or being ignorant of the pain they may have caused. Sometimes, they simply do not recognize that they are harboring ill feelings or even ill will. Christian mindfulness gives God the space to sift their hearts and promotes a change away from unrighteous behaviors or patterns. Mindfulness, in the Christian life, has practical benefits and spiritual implications. We hope that as you read on, you also begin the practice and note the changes taking place—to taste and see that the Lord is good, and that he is at work at all times, for all days, in your life here on earth.

Mindfulness and Behaviorism

Mindfulness is useful in therapy and has been described by researchers and practitioners alike, part of an evidence-based practice tied to behaviorism. Cultivating a state of mindfulness is a skill that is part of the third wave of behavioral interventions: acceptance and commitment therapy (ACT), dialectical behavioral therapy (DBT), and mindfulness-based cognitive therapy (MBCT). To understand what we mean by third wave, it's important to be reminded of how behaviorism has shaped modern psychotherapy and counseling in the modern and postmodern eras.

The first wave of behaviorism was standard behavioral therapy pioneered by the behaviorist B. F. Skinner of the famous Skinner box and focused on behavior-response. Behavior is shaped by a system of rewards and punishment, including Pavlovian responses. Learning, therefore, is a result of instinct and motivation through reward.

The second wave of behaviorism is more familiar to most therapists, counselors, and other mental health professionals, which consists of Aaron Beck's cognitive behavioral therapy and Albert Ellis's rational emotive therapy (Brown et al., 2011). The overview of each therapy mentioned is outside the scope of this book. However, the key difference between second-wave and third-wave behavioral therapies is that the latter emphasizes the role of awareness and acceptance related to cognitions. In addition, the alignment to values as part of third-wave behavioral therapies provides an entryway for Christian faith integration.

Mindfulness has been enfolded into third-wave therapies and has shown to be quite useful. What follows is a brief summary of three mindfulness-based therapies in the third wave.

1. Dialectical Behavioral Therapy (DBT)

The first is dialectical behavioral therapy (DBT), which is a mindfulness-based therapy used in a number of clinical situations including addressing the emotional dysregulation present in survivors of trauma and persons diagnosed with borderline personality disorder. Dr. Marsha Linehan is the key founder of this therapy. DBT is often used in group settings and has been shown to be effective in the treatment of post-traumatic stress disorder, borderline personality disorder, and eating disorders (Chen et al., 2008; Harned et al., 2012). DBT practitioners integrate mindfulness to help with emotional regulation amid rapid mood fluctuations.

2. Acceptance and Commitment Therapy (ACT)

Likewise, the intervention construction of acceptance and commitment therapy (ACT) features mindfulness as an awareness tool. Dr. Steven Hayes is the founder of this method. Acceptance is a key part, which includes a mindfulness-based outlook that moves awareness into values. Hayes describes awareness as a way to connect our values with thought and action, and therefore, the progression is outward-facing for the client (Rousmaniere, 2020). Clients are encouraged to live out those values with awareness and observe when their thoughts do not align. ACT is known to be effective in the treatment of stress and obsessive compulsive disorder (Brinkborg et al., 2011; Twohig et al., 2010).

3. Mindfulness-Based Stress Reduction (MBSR)

Last, Dr. Jon Kabat-Zinn's mindfulness-based stress reduction (MBSR) is employed to help clients tune in to the present moment, identify their emotional states, and avoid or address ruminative and negative patterns of thinking, and has been documented to be effective in the treatment of PTSD and chronic pain, among many other mental health ailments (Baer et al., 2012; Crisp et al., 2016; King et al., 2013).

Christian Integration of Mindfulness

There are some studies that point specifically to a Christian integration of mindfulness. In my (Regina's) research, I have tested a Christian mindfulness intervention (many parts of which are included in this book) and have found significant increases in participants' ability to attain a mindfulness state before and after the Christian mindfulness intervention. The meta-awareness of our own thoughts is the key process to distill Christian mindfulness to its most effective basics. Results were similar with participants' self-reports of perceived stress, reflecting a decrease in stress after the intervention (Trammel, 2018). Another study I conducted used heart rate variability, which helps measure parasympathetic responses (the body's calming response), and the Christian mindfulness intervention, and found it improved emotional regularity functioning as well as reduced burnout (Trammel, Park, & Karlsson, 2021).

Many other researchers have also used forms of Christian mindfulness practices included in this book to demonstrate the intervention's therapeutic benefits and relevance (Ford & Garzon, 2017; Fox et al., 2016; Rosales, 2016). Others have also described how third-wave mindfulness therapies can be integrated with the Christian faith (Wang & Tan, 2016). Thus, you can be confident that the exercises and scripts contained in this book are established, well studied, and based on a sound Christian foundation.

The Upward Spiral of Mindfulness

The strength of any mindfulness practice, including a Christian mindfulness practice, is the way it helps us tolerate emotional upheaval and to take a step back in our thought patterns. Garland et al. (2017) explains that those who practice consistent mindfulness meditation are more likely to integrate a nonjudgmental stance to understand distressing events in a more positive and acceptance-based way. They call this process an "upward spiral" toward improved well-being through this constant reappraisal of their thought life. In their results, the researchers discovered that participants who displayed the highest increases in state mindfulness also showed the highest increases in the use of positive reappraisal (Garland et al., 2017). That means that as we practice mindfulness, we are more aware of where our thoughts are taking us. Disciplining the mind as in 1 Corinthians 2 means that we can evaluate, appraise, and reappraise how our thoughts line up with the truth of Scripture, which, as Christ followers, we know leads to hope. Our upward spiral, as Christians, is centered on God's provision,

God's hope, God's restoration, God's will, God's purpose, God's meaning. We partner with God, knowing that our upward spiral lifts up our minds and our spirits.

Thus, the upward spiral idea is important because it points to hope—a hope that our minds can be shaped, strengthened. It is hopeful for our clients because they can improve the way they process experience through their minds. This means that the mental health struggles they battle are not immune to interventions and can be tailored to their experiences through reappraisal. For us as Christian counselors, therapists, and other healing professionals, we can be confident that a mindfulness intervention will help our clients attain this hope.

Basic Steps of Mindfulness

Mindfulness as we know it in the therapy and counseling world has been established as useful and helpful. In order for us to integrate foundational Christian thinking and practices, it's important to get the basic outline of mindfulness practice, which we will build on in part 2 and then help you apply in part 3.

These basic mindfulness steps are nearly universal. Obviously, there is much more instruction to be given, much more detail for each step, but we thought a basic nuts-and-bolts overview would set you up to practice skills for you and your client or counselee to hone.

Breathe Deeply while Noticing and Observing

The first step of mindfulness practice is to begin lowering our heart rate, by breathing and letting our thoughts settle. We breathe to focus our thoughts toward something tangible and steady. Paying attention to what our bodies are doing is a way to focus. Though our thoughts bounce around at first, the rhythm of our respiration can give them something to hang on to. Our bodies respond with a calming effect triggered by our vagus nerve as well as our lowered heart rate (Park & Thayer, 2014).

There is a relaxation that we can access through this body-based focus. We notice this relaxation and notice the way our minds work: how they bounce, how they are easily distracted, how our thoughts go a mile a minute. Noticing requires little more than attunement and attention. Our clients will notice themselves and build the capacity for self-awareness with guidance and a practical approach. With this book as your starting point, there are many exercises intended to help your clients simply notice.

When we notice, the sky is blue, the earth and nature feel like a healing balm, and God's presence seems ever flowing and abundant. When our clients build noticing skills, they can receive these gifts and blessing that God has provided: they can inhale and notice the smell of the flower nearby, the sensation of warm water on their skin, the way sunlight opens up their sight and viewpoint. When our clients notice, they notice their heart rates slow, their breathing steadies, their thoughts slow down to a quieter simmer. As therapists, counselors, psychologists, and healing practitioners, we can also notice for them to build that metacognitive awareness. We can help point out to them when we see that change. The path opens up, the therapeutic work more easily travels into mind, psyche, soul. Noticing is the pathway; observation is the next step on that road.

Observe

The next step of mindfulness practice is to observe our thoughts and body responses in a metaobservational way. René Descartes, many centuries ago, said, "I think, therefore I am." The truths of what we think about is the step in mindfulness that helps to really change things. When we are thinking, we observe our thoughts. In mindfulness, we are observing our thoughts with a curiosity, with a distance, so that we can step outside of our usual inner vantage points and see ourselves a bit more clearly. We can begin to ask ourselves, What do I think about? Why do I think about this and ruminate often about [enter rumination here]? What is it about my experience right now that makes me think this thought?

The power of observation is that we can begin to be better aware of not just our thoughts but also our present moment. When we observe, we don't drive our cars and forget where we are going. We don't think about our myriad to-dos while in the midst of reading a book to our little ones. We don't zone out on the boring details of a meeting, missing out on connection with others. Observation means that our minds, our thoughts, and our bodies are right here, right now, fully present to the changing moment and responding in kind.

Observation of our bodies' reactions is key here as well. Sometimes our thoughts get stuck in patterns while our bodies tell another story. When we observe our bodies, we see when our palms get sweaty, when and why our hearts begin to race—for good or for ill. We see the toxic effects of conflict in the knots forming in our stomachs, in the stiffness of our necks, in the tightness of shoulders.

Observing our thoughts and feelings gives us great insight into what we think about, how we react, providing some key tools to understand who we really are. Beyond that, when we get to know what we think about, we can make corrections, we can act with intention. We also begin the process of seeing outside of ourselves. When we observe ourselves, we can also begin to turn outward and observe others, how they react to us, evaluate how responsible we are with others' feelings, actions, emotions, and where our boundaries with them should lie. Mindfulness gives us tools to relate better with ourselves and others, especially as they interact with us.

Name Values

The next step of a general mindfulness practice is to identify and name values. This is what helps pull together the actions of noticing and observing with beliefs. Our outlooks, our values, the things we hold dear, the systems of thought that do not serve us—mindfulness practice helps us align ourselves better to the sacred. This step is where faith and our Christian values come into play, where we can align thoughts, behaviors, motivations, and temptations with values based on Scripture.

For the general mindfulness practitioner, this step opens up a conversation about values and about how our clients are living and making choices in alignment. We know that part of mental health well-being is to evaluate thoughts and observe the consequences of thoughts and feelings.

When folks notice what is happening internally, there is a system change. One's mind, body, and soul are activated. The contemplation point moves from the internal to the outward by considering the question, What do I stand for and why? The naming of values moves our clients and counselees toward right relationship with others, and toward ethical, honorable thoughts that take responsibility, and rewards right action as they interact in the world.

Rehearse

When we are able to be still in mindfulness, many thoughts bounce around. We breathe and notice, we observe, we name our values, and then we rehearse our responses. Life is often complex. Relationships need upkeep, and conflict, too often, seems inevitable. Rehearsing a right way to act is part of a general mindfulness contemplation. We look inward so we can live right patterns of healthy thought, say the secularists and other mindfulness practitioners. Hopefully, a healthy thought pattern emerges. It may sound something like, "I do not need to be afraid because I can do as much as I can to be healthy in my thoughts and act justly for the good of everyone." Rehearsal of thoughts and planned action acknowledges the good and bad thoughts we are having, and the awareness of what is most honest and true about our situation in the present moment. Rehearsing means we stay in the present, we stay aware, and we flex our skills to expand our compassion for ourselves and others.

For the Christian, this mindfulness step is a wonderful opportunity to rehearse those things that are beyond us, and where we need Christ to dwell. We rehearse understanding his will, the Holy Spirit's guidance, the Scripture that makes the truth clear to us. We rehearse so that God's truths and his plan sink deeper into our psyches, our souls, our bodies. It is not only our truth and right action, according to what we value, but it is also God's truth and what he may be stretching our clients toward.

Thus, the basic steps of mindfulness, including one incorporating faith, is a place to look inward in order for us to turn our attention to God's presence, and ultimately to look outward, toward others.

Short Contemplation Practice

Let's end this chapter with a short general mindfulness practice. Then please keep reading for more on Christian mindfulness in part 2 as we explore some basic practices and concepts and work together on some exercises drawing from the Lord's Prayer.

> Have you taken a few minutes to breathe today?
>> If not, there is always time to do so.
>> God is present each time you make space for God's presence.
>> What do you observe today in your thought pattern? In your body? In your emotional state?
>> What do you anticipate will be easy for you today? How about what will be complex or difficult?
>> Take some time to breathe, notice your thoughts, feelings, and actions thus far. Rehearse in your mind a response to those thoughts, feelings, and actions that aligns with your faith today. In God's presence, what do you feel is stirring inside of you as a response to your mindful contemplation?

References for Chapter 2

Baer, R. A., Carmody, J., & Hunsinger, M. (2012). Weekly change in mindfulness and perceived stress in a mindfulness-based stress reduction program. *Journal of Clinical Psychology, 68*(7), 755–765. https://doi.org/10.1002/jclp.21865

Brinkborg, H., Michanek, J., Hesser, H., & Berglund, G. (2011). Acceptance and commitment therapy for the treatment of stress among social workers: A randomized controlled trial. *Behaviour Research and Therapy, 49*(6–7), 389–398. https://doi.org/10.1016/j.brat.2011.03.009

Brown, L. A., Gaudiano, B. A., & Miller, I. W. (2011). Investigating the similarities and differences between practitioners of second- and third-wave cognitive-behavioral therapies. *Behavior Modification*, *35*(2), 187–200. https://doi.org/10.1177/0145445510393730

Chen, E. Y., Matthews, L., Allen, C., Kuo, J. R., & Linehan, M. M. (2008). Dialectical behavior therapy for clients with binge-eating disorder or bulimia nervosa and borderline personality disorder. *International Journal of Eating Disorders*, *41*(6), 505–512. https://doi.org/10.1002/eat.20522

Crisp, C. D., Hastings-Tolsma, M., & Jonscher, K. R. (2016). Mindfulness-based stress reduction for military women with chronic pelvic pain: A feasibility study. *Military Medicine*, *181*(9), 982–989. https://doi.org/10.7205/MILMED-D-15-00354

Ford, K., & Garzon, F. (2017). Research note: A randomized investigation of evangelical Christian accommodative mindfulness. *Spirituality in Clinical Practice*, *4*(2), 92–99. https://doi.org/10.1037/scp0000137

Fox, J., Gutierrez, D., Haas, J., & Durnford, S. (2016). Centering prayer's effects on psycho-spiritual outcomes: A pilot outcome study. *Mental Health, Religion & Culture*, *19*(4), 379–392. https://doi.org/10.1080/13674676.2016.1203299

Garland, E., Kiken, L. G., Faurot, K., Palsson, O., & Gaylord, S. A. (2017). Upward spirals of mindfulness and reappraisal: Testing the mindfulness-to-meaning theory with autoregressive latent trajectory modeling. *Cognitive Therapy & Research*, *41*(3), 381–392. https://doi.org/10.1007/s10608-016-9768-y

Harned, M. S., Korslund, K. E., Foa, E. B., & Linehan, M. M. (2012). Treating PTSD in suicidal and self-injuring women with borderline personality disorder: Development and preliminary evaluation of a dialectical behavior therapy prolonged exposure protocol. *Behaviour Research & Therapy*, *50*(6), 381–386. https://doi.org/10.1016/j.brat.2012.02.011

King, A. P., Erickson, T. M., Giardino, N. D., Favorite, T., Rauch, S. A. M., Robinson, E., Kulkarni, M., & Liberzon, I. (2013). A pilot study of group mindfulness-based cognitive therapy (MBCT) for combat veterans with posttraumatic stress disorder (PTSD). *Depression & Anxiety, 30*(7), 638–645. https://doi.org/10.1002/da.22104

Park, G., & Thayer, J. F. (2014). From the heart to the mind: Cardiac vagal tone modulates top-down and bottom-up visual perception and attention to emotional stimuli. *Frontiers in Psychology, 5.* https://doi.org/10.3389/fpsyg.2014.00278

Rosales, A. (2016). Acceptance and commitment therapy (ACT): Empirical evidence and clinical applications from a Christian perspective. *Journal of Psychology and Christianity, 35*(3), 269–275.

Rousmaniere, T. (2020). Steven Hayes on acceptance and commitment therapy. Psychotherapy.net. https://www.psychotherapy.net/interview/acceptance-commitment-therapy-ACT-steven-hayes-interview#:~:text=Acceptance%20and%20Commitment%20Therapy%20(ACT)%20founder%20Steven%20Hayes%20discusses%20the,and%20pain%2Dfilled%20modern%20world

Trammel, R. (2018). Effectiveness of an MP3 Christian mindfulness intervention on mindfulness and perceived stress. *Mental Health, Religion & Culture, 21*(5), 500–514. https://doi.org/10.1080/13674676.2018.1505837

Trammel, R. C., Park, G., & Karlsson, I. (2021). Religiously oriented mindfulness for social workers: Effects on mindfulness, heart rate variability, and personal burnout. *Journal of Religion & Spirituality in Social Work: Social Thought, 40*(1), 19–38. https://doi.org/10.1080/15426432.2020.1818358

Twohig, M. P., Hayes, S. C., Plumb, J. C., Pruitt, L. D., Collins, A. B., Hazlett-Stevens, H., & Woidneck, M. R. (2010). A randomized clinical trial of acceptance and commitment therapy versus progressive relaxation training for obsessive-compulsive disorder. *Journal of Consulting & Clinical Psychology, 78*(5), 705–716. https://doi.org/10.1037/a0020508

Wang, D. C., & Tan, S.-Y. (2016). Dialectical behavior therapy (DBT): Empirical evidence and clinical applications from a Christian perspective. *Journal of Psychology and Christianity, 35*(1), 68–76.

CHAPTER 3

The Gifts of Christian Mindfulness

If you, then, though you are evil, know how to give
good gifts to your children, how much more will your
Father in heaven give good gifts to those who ask him!
—Matthew 7:11

There are truths of Christian mindfulness that are universally experienced by both client and therapist, counselor, psychologist, practitioner. We as practitioners experience the gifts of Christian mindfulness because God is in those moments. We can be confident that God is present even when we are with our clients. As we lean into his presence, those gifts we receive from him are more easily passed along to our clients and can affect our work with our clients in a positive way. In addition, the more we can experience these gifts, the more fluid and competent we will feel in infusing Christian mindfulness into our therapeutic work.

In support of our counseling and therapeutic work, Christian mindfulness practice offers us space to evaluate what is happening around us, inside of us, and between us and others. When we take a moment to pay attention to the present and invite God into that mental space, we become more aware. This awareness makes us more available to serve God's work through us in home, relationships, work, and self. Our availability is mental, emotional, and spiritual. A virtuous cycle ensues. We are more available to serve, we can reflect on and feel good about being aligned with God's purpose, and we become more aware of these good things through practice, leading to more availability.

Awareness of the Presence of God

In Christian mindfulness, the origin of our awareness is Christ, through the work of the Holy Spirit. The aim of our awareness is to be more like Christ. How many of us find ourselves going through the day without an awareness of God's work in our lives? Usually, in times of distress, do we seek him in our day-to-day, or do we try to control our circumstances? As Christian counselors, therapists, and other healing practitioners who work with clients in distress, how many of us invite God's presence into the counseling or therapeutic space with us? Are we aware of him, do we tap into his wisdom while we work? Some of us may do this, some of us may not.

We hope that through Christian mindfulness, you can build a base of practice around this awareness. When we ourselves are aware, we build in a safe place that our clients can sense, because we are authentically in God's presence. Our clients are sophisticated and complex. They can pick up any emotional shifts from us. The mental, psychological, and soul-based shifts we experience ourselves when we practice mindfulness help us approach our work with our clients with resilience, a greater capacity for empathy, and an unending resource for us in the presence of our eternal God. Acknowledging that God is at work during the day-to-day of our clients' lives can change our perspective and our capacity to help heal others quite dramatically.

Therefore, we must identify the mechanism for such awareness, which is our thoughts and cognitions, as they are the most accessible to us as we begin a Christian mindfulness practice. Our daily thought habit—conscious and unconscious—can easily become our narrative. The way we view the world, the way we view our clients, the way we view ourselves—thoughts are powerful vehicles for decision making, our emotions, and even the intuition that guides our therapeutic work.

In Christian mindfulness, we work out our thought lives by observing them with nonjudgment. Nonjudgment does not mean we don't care about sin, because God does care. No, it's much the opposite. We do not put much stock in our thoughts because they come from our sinful being. We know that thoughts come and go. What truly matters is God's thoughts for us in the present moment. God's truths are gifts to us in moments of stillness. We receive his thoughts wholeheartedly by allowing them to inhabit our very being in that silent time of attention to him. We can do so only when we are not so caught up in our thoughts that we lose the space we need for him to move in our minds and hearts and to stir our souls. When we grasp every thought, analyze them to death, we are preoccupied with self. When we give up our thoughts, look at them, observe them, we ask the Holy Spirit to reveal our inner thoughts in light of God's truth. Psalm 139:1–3 reads, "You have searched me, LORD, and you know me. You know when I sit and when I rise; you perceive my thoughts from afar. You discern my going out and my lying down; you are familiar with all my ways."

God knows us better than we know ourselves. Christian mindfulness is a mind-body-soul practice that creates stillness, silence, time to pause, and a place to be ourselves in the presence of God. "Search me, God, and know my heart; test me and know my anxious thoughts. See if there is any offensive way in me, and lead me in the way everlasting" (Ps. 139:23–24).

We, as Christian counselors, therapists, social workers, psychologists, and pastoral and lay counselors, can embrace the practices of mindfulness in Christ because he is the only one able to transform our thoughts from selfishness to selflessness. As we surrender to God's will and desire for us, we can focus on the healing aspects of our work more thoroughly. What do our clients need from us in this moment? What do we sense God is working out in their lives? How can we attune to their suffering and provide hope and glimpses of healing that come from them?

In our roles as healing professionals, we must remember that this work is not about us—our victories, our words, our intentions. The work is about our clients and counselees. They come first when we are in service to them. Our clients sometimes need more insight, more commitment, and more practice of the skills or insights we can provide them. In Christian mindfulness, we become more aware of their shifts in attitudes, their abilities to see themselves as who they are from a more honest place. Sometimes our clients defend their thinking, defend their actions, and make little commitment to change. Let's remember together that rigidity and defensiveness come from a place of pain. Maybe it's shame or rejection or fear of transformation. We, as healers, understand that their powerful experiences in suffering—whether from mental health, trauma, or just daily life—are influencing them and can diminish their ability to see themselves accurately.

Jesus is the most real thing, not our thoughts, even if they are powerful thoughts. We align our thoughts with our Lord, and we do so by settling into nonjudgment to give space for the Holy Spirit to speak into our thoughts. Our clients begin not only to reframe the negative self-talk that rushes through their mental space, they begin to inhabit a different way of thinking that is healthier and truer. Instead of hardness of hearts toward their suffering or others', they tear down walls of relationship because they begin to see and observe how they are feeling.

When clients can begin to have space to review, and to renew, with your help and guidance as a Christian mindfulness practitioner, their sufferings take a vacation. Our clients can begin to think again, to problem-solve, to see the patterns that trip them up. When they are caught up in reactivity and powerful emotions in the counseling office with you, they are in a heightened emotional state.

As you help acknowledge Christ's work in the therapy or counseling room together, you make space for a renewal of the mind. Awareness is the first step. Honing the tool God made (which, in our case as Christian counselors and therapists, is us) is the next step.

Mindfulness for Self-Care for Healing Professionals

Awareness begins with you. When we begin to work in the counseling or therapy room, we are trained to be aware of our clients—how they feel, how they present, their mood, affect, energy level. We make all kinds of assessments quickly, based on our training and practice. With experience, we are more attuned, more aware of our clients' shifting moods, wounds, triumphs, victories. We will unpack Christian mindfulness not only as a therapeutic skill for you to use but also as a practice for yourself. This will enhance your ability to teach your clients the skills as well.

Practicing mindfulness is also an opportunity for spiritual growth. Oftentimes, we neglect our own care. This book is a tool not only for learning but also for discipleship and growth. Think of it this way: if you are called to bring healing to others, then you are in need of God's consistent healing presence yourself.

The analogy you have likely heard is that you cannot pour from an empty cup. When we are poured out for the sake of our clients—emotionally, spiritually, even physically—we become less effective. Our listening skills can be diminished. Here's another one: like a piano teacher, we can hear the notes that our clients play, but we may hear them off key or out of tune. When we are not filled up by the Spirit or simply lack the mental space to be intentional in our work, we can become tone deaf to our clients' real needs, spoken and unspoken. As healing professionals, it is not just about self-care but about living within our limits. We are human, but we are tools. Our work is even more needed during these anxious, uncertain, and unsettling times. The hope is that we all will come out more aware, understanding our need for each other as God's creation and focused on the most important things. As healers, we create more heart space when we feel our own humanity. That is a good thing.

Sometimes we sacrifice our self-care and needs to take on the suffering of others. This is why we feel called to the counseling professions, such as social work, psychology, marital and family therapy, and the pastorate. However, our neglect of our bodies, minds, and spirits comes at a cost. The rate of burnout for mental health professionals (social workers in particular) is quite high and leads to emotional exhaustion, disillusionment, and the intention to quit (Acker, 2012; Hamama, 2012). I (Regina) have recently conducted a study using a Christian mindfulness intervention for social workers and found that Christian mindfulness decreases burnout and increases heart-rate variability, which is an indicator of emotional flexibility.

The Gift of Nonjudgment

God has made humans complex creatures, so there is usually a mix of good and bad when we practice Christian mindfulness. Understanding and practicing mindfulness as a Christian is uncomplicated. The skills that are built in the area of nonjudgment are also uncomplicated, but they can be revealing. When we practice mindfulness ourselves, judgment simply means not hurting ourselves when we observe our thoughts. We do no harm when we sit still to observe our thoughts. We invite God with us into those moments when we can observe and reflect on our thought lives. Thoughts come and go. That's naturally how the mind works. We see them, we hear them, we name them. That's it.

What becomes destructive is when we let unhealthy and sinful thoughts take hold. Simply observing these toxic thoughts in the mind makes them smaller. Being angry at ourselves for having a sinful thought actually gives that thought staying power. Feeling ashamed and obsessing about why we have a sinful or destructive thought gives it power. In Christian mindfulness practice, we simply sit in those thoughts, place them in front of God's gracious presence. Understanding that thoughts are just that—thoughts—roots them out. We line up our thoughts in light of Scripture. When they don't align, we let them pass, as they should. In Christian mindfulness, God's Holy Spirit can convict, and we allow that process. So for our clients, as they sift through what they think or feel, they do so in a place of nonjudgment so that God's truths shine through. Our clients are more empowered to invite God into the stillness, to help them hear clearly what emerges in their minds, what manifests in their emotional lives. In mindful silence, our clients begin to break away from perfectionism, deal with their addiction, reckon with their history of abuse. All the challenges of life are to be dealt with because we all are under the curse of sin this side of heaven. However, we can empower our counselees to gain the strength to tolerate the truth of what assails them, because in Christian mindfulness, the gift of nonjudgment sets them free as they embrace Christ's conviction, grace, and restoration.

The gift of nonjudgment, therefore, relays the power of a thought-life centered in Christ. Whether for your own well-being or for your clients' therapeutic work, you can approach the counseling room with focus, disciplined by God's eternal love, forgiveness, and truth. We welcome our clients in that vein; we offer them the best we can because we are aware of the sameness of our struggle, that our judgment toward ourselves and each other must come under obedience to Christ and God's Word. What a relief. Nonjudgment frees us from our destructive thought patterns, our poor view of reality, and offers us a hopeful vision grounded in the truth that God is here. He really is present. He will sift our thoughts and use what is needed toward health, healing, and holiness.

The Gift of Listening

Christian mindfulness is a practice of listening to God's voice as well as to the internal narrative that warps God's voice. We also listen to others better and become more present to their pain and hurts when we practice Christian mindfulness. This gift of listening is essential to our work in the counseling room. We listen well when we can fully embrace and lean into the voice of the person who needs our empathy and listening ears. We listen with presence. As healers of all professions, we embrace this listening gift and home in on all of the parts of our clients that sound alienated from one another. Inherent in Christian mindfulness practice is the way we can listen to the cries of our clients' souls, anxious minds, and neglected bodies. Our own Christian mindfulness practice fine-tunes our listening so we hear the things our clients may not verbalize. We also must listen with our whole bodies, minds, and spirits. With the help of the Holy Spirit, our listening is not limited just to the psychological. What is tied to the mental health issues or emotional anguish presented to us? What purpose do we have in that role God has placed us in right here, right now, with our clients?

The gift of listening is a sacred one. We are entrusted with the well-being of another person who is God's created one. It is so easy to forget to listen, especially when we are harried, hurried, and worn out. So when we take a breath, when we take a moment, when we sit still and notice, the listening gift is refreshed. Take a beat and listen in. We hear his voice in the desert, we hear his voice in the wilderness, we hear his voice again as the roaring waves. God is listening to us as we listen for his voice. He calls us toward truth, toward our salvation in him. We extend to others the grace we receive. We heed his call and dive deeper into the mystery of his goodness and grace. We listen because we don't know what to do without him, and he offers us direction, assurance, hope, healing, grace, eternity in his presence.

When our clients practice Christian mindfulness, they listen to a new song. The song they used to hear was oftentimes full of judgment, shame, or self-hatred. The tune they used to sing was alienation from themselves (their emotions, their sense of self), from others, and from God. When they listen in Christian mindfulness, they hear the deep, clear, and gentle voice of God calling to them, through the Holy Spirit, full of forgiveness, acceptance, and love—a call that is the deep calling to deep. When our counselees can sit and listen, they learn to adjust their songs, and they call back to God, ultimately finding him, and therefore finding themselves. They can listen for his voice to guide them. When our clients are mindful, they may sense him more, hear him more, trust him more. Listening is a gift that draws our clients closer. Closer to peace, closer to healing, closer to themselves, and closer to others. Listening is a gift that provides them stronger relationships with others because our clients are no longer listening to the warped music that drew them farther away from those who offered healthy relationship and closer to those others who offered abuse, trauma, judgment, or pain.

For our clients, the gift of listening is also of presence. They begin to understand that their voices also matter, their feelings matter, their thoughts matter, and the song they sing in their lives gets heard. Boundaries are kept, equanimity prevails, their strength and confidence are built up by the Lord. When our clients feel listened to, they feel they matter. They feel heard but also seen. In Christian mindfulness, they can rest in those facts, that they do matter. If they listen to their God, they know they are worth being listened to—in their bones they know it. They know it also in their hearts, and they will choose to repair those broken places and relationships and move forward because they know they are worth it. Listening is a gift of our clients' presence in their world. They no longer just exist, but they show up, and others notice them hearing the song God has sung for them.

The Gift of Authenticity

Authenticity is about living honestly and congruently, and this gift is powerful in the healing process. Specifically, for us practitioners, the gift of authenticity is about understanding who we are in Christ and then living out that understanding truthfully and genuinely in all aspects of our lives, personal and professional. Authenticity means we sense, feel, cognitively and analytically know what makes us tick and how we want to live. We understand who Christ has made us to be and for what purpose. We each have a way with a client that is uniquely suited. When we practice Christian mindfulness, the gifts of authenticity we receive are about understanding the use of self. How we integrate who we are in Christ with our theoretical approach in therapy and counseling is powerful. Research shows that this mix of use of self with evidence-based practice is most effective. We fluidly access those parts of ourselves that were knit together by God by experience, the truths we have learned, and the cognitive shifts we have made.

The gift of authenticity helps us receive the wins that we witness in our clients' lives. Small or big changes, success in their treatment or relationships or ability to function—we can celebrate those wins with each of them. We can also receive the gifts of authenticity from Christian mindfulness practice that helped our connection, our care, and our support for them.

For our clients, the gift of authenticity is freeing. There is no need to perform anymore. As we know, our clients are learning how to heal in a way that helps them peel off the protective masks that many of them feel they need in order to be accepted. When our clients understand Christ's love and acceptance of them, they feel safer to risk being more honest with themselves and others. They can live congruently with the values they hold dear. Authenticity for our clients is identifying how they feel, how they discern between what among their choices is healthy and unhealthy, what is holy and unholy, what is well and unwell. What gets in the way of our living into who we are is that oftentimes we are not even aware of how we are living. Our clients' choices become more conscious. Instead of reacting mindlessly, they notice how various factors impact them, and they can deal with these impacts more honestly, take responsibility, and repair when necessary. They move into a more conscious awareness of God, who is cheering them on toward holier lives, more abundant and healthier lives.

Authentic living is a gift the breeds improved mental health. When our clients deal with themselves honestly, they can assess themselves, their strengths and weaknesses, and make necessary adjustments. For instance, when our clients feel accepted by God, they can face their mental health diagnoses with more ease and authenticity. Authenticity also allows them to accept the exiled parts of themselves, whether past trauma history or neglected aspects or shameful parts, integrating these parts as an outflow of authenticity.

Emotional health and stability are born of our clients' authentic selves. When they can discover the core of who they are, accepted, flawed, forgiven, and desperate for God, our clients are powerfully served by a great and generous God. His abundance is so much clearer for them. His nature is so much more grace filled than they know. His ways are good and right, and God calls them to much more than hiding who he has created them to be. Christian mindfulness practice puts our clients more in touch with these truths so they can embrace, love, and live a life of grace and forgiveness.

The Gift of Joyful Awareness

There is joy in the Lord, in his presence, in seeking his face. In Christian mindfulness, we practice how to be in God's presence. We notice, we are more fully awake and aware of, God's hand in our lives. No wonder joy becomes present. There is an awareness that comes with Christian mindfulness because joy rains down on us from heaven. It is an everlasting joy that does not ignore pain but steadies us under it. This joyful awareness does not mean there is an absence of suffering, but in that suffering there is hope for endurance. Joyful awareness is not even about happiness, though folks often get joy and happiness confused. Joy is experienced in the present, cultivated by being aware of God's faithfulness in our past and seeing hope in the future. Joyful awareness is therefore informed by the past but lived in the present, with an orientation of flourishing toward the future.

As we write this section, there is a global pandemic, and we have endured injustice and protests as well as chaotic violence. Now there is smoke in the air from wildfires in the West. Simply put, it feels as if our world is under siege. 2020 has been more than challenging. It has been full of suffering and loss. Nevertheless, there is a joyful awareness of how we are getting through it all day by day. We endure under the strength of God's assurance. We are joyfully aware that there really is an end to suffering, because we are dust—we are created from dust and will return to dust some day. There is a joyful awareness of the peace of God because of this knowing, because we know our destiny as Christians.

As counselors, therapists, psychologists, healing practitioners of faith, we witness great suffering and great loss as well as despair, but we have the joyful hope that all of our clients who know him will be lifted from their burdens one day in Christ. In Christian mindfulness, we are aware of the impermanence of life. We have a joyful awareness both of the now and also of what is to come: we have joy even amid suffering now, and we have witnessed when God has walked with us in the past. The gift of joyful awareness that comes from Christian mindfulness brings us wisdom and a wise way of living that is knowledgeable of God's truths.

As they are joyfully aware, our clients gain the knowledge of skills they have used in the past and of skills that will work in this present moment. Our clients stop basing their thoughts and behaviors on fleeting emotions, and they become joyfully aware of how their emotions and actions impact them. They notice, they build awareness because they are curious where those emotions come from, not in a nihilistic way but in a way of joy. There is no nihilism with God. He promises a hope and a future, but we get to that when we can live in joyful awareness of his presence in this present moment. That really is all we can do—live presently, purposefully. Our clients begin to get this and live it out when they are joyfully aware.

Joyful awareness is also the opposite of toxic positivity. The awareness part means that we face the suffering head on, with eyes opened wide, with acceptance, knowing that not all things will go right and that many things may go wrong. We are not immune to pain, but we can be aware of beauty and joy amid pain and even grief. We accept that all glory is God's and that all pain can be endured when we hang on and Jesus hangs on to us. Joyful awareness is the gift that keeps us hanging on.

Questions for Reflection

1. Of the gifts of Christian mindfulness described in this chapter, which ones seem most resonant to you? Why?
2. When you listen in Christian mindfulness, what is an example of what you hear about your thoughts?
3. Describe at least one way you experienced living more authentically recently.
4. Do you find yourself challenged to stay in the past more than being able to live in the present moment with joyful awareness? Why or why not?

References for Chapter 3

Acker, G. M. (2012). Burnout among mental health care providers. *Journal of Social Work, 12*(5), 475–490. https://doi.org/10.1177/1468017310392418

Hamama, L. (2012). Burnout in social workers treating children as related to demographic characteristics, work environment, and social support. *Social Work Research, 36*(2), 113–125. https://doi.org/10.1093/swr/svs003

PART 2

BASIC STEPS
OF CHRISTIAN
MINDFULNESS

You may be familiar with the Lord's Prayer. Perhaps you learned it in Sunday school or recite the prayer weekly during church services. The Lord's Prayer might even be so familiar to you that you do not recall when or where you learned it or who taught you to recite it. The beauty of the Lord's Prayer is that Jesus himself taught it to his disciples and teaches us in God's Word that this is the way we should pray. Reciting these familiar words puts many of us into a mindset of readiness to worship and to receive God's teaching. In this book, the words of the Lord's Prayer also offer the perfect structure for us to explore some basic skills in Christian mindfulness.

In the next few chapters, we'll contemplate the Lord's Prayer in small bits, allowing our minds to marinate in the prayer so we can take in its deeper meaning. More than just a rote way of praying (especially for clients with some sort of Christian or Catholic background), the Lord's Prayer offers ample direction to help our clients practice some basic skills in Christian mindfulness.

In each of the chapters in part 2, we home in on a specific part of the Lord's Prayer. Then we introduce and unpack a mindfulness practice skill. Please take the time to orient yourself to the concepts, practice them yourself, and then, after a good clinical assessment, see whether these concepts and skills can be applied in your counseling or therapy sessions. Each chapter contains a specific exercise you can use under the heading "Contemplation Exercise." We hope that you will find the guided language in these exercises useful for your work with counselees and clients. It is important that you adapt the language and lead your client or counselee through the Lord's Prayer with their therapeutic goals in mind. Tailor the specifics as part of your debriefing from the exercises.

The hope we have for you as you work your way through part 2 before leading your clients through many of the exercises in this book is to adopt a basic Christian mindfulness practice yourself. Then it will be easier to understand firsthand what your client or counselee will find helpful.

We will begin with inner silence, which will help you to create space for your clients to ponder the verses in the style of *Lectio Divina:* with a time to read each verse, to pray and meditate on the verse, and then to contemplate it so that the Holy Spirit can move them to a deeper relationship with Christ and possibly into action. The efforts we, as counselors, therapists, and healing practitioners, make to understand these verses will inform us on how our clients might understand them as well. In the process of discovering new or deeper meanings of the Lord's Prayer, be open to helping your clients by noticing how they are impacted either by reinforcement, challenge, or metamorphosis. You are a witness to their growth, which is such a gift. And to share in that growth through the Lord's Prayer is a sacred space that clients can use daily.

Your familiarity with your clients will inform your prompts and discussions. We hope you will build off of the concepts and skills presented in each chapter of part 2. The basic yet effective Christian mindfulness skills in each chapter can help effect change for your clients' or counselees' minds, bodies, and souls. We know this because we believe that God is more than capable to help your people thrive, even in the midst of suffering. He is a shelter and refuge from the storm (2 Sam. 22:31).

CHAPTER 4

The Practice of Silence to Cultivate Awareness

Our Father in heaven,
hallowed be your name.
—MATTHEW 6:9

Mariah is a new mom. She recently gave birth to a baby girl. Before motherhood, Mariah would have described herself as organized, fastidious, thorough, and accomplished. She and her husband of five years decided that it was best for her to move to a part-time job in her company as a consultant. She reports feeling fully engaged and behind making this career choice, and her husband, Ben, is very supportive of the move. Recently, however, Ben is noticing a growing level of anxiety and stress that Mariah seems to be experiencing three months after giving birth. Mariah is hard on herself and is feeling more and more like a failure. She reports that she does not sleep very often and worries constantly about her baby girl's well-being and has enough insight to recognize that her anxiety is worsening.

Becoming a parent is a wonderful change. The joy and love of having a child is special, truly life-giving. However, there's no discounting how drastic of a change it can be. New parents find themselves with new responsibilities, new schedules, and new worries. If they have made a career change, like Mariah did, they may also find themselves with a new identity and a sense of loss for the person they used to be. Individuals like Mariah often feel anxious, exhausted, overwhelmed, distracted, and lost.

These feelings of stress amid change are not confined to new parents. Our world can be a noisy place. Change comes fast. Job changes, the building or breaking apart of relationships, even simple, everyday messages, emails, and problems to solve deluge our thinking space throughout the day. Often, our clients come to us when they are overextended, burdened, experiencing conflict or traumas, or struggling with addictions. When clients suffer many impinging factors, they come to us for help and support.

A key starting point for Christian mindfulness is the practice of silence and awareness. Silence is a purposeful retreat from the daily rhythms of life. In Christian mindfulness, silence is also a pathway to transcend and commune with our savior and receive the love of Christ.

Biblical Basis for the Practice of Silence

In our demanding world, finding time to indulge in silence and solitude may seem selfish, frivolous, or even self-centered. A new mother like Mariah might struggle with the fear of being a self-centered mother. Her anxiety about whether she is doing enough as a mother or is a good enough mother can be overwhelming and easily distorted.

Over and over again in Scripture, however, we see Jesus taking himself out of the crowds to be in silence with God. Mark 1:35 says, "Very early in the morning, while it was still dark, Jesus got up, left the house and went off to a solitary place, where he prayed." Jesus sought time to be quiet and alone. Jesus identified times when he needed to be in silence with God the Father, and when he needed to be with the crowds teaching, healing, being in community with others.

We too can seek time to be silent in God's presence. In the Lord's Prayer, Jesus instructs us on how to pray about stressors and worries we experience daily, starting with the words, "Our Father in heaven, hallowed be your name" (Matt. 6:9). Matthew 6:9 suggests that we can use mindfulness practice to deepen our awareness of God in our lives and in our clients' lives, and experience deeper peace.

The Benefits of the Practice of Silence for Clients

When our clients walk through their daily lives unaware of their feelings or thoughts, they are not grounded in the truth. They may also experience intrusive and judgmental thoughts about themselves and hold harsh or rigid judgments toward others. For a young mom like Mariah, new motherhood brings with it expectations of what a good mother should look like. Is it better to breastfeed or bottle feed? Should she still work or mostly stay home? Is attachment parenting better or should she let her baby cry it out? Many more questions could be added to this list, but the sum of it is this: how Mariah judges herself as a good enough mother depends a lot on the messages she values from her mother, key relationships, and society.

Whether or not they are aware of them, our clients often hold on to old messages from dysfunctional or codependent relationships and have a negative mental schema that inflicts emotional pain or even physical pain. Many of our clients with other mental health presentations are not aware—or perhaps are in denial—of the stress they carry in their bodies. An elevated heart rate, perspiration, and shallow breaths are bodily symptoms that many of our counselees have learned to live with as normal. Practicing silence helps bring down our clients' or counselees' parasympathetic responses, especially for those whose stress and anxiety levels are high. Additionally, the practice of silence is an important way to help our clients identify what is at the heart of their hurts, struggles, or need of support, healing, and guidance. Clients who are open to building a practice of mindfulness can become aware of what they need in the quiet space of the therapy office.

The benefits of a practice of silence are amplified when they are part of Christian mindfulness. Silence is a way to listen. It helps our thoughts to sharpen. Without language, distraction, or rumination, God's still small voice becomes louder, and we can hear him, our shepherd, more clearly. For someone like Mariah, spending time alone in God's presence can solidify the work she does in the counseling office. She can take in the message that she really is good enough, that in the silence is the place she can hear God's call on her life as a mother and the reassurance she needs, as well as the rest her body, mind, and soul crave.

When we and our clients can sit in silence without the cacophony and pulls from the world's priorities, we can understand when we have wandered away from truths or actions that can anchor us. We can come to realize that Jesus' yoke is easy and his burden is light. When we are steeped in a silence built by a Christian mindfulness practice, we can hang on to these truths more readily and turn truths into action steps.

In the following paragraphs, we'll explore a few additional benefits the practice of silence can offer our clients.

Silence Exposes the False Self

In Christian mindfulness, the practice of silence can help our clients out of their false self-ideals. Prominent philosopher and theologian Moreland (2007) describes the "empty self" or "false self" as the self that is focused on hyperindividualism, pleasure seeking, and relationships that are shallow, and that is based on viewing people as objects (pp. 141–47). Some of our clients have never known the embrace of empathy and love from a fellow human being or from God. If our clients have built their identities around external and superficial ends, then part of their healing in our counseling and therapy spaces must deal with the emptiness that surely these things have provided. The practice of silence is to recall again their values and judgments and to hold them to their God-given values and God-given dignity.

Silence Cultivates Awareness

Silence cultivates awareness as it provides space for our clients to mine and explore the inner workings of the thoughts, feelings, and reactions that they normally would not spend time thinking about. The metacognitive tasks of any mindfulness practice are the seat of awareness. Counselees begin to develop what is called meta-awareness, which means they not only observe their thoughts but are curious enough about them to put them in context with their beliefs and faith. They are metacognitively aware that their thoughts may or may not line up with what is true in Scripture or in what they sense is true through the Holy Spirit.

Silence Makes Space for the Holy Spirit's Promptings

Silence and awareness in Christian mindfulness is a space where counselees can hear the corrections and promptings of the Holy Spirit. It allows them to cultivate that thought muscle and to explore questions such as, What are my thoughts? What do I think about my thoughts? How do I feel knowing that this is my thought right now? How does God's presence in this awareness make me feel? Does knowing that God is always with me shift the way I think and feel about my thoughts? How do my thoughts compare with what I know God's thoughts to be about me, my situation, or the problem that I'm mulling over?

Notes for Mental Health Professionals

As practitioners, we must recognize that, in Christian mindfulness, we are silent but not alone in our thoughts, that God is with us in our thoughts. That can cause an inner sense of shame or judgment. Therefore, it is important that, as you lead your client into a moment of silence, you ask God to redeem them and help them to feel embraced and loved unconditionally and to experience what it's like to dwell in his presence during therapy.

We must further understand that the goal of practicing silence is not to foster denial. Our clients need to continue to face their issues head on while being bathed with empathy, compassion, and a high value for justice. Christian mindfulness practices should not explain away injustice, trauma, pain, and hurt. On the contrary, one goal of practicing silence is to remind our clients of their dignity as children of God.

Silence centers our thoughts, and in the therapy and counseling room, our ability to stay in silence and to teach the skills of silence is predicated on our own practice. During our therapy, counseling, and healing interactions, we must remember that, in God's eyes (as well as in our own), our clients are no less capable, no less worthy, no less dignified and respected than anyone else. When we are able to sit in the presence of God ourselves, we come to realize this truth more and more: that all of God's children are precious and that our value is not based on the material world and matters our clients face daily.

Our clients often have outsourced their thinking to others. It is both in the silence cultivated by the individual and in their relationship with God that the magic of mindfulness happens. We are the third party that explores our clients' experience of silence. In the treatment space, we help our clients use this silent space for deep contemplation in which they can hear internally and become aware of God's desires for them. As counselors and therapists, we trust that, given the space that silence creates, our clients will meet God where they are because God is with them wherever they go in their thoughts.

Contemplation Exercise

MATTHEW 6:9

The practice of silence is a place to listen to our thoughts and to seek God. Take a few minutes to sit still with your eyes closed in the quietness of your thoughts. The quietness is to help settle your mind. The silence is to help tune your internal ears for listening. While you are silent, contemplate the first part of the Lord's Prayer: "Our Father in heaven." Pay attention to the quiet and note any feelings that come up for you, what this time in silence brings to mind. Identify what you might hear or see in this inward time. Then take a couple of breaths and stay silent as you prepare to meditate on the first part of the Lord's Prayer: "Our Father in heaven."

Now, in this moment, with your eyes closed so you can dwell in the concept of the verse, take the word "our." "Our" might be a distant concept or a word that brings up images of folks who are the "our" in your life. Just note who may or may not come to mind and observe what comes up for you as you ponder the word. What is your thought about "our"?

Next mull over the two simple words "our Father." Continue to observe your thoughts and where they go when you put these two words together. Who is the "our" when you think of "our Father"? What does the word "Father" bring up for you? What feelings do you experience as you ponder the word and concept? Continue to mull over these words, but, as if using a bookmark, mark where you left off so we can discuss it together after this experience.

Picture what it means to combine "our Father" with "in heaven." Does "our Father" change when you contemplate "in heaven"? In this quiet space, you can practice seeing with new eyes—eyes that are focused on heaven. As we calm our bodies through our breath, our senses become more attuned to him. As we close our eyes, we engage our minds to focus on God's rightful place in heaven. Christ is on God's right hand. Picture God in heaven. What do you see? What do you hear? What colors surround our Father in heaven? Reflect on these sights. Let them sink into your mind's eye. We don't force these images, we simply reflect and give space for God to work. Focus on your thoughts regarding the whole phrase "our Father in heaven."

Breathe in three deep breaths. Sit for another minute in silence to let your thoughts settle. Let the poignant moments of this quiet time reach farther into your conscious thoughts to prepare for the next part of the verse.

Hallowed means "holy." Use this time of silence to look at the concept of hallowed or holy in your mind. Does hallowed or holy have a definition? What makes hallowed or holy easy to think about? Is it difficult to think about hallowed or holy? Why or why not? Chew on the concept of hallowed and holy and consider where these thoughts might come from. Notice anything you might want to explore further.

Take the last part of the verse: "be your name." Think about the significance of a name. What is your thought on God's being named and how God's name is holy? Observe any reaction or feeling that might come up for you. Remember there is no judgment in this silent space. The silence is simply a place where you get to observe and mull over your thoughts in God's presence.

To close this practice, spend another minute with the entire verse. Inhale a deep breath and say aloud, "Our Father in heaven, hallowed be your name." Let the prayer soak into your mind, lingering there, assisting you in recalling your place in this world, with your Father, holy is his name.

To end, let me offer up the words of John of Damascus, a monk living in Jerusalem around 700 AD, who envisioned the Father as the Lamb:

> While we embrace the ancient figures and shadows handed down in the Church, as symbols and foreshadows of the truth, we prefer grace and truth, which we receive as the fulfillment of the Law ... in icons the Lamb who takes away the sins of the world, Christ our God, is to be presented in his human form instead of as the ancient lamb, so that, coming to understand through his humility the greatness of God the Word, we may be led to a memory of his life in the flesh and his passion and the redemption of the world that consequently came about. (Louth, 2003, p. 158)

References for Chapter 4

Louth, A. (2003). *Three treatises on the divine images: Apologia against those who deny holy images.* St. Vladimir's Seminary Press.

Moreland, J. P. (2007). *Kingdom triangle: Recover the Christian mind, renovate the soul, restore the Spirit's power.* Zondervan.

CHAPTER 5

Reading God's Word Slowly

Your kingdom come,
your will be done,
on earth as it is in heaven.
—MATTHEW 6:10

John is a freshman who moved out of state to attend college. He is enjoying meeting new people, living in the dorms, getting to know his professors. However, every morning, he wakes up with a feeling of dread that is new to him. Being far from home is difficult, and his sleep patterns have changed. His eating has been uneven because of the new foods he is encountering. Feeling alone and isolated, John is both struggling emotionally and succeeding in his transition to a more independent life.

He has been struggling to get up each morning, and to eat his daily meals at the cafeteria. Some of this is simply because of his lack of energy. Other times, he is intimidated by the crowds of people. He has not taken part in any dorm activities, which would be good opportunities for him to form supportive relationships. Part of his treatment plan addresses these important steps to not only provide a routine but also focus on the daily work he will do with support. One aim is socializing at mealtimes. The support John is receiving in therapy provides accountability for these solution-focused goals to address his depression.

It also uses Christian mindfulness practice to help him align his values with his behaviors, for the benefit of himself and his college community.

John makes progress in therapy and is now taking some ownership to determine his next action steps to work on this month. John determines that his focus will be on making new relationships. Part of his struggle has been the emptiness he has been feeling and the loneliness he has been experiencing. In therapy, he is making the connection that the loneliness comes from some family-of-origin issues because of what can best be described as his parents' negligence. He indicates over time in therapy that he felt as if he was invisible, that his parents were more about order and control than warmth and acceptance. His value as a person was tied up more with achievement and independence than with feeling a part of his family. He is realizing that taking initiative in social relationships and not following through with them is a pattern to protect himself from being lonely again.

In John's case, his idea of his value was tied to the subtle message that he absorbed from his parents: he was not valuable enough to spend time with, to get to know. It was easier for him to withdraw than to risk rejection and the subsequent feelings of loss and loneliness. It was much easier to retreat and stay in that aloneness than risk emotional abandonment again. For John, the therapy process has been about unlearning lies about his value and worth. His developing insights into those lies were like little lightbulbs going off, and he began to make the connection between his present behaviors of retreat and withdrawal to those childhood experiences of feeling alone.

Have you ever had a client came back to a counseling session with an insight that helped them change their perspective? Perhaps they finally grasped a certain truth or maybe they finally accepted that they cannot control a certain person or situation. In therapy, we reach for those points of connection with our clients not just through thinking and reframing but through a deep-seated knowing. What if, in incorporating Christian mindfulness, this deep-seated knowing were informed by Scripture? Sometimes the knowing comes from the insights that develop as we read Scripture in different ways. A verse or truth can be unpacked when we look at the words, think through the ways our minds, bodies, and souls are responding through the prompting of the Holy Spirit. For instance, in John's case, Matthew 6:9 can be quickly read and overlooked. With a slow, deliberate, reflective reading, the "our" can help John feel like he is not alone, that many folks understand what emotional abandonment by a father or mother feels like. And then the corrective, "our Father," for John can open up a whole new insight as he ponders what a father would do and say and how a father would love him. The power of reading Scripture in the *Lectio Divina* practice is that knowing, that slow, reflective, pondering way in which God's words can truly become the living Word for our clients and their healing.

In this chapter, we will discuss the practice of reading God's Word slowly, which is a basic building block of the practice of Christian mindfulness. Reading God's Word slowly helps us and our clients gain a deeper understanding of Scripture so that it reaches into one's spirit and psyche. The reading of God's Word in this way not only sheds light on our thoughts but also allows the Holy Spirit to speak to us, and to our clients.

The style of reading God's Word slowly that we recommend for our clients is based on the *Lectio Divina* ("divine reading").

The Basics of *Lectio Divina*

According to Howard (2012), *Lectio Divina* originated in the Benedictine monastic tradition. Practitioners set times for manual labor as well as divine reading of the Scriptures. The practice includes (Howard, 2012):

- Reading the biblical text, or Scripture (*lectio*)
- Meditating on Scripture (*meditation*)
- Praying (*oratio*)
- Contemplating (*contemplatio*), or pondering Scripture slowly with the assistance of the Holy Spirit

We can see how the practice of *Lectio Divina*, with its periods of quiet reflection, meditation, and contemplation, aligns well with Christian mindfulness. The essence of the work is to absorb God's Word slowly and with humility.

The person who practices *Lectio Divina* encounters Christ through the Scriptures. Thus, it is a divine encounter, not an intellectual reading. Self-examination and reflection on thoughts and behavior is enfolded into the practice, however. The last part of *Lectio Divina*, *operatio* (action), is about taking action. This last part naturally lends itself to the use of this spiritual practice in therapy, which is for our clients to head toward growth and healing and for their flourishing. We know, as Christ followers, that God's Word does not return void, and therefore we trust that the divine reading is a divine encounter with the ultimate counselor, therapist, and healer of us all.

The Benefits of Reading God's Word Slowly for Clients

If we take a therapeutic intervention, such as cognitive behavioral therapy, we understand that the impetus of change will be in how our clients can think about their thoughts. This ability to be objective is a helpful first step. We help our clients make space for nonjudgment, for reframing, and we do so in an often verbal, language-based method—hence why many of us are trained and licensed to do talk therapy. However, the integration of spiritual practices with talk therapy can promote our counseling and therapy efforts because the practices allow our clients to tap into resources they already have, especially if they are able and willing to come before the Lord.

Incorporating *Lectio Divina* into counseling helps our clients address their struggles, with the assistance of the Holy Spirit. Part of the value of this practice is the instruction of examination, especially with the assistance of the trained counselor or licensed therapist to ask questions empathically and to help our clients dig into the material that surpasses human language. The beauty of this practice is that it provides a practical example of a Christian mindfulness intervention at work. Paired with the counselor's skills, dwelling in God's Word can lead to insights that both the client and the counselor, therapist, social worker, or psychologist could never get to without the work of the Holy Spirit.

Notes for Mental Health Professionals

Think about how little time we spend in Bible reading, especially when pressed or busy. For our clients, the time to marinate in Scripture while they are working on their therapeutic issues is a gift of space and time to read, ponder, feel, and think. It is also a place where our clients can meet God: in the divine reading, wherever you go, there God is. Thus, the *Lectio Divina* is a focused practice where the Bible provides both instruction and spiritual food, and serves as a true resource for healing.

In the following sections, we'll explore a few important points we as practitioners must keep in mind when we are helping our clients incorporate the Christian mindfulness practice of *Lectio Divina*.

Be Open to Any Possible Result

In Christian mindfulness, we ask our counselees to ponder things they have not thought about or have not had the time to turn their attention to. For instance, a question that we often ask when using Christian mindfulness is, What are the emotions or thoughts that come up within? For our clients, over time, as they read slowly in the style of *Lectio Divina*, they ingest the Scriptures into their minds, make internal connections and application points. Not only are our clients' and counselees' minds impacted by the Scriptures but also they are moved emotionally or spiritually when they can connect with them.

As counselors, therapists, and healing practitioners, it is important that we allow for those deep moments of change even through the simple reading of the Scriptures. Verses might wash over them, and in their minds and hearts, they might be doing a holy work, or there might be moments of deep soul-searching, or moments when they are really hearing God speak to them. This kind of spiritual work pays dividends in our clients' emotional and psychological work. We must be open to all of those possibilities.

We must also acknowledge when those verses and words may not be impactful. There may be moments when the words of Scripture come across as just words. It is important to keep the space open for those two ends of the spectrum. One moment, your client may be deep inside the verse; the other, they may be utterly distracted. However, most of the time, we find that counselees will likely be somewhere in between. We simply encourage you to acknowledge that there will be sacred moments when your client's mental health need meets a verse in the Lord's Prayer. The contemplation point can be a moment when your client's deeper unknown and mysterious need weaves beautifully with an insight or word from God.

The weaving together of faith and the healing work in counseling, therapy, or other healing methods can uplift our clients' souls as well as their psyches. Thus, the opportunity for healing and repair comes with giving clients some space to develop insights into their presenting issues not only through talking but also perhaps through the Holy Spirit's groaning on their behalf (Rom. 8:26–27).

Consider Using Lectio Divina in Community

The modern Western church overemphasizes the idea that Christian life and faith is a private and individualistic practice. In their groundbreaking work, Markus and Kitayama (1991) compared Western notions of the individual with Eastern notions of the collective self, whereby the self in relation to others can be contrasted. With the former, the individual's identity and value are independent, while those in collectivist cultures value harmony of the self in relation to others. In collective cultures, the individual's self-concept is in submission to the family or community.

In the practice of *Lectio Divina*, our clients do not read in isolation. They should read within their relationship with God in Christ. We also have a part to play, because our relationship with our clients is key to their growth, healing, and wellness. Additionally, the *Lectio Divina* could be integrated into a counseling or therapy group. There is historical precedent for this. In the monastic tradition, the *Lectio Divina* was a community practice. We know that our clients' relationships with others can further help illuminate God's truths in the Scriptures. In John's case, imagine that you are the counselor reading Matthew 6:9 with him in the room as you process his pain and childhood wound. The "our" in "our Father" is much more poignant. John senses that you, the counselor, the therapist, the healing practitioner, are part of this experience. There is an opportunity for a correctional emotional experience simply in that part of the divine reading. In a group setting, the readings might address clients' deepest wounds and needs in a way that even more powerfully feels less isolating. Sharing a portion of Scripture that speaks to the needs of all clients can not only normalize their experiences but also provide new insight for their healing journey.

Recall that one of the main diagnostic criteria for any person with a mental health disorder, as defined by the *Diagnostic and Statistical Manual 5* (DSM-5), addresses the individual's occupational and social-relational functioning. Thus, it seems that for our clients to fully realize a remission of a mental health disorder, their ability to have relationships with others points to the way God has made all of us.

Contemplation Exercise

MATTHEW 6:10

You can use the following contemplation exercise as a way to foster your own *Lectio Divina* experience. Once you understand the concepts, you may then feel comfortable working through this exercise as an adjunctive part of your therapy and counseling skills with your clients and counselees.

The verse for contemplation begins with "your kingdom come." This section of the verse is a truth-telling fact. We understand that there is something more than what the world is offering. This idea can be comforting when what we experience is not what we hoped for. Thus, when we think about what "your" means, this idea can be a loaded concept. As in the contemplation of "our Father," the "your" may be distant. If it feels distant, first read aloud the phrase "your kingdom come," then meditate on the phrase "your kingdom."

Take some time to contemplate "your kingdom," contrasting it with life on earth as it is now—the good and the bad. Identify both. There is no judgment as to what you include in the good. Identify honestly the bad that, according to the Scriptures, is opposite of God's kingdom. Pray now and ask for "your kingdom come" into your emotions, into your pain, into your trauma, or into whatever you feel needs the healing, grace, and warmth of God's kingdom in your life.

In hurts or painful memories, the light opens up when we can invite God's kingdom into our minds, hearts, and souls. We interact with Christ, knowing that our humanity is limited by time, space, sinfulness, and separation from the incarnate God. However, we also know as Christians that the Holy Spirit sees us. When we can think through and determine the differences of the world's ways versus God's kingdom ways, the truth opens up.

If your challenge is with anxiety or low self-esteem, then remember that when God instructs you to pray "your kingdom come," that means that you are God's child. You are not alone. God is really the provider of good things. And even though your struggle is real, your present reality and feelings about the struggle are all tools that God can use to bring about God's "kingdom come." You have a key role to play in the kingdom, and your life will help bring about the reality of God's goodness, peace, justice, and kindness to you and to the world. We might not feel or understand it day-to-day, but when we recall that Jesus asked us to pray this prayer, we dig into his purpose and plan daily. He most certainly has a plan, and we are part of his kingdom.

After "your kingdom come," the next part of the verse is "your will be done." With eyes closed, say aloud "your will be done" three times, slowly. Each time you speak this, let these words soak into your soul, absorbing this prayer to God into your heart. It's all right if you do not believe this or want this completely, but reading the Scripture out loud alone will do its job. As Hebrews 4:12 states, "For the word of God is alive and active. Sharper than any double-edged sword, it penetrates even to dividing soul and spirit, joints and marrow; it judges the thoughts and attitudes of the heart." So take a few minutes to contemplate "your will be done."

Contemplate these questions: What is God's will for me today, in this moment? Where does my mind go to? Continue to explore what comes up for you with your counselor, therapist, or healing professional. Determine what parts of your life you will allow to undergo growth and grace, and determine which parts need pruning, which ones do not align with God's will for you. If addiction is a pattern, allow God's will to come, which is for you to work on letting go of addictions. Continue to process and find support through your counselor, twelve-step program, and other interventions your therapist recommends for you. Acknowledge today where God's will needs to be reclaimed in your life. Confess those areas to someone; process this action with your therapist or counselor.

"Your will be done" is a verse about submitting and letting go. If it's helpful, with closed eyes, you can breathe and use your hands as a symbol of this letting go through this Christian mindfulness exercise. Hold your hands out in front of you, with palms out, as you take a deep breath in and say in your mind or out loud, "Your kingdom come." Then turn your palms down and exhale with the words, "Your will be done." Do this at least three times. Engage your body through your hands. Be mindful of the words you speak. Let your soul assent and agree.

Continue to use this verse as a point of focus for your thoughts and regulate your breathing so the inhalation is the first part and your exhalation is matched with the phrase "your will be done." Now, again, add some hand movements to symbolize the action. Sit up in a comfortable position, feet on the ground. Close your eyes and focus on the verse. Place your hands with palms up on your lap, and with a deep inhalation say the verse "your kingdom come." Gently form your hands into loose fists so you are taking in "your kingdom come."

On your exhalation, say, "Your will be done." Unfurl your hands so your palms are up again.

Do this again. You are breathing in and welcoming with your hands to "your kingdom come." You are breathing out and letting go, unfurling your loose fists to "your will be done." Try doing this at least three times again. Focus on each word. Be slow to breathe in and out. Be slow and deliberate in closing your hands and then opening them up as a gesture of letting go.

The last part of this verse reads, "On earth as it is in heaven." Life on earth can be unpredictable. That means the bad times will end. However, God's purpose for you here on earth is alive and well. You are loved here on earth. Breathe in and focus on the words "on earth." Picture earth, your place on the earth, God's will for you on earth. If you are going through challenging times, remember that any suffering you experience on earth will pass. The difficult emotions will smooth over (more quickly when you have the support and help of those who are trained to help). Therapy and medications are useful and helpful when dealing with mental health issues and can be integral for mental health recovery here on earth.

Read aloud again "on earth as it is in heaven" three times, allowing each word to absorb into your mind, into your heart. Pray through the phrase "as it is in heaven," as Jesus instructs us in how to pray. Contrast what it means to pray for things to be on earth as they are in heaven. Meditate, contemplate, turn these words and concepts over in your mind at least three times. We do not obsess on these words, but we take them in so they reach into our intellect and our emotions. This *Lectio Divina* practice is soul work. We hope you are reaping some benefits of this work thus far.

Finally, in the practice of reading, praying, and contemplating, put all the words of this verse together: "Your kingdom come, your will be done, on earth as it is in heaven." Read the whole verse at least three times. Pray this verse, asking God to search you and teach you through it. Contemplate the whole verse again, putting together the thoughts and concepts of each part as a whole. Notice how each portion of the verse coalesces and attend to how God may be speaking to you. Receive and bookmark any insights you gain through this time. Breathe in the words again: inhale and receive God's word through the phrase "your kingdom come, your will be done," and exhale as a way of letting go through "on earth as it is in heaven." Receive God's kingdom, his will for you to be done on earth as he deems it in heaven.

References for Chapter 5

Howard, E. (2012). Lectio divina in the evangelical tradition. *Journal of Spiritual Formation & Soul Care*, 5(1), 56–77. https://doi.org /10.1177/193979091200500104

Markus, H. R., & Kitayama, S. (1991). Culture and the self: Implications for cognition, emotion, and motivation. *Psychological Review*, 98(2), 224–253. https://psycnet.apa.org/doi/10.1037/0033-295X.98.2.224

CHAPTER 6

Set an Intention of the Day

Give us today our daily bread.
—MATTHEW 6:11

Gabby and Dan have been married for more than three years and have recently begun *in vitro* fertilization (IVF) treatment. Their desire to bear a child has been strong, and their experiences with IVF treatment have so far been unsuccessful and painful. They are dealing with feelings of hopelessness, and the stress of treatments yielding negative results has been a strain on their marriage. They are seeking counseling to find support and to help them sort through their marital conflict. They are willing and able to express the feelings of emptiness they face as they fight against jealousy whenever anyone in their Bible study group shares their good news. Overall, Gabby and Dan simply feel left behind by God and his promises. They wonder why their prayers are going unanswered.

Gabby and Dan have expressed not only the expectations their families have placed on them to begin having children but their own timeline of life events. They feel they ought to have children and feel compelled to move on to the next stage of life because they have been diligent financially to prepare for the transition to parenthood.

In counseling, the focus of their sessions has been to get an update on the progress of treatments and to have an honest discussion with both of them in the room so they can process the impact of IVF on Gabby's body and the impact of receiving the injections. The sessions have been helpful in giving them the space to fully talk through expectations of treatment and the financial strain it is causing, which they both now understand to be a big trigger for their stress. Dan has become a source of emotional support for Gabby, rather than Gabby's feeling left alone. He is reassuring her that she is not a failure, that her body is not a failure. They have a couple more rounds of treatment to go and will evaluate whether they will seek more treatment or consider adoption.

Oftentimes, our clients become upset with the circumstances they have been given. Like Gabby and Dan, they might lose hope, they might feel regret, they might be angry. They might even blame God. Many of these feelings, as we know, come from a place of hurt and the pain they have had to carry.

In this chapter, we will talk about the gift of setting an intention. This practice can help our clients explore the situations they find themselves in and wish to get out of. Setting an intention means that they begin the process of surrender, and then hope again. Surrender comes first because clients must understand that life is not always what they hope or plan it to be. Fortunately, our clients are capable of holding the two truths—life is hard but there is hope—and finding in God the source of hope in difficult circumstances. For Gabby and Dan, the intention that they could set might be to find clarity in God's purposes. Another might be to find hope in God. Depending on the day, setting an intention means that we listen for God, that we hold our prayers and requests loosely so we can hear from him and gain hope.

Biblical Basis for Setting an Intention

Setting an intention of the day is encapsulated by the third verse of the Lord's Prayer: "Give us today our daily bread." An intention is the merging of goals with God's wisdom. It is not something to strive for but rather a prayer and hope. Christian mindfulness is about sitting in a learning, reflective stance at the feet of God. As Keating (1992) puts it, "Listening is a skill to deepen the relationship of the self to God contained in Christ, the Holy Spirit and God the Father." We listen to God before we set our intention. We allow him to search our hearts and minds and guide us in the path everlasting.

When we lead our clients through an inner search for God's voice, we ask them to approach themselves as fallible, with humility to learn and receive. In the following sections, we'll break down Jesus' words in Matthew 6:11, "Give us today our daily bread," to explore the concept of setting an intention.

Staying in the Today

It is a challenge for any of us to stay in the present moment, day by day, amid the hardscapes of life. We often look to our past in order to compare it with our present circumstances or future longings. For many of our clients, however, the past is a trauma they are trying to reconcile with their current experience. To lead our clients into a more present-oriented outlook, the place where healing can most effectively begin to take place, we need to arrive ourselves in a mental space that is current with our clients' needs.

We and our clients often look to the future in different ways as we age. If we are young, the future is usually full of hope and adventure and goals to be set. If we are in midlife, then the future is still open, but we realize now that we are limited by time. If we or our clients are much older, then the future no longer awaits us. We have only the present and the memories of our past.

Today is life. Life's paths are paved day by day, the patterns of our lives etched in our daily patterns. We know that our clients' mental health is best healed when they can grasp the challenges in bite-sized pieces, not trying to cram in too much. We know as therapists and counselors that change comes with consistency; intensity is overrated. As we walk our clients through mindfulness-based interventions, we always need to keep in mind the treatment goal. If our clients are struggling with depression, anxiety, or other mental health issues, the purpose of remaining in the present is to be able to do the therapy work with a less reactive response. When our clients retreat into defenses because the work we are guiding them to becomes difficult, it is important to ground them in what existentialist Dr. Irvin Yalom calls the here and now, because what comes about is a microcosm of what our clients experience outside of the therapy office (Yalom, 2020).

Receiving Our Daily Bread

Day by day, we as counselors and therapists are led by God to do his work. In our case, that is opening up our clients to managing their mental illnesses or family issues or past traumas. We offer and bring resolution or solution, insight and awareness, which lead, more often than we think, to healing and hope for them. In the safety of our presence, our clients can be emotionally held, then encouraged to venture out, applying the skills we teach and coach them through, into their real circumstances in their everyday relationships and in cultivating a healthy support system.

We as Christian counselors and therapists must first receive God's daily bread. It is our sustenance for the work we are called to do. We must be aware of God's gifts to us for our nourishment: body, mind, and soul. Our work with clients demands all those parts of us. We rely on our bodies: health, energy, stamina. We rely on our minds: focus, insight, awareness. We rely on our souls: dignity as a part of creation, lament, hope, deeper wells of empathy. So for us, "give us today our daily bread" is about asking God to give us sustenance just for today. Today is all we have to give to him. We receive from God his provision. Just as the Israelites could not hoard their manna, we must go to God each day. Yes, we must go to him even moment by moment. Receive from Jesus the daily bread that he gives out of his perfect, sinless example. Move forward in your work with the confidence that God is the giver of good gifts to all of us.

The Benefits of Setting an Intention for Clients

When we ask our clients to first set an intention for their time in Christian mindfulness, it is to help them let go of controlled responses, to open them up from a rigid mindset and into a place where they can be receptive. It is far from goal setting but keeps in mind clients' desires for improved mental health or well-being. There is a detached stance or outlook on goals themselves.

Intention setting can assist your counselees in evaluating where they want to land and how they want to deal with their present suffering. The mindset change is important here. Many of our counselees are victims or survivors, ones who can be empowered despite their histories. We might need to help them sort out what parts of themselves remain victimized, what parts are girded for survival, and what parts are prone to thrive while in the healing process or when healed. Setting an intention is one way to help them move toward thriving. That itself can be the intention.

Notes for Mental Health Professionals

Part of the counseling or therapeutic use of this part of the Lord's Prayer is to center clients' or counselees' thought patterns on the transcendent. Not to be stuck in an old, unsatisfying worldly pattern means that they give up toxic things or places or people and receive of God's goodness—his manna, his daily bread for life. In those moments in Christian mindfulness, when the lightbulbs go off and our clients realize what they truly need, they begin to live out and understand that wherever we go, there God is as the giver of daily bread, today, as he always has been and will be forevermore.

In the following sections, we'll explore aspects of setting an intention that we need to remember as we work with clients.

Lead with Prayer, Then Follow Your Client

Separate from a treatment-plan goal, intentions are a way to help our clients receive what they do not know, what they are not aware of consciously. Intentions are accessed not just cognitively but require an engagement at the soul level as well. As therapists and counselors, we might pray with our clients (with their permission) even before they set an intention: "Lord, we ask that you help set up the intention for our time together in counseling."

You can prompt the client by saying, "What would your intention be?" and again pray for your client by name: "Lord, help [client's name] be aware of the intention you would have us set for this time in therapy." After a short time in prayer, either silently or led by you, you can prompt your client to speak their intention to God. They might opt to share it and speak it aloud; others might just speak it to God. Either way is okay. It's important to reassure them that you hold no judgment as they speak their intention.

Some might set an intention of more peace, or relief from their anguish or suffering, or being in God's presence, or using time in therapy well. It could be none of these. Go with your client and begin where your client is. If your client states that they feel stuck, reassure them that this is normal. Remind them that it is not required to set an intention. You are simply opening up a couple of minutes for them to ponder what they might not usually have time or space for.

Work with Clients to Know and Receive from Our Giver

There are times when we and our clients—in our common humanity—struggle to receive from God. We ask God for peace and nourishment in our lives, but it is hard not to seize control or give up. Receiving God's daily bread is a practice of recognizing not only that Jesus is the only giver of daily bread but also that he is the master baker, so to speak, and we are not capable of rising until he kneads us into the shape he must make for his glory, kingdom, and promise. It is in the daily faithfulness of living into God's desires that makes the most difference. What can our clients let go of? What parts of their thinking are distorted and remain stuck in a pattern of unhealthy thinking that diminishes their need to relinquish control?

Or perhaps we must explore with our clients the secondary gains in a gentle, humble, Christlike manner to help them recognize that their seizing of power will lead only to more suffering, heartache, or destruction. The receiving of God's daily bread means that our clients work on making a plan for the day, just today, just this moment, that reaches into God's intention for their lives. This takes wisdom, patience, mindfulness.

Our clients must be tuned in to God and tuned out of the expectations of the world or of others. Receiving God's daily bread might be our clients' contemplating this verse when they wake up. No matter what happened yesterday, no matter whether they feel like peeling themselves out of bed when depressed, no matter the anxieties they might be dealing with, we can reassure them that, moment by moment, God is there.

He is the good giver, he is part of the "us" because he knew suffering—anguish, pain that is physical, mental, and spiritual. So he really knows what our clients need. We can encourage our clients that all they need to do is focus on receiving God's daily bread just for today. Maybe this moment, they relinquish, they open up their palms, they look up to the sky. They can say, "Give me today my daily bread, Lord." Support and encourage your client to live into the day in the fullness of what God may offer them. Help them sit in a receptive posture. Support their peace by helping them use their breath.

As counselors, therapists, and healing practitioners, not only should we model this type of "letting go and letting God" to our clients in our responses, our manner, our guidance, our way of keeping them on a safe and healthy path, but also we should live this out as well. It is a good practice for us to utilize in the everyday. The plan for our day is to support, empower, bring healing and hope, and help our clients break unhealthy patterns of thought and behavior. They may need medication to assist them in their healing. They may need to build healthy Christian mindfulness practices in their lives. They may need to step into or out of areas of their lives to support their mental wellness.

Contemplation Exercise

MATTHEW 6:11

As you begin this contemplation of Matthew 6:11, start with setting an intention for this time. This is not a goal but a chance to tell God what you need or what you hope to accomplish during this time. It can be something like, "I want to rest in your presence, God," or, "I would like to gain your peace," or even, "I need your perspective, Lord." Anything that comes from an honest place. Again, an intention is not a goal, it is simply a way to focus on your Christian mindfulness practice in God's presence.

As you move into a time of pondering Matthew 6:11, which begins "give us today," contemplate the verse using these questions: Who is the giver? Is it God? Think about who was a giver to you in the past. Was the giver one or both of your parents? Or was it someone else? Think about: What does God give? What did your parents or someone else give to you? If it was someone close to you, was the giver flawed? Did the gift have strings attached? Was it for ill or toxic reward? Contemplate: What is different, if anything, between what God gives you and what the person you identified gave you?

Sometimes "give" is loaded because it can have malevolent ends. In contrast, maybe you were given a lot of things, but not love, acceptance, or forgiveness, and you have ended up with a low self-concept based on what you did to perform rather than who you are or were to those givers. To know God as a giver may be different for you as a recipient of unconditional love and good gifts that come from a giver's heart.

After you have explored those earthly givers, think about the object of this verse: the ultimate, flawless one who gives. The verse is a prayer: "Give us." We need God to give to us. That is okay. He gives of himself on the cross, and he gives to you out of his perfect will and plan. Notice how this is a declarative statement to God. It is confident and bold: "Give us."

Next work on becoming aware of a short but perhaps complicated word in this part of the verse. Contemplate the "us" in "give us." Ask yourself, Who is "us"? Who would you like to include in "us"? How is "us" true or untrue in your life? Again, embrace the honesty of where you can begin, who is a part of your life, who is in your corner. Think about these folks. Even if you have not seen certain people lately, include them in the "us" as you sit with this part of the verse. If it's helpful, you can visualize in your mind who you are with in "us." If you are struggling with this or if it feels too difficult, simply go back to the intention you set at the beginning of this exercise. Return to the verse and read it aloud, seeing "us" as all those who read the Lord's Prayer. That is who the "us" relates to as well.

The next part of the verse is "today our daily bread." Today is the day for the work of counseling, therapy, the healing path. You can embrace the power of living in God's presence today. Sometimes, we take our days for granted. We know this because life is complex and difficult at times. A focus on today is not merely a way to absolve us from the labor of therapy or counseling; it is to provide space to expand on the way you tackle your counseling issue or mental health challenge. Daily life and the tasks, expectations, and tools for getting through each day can be burdensome when we look at all of the challenges ahead. It is best to tackle the complex by breaking it down into smaller pieces of the puzzles that can be dealt with only day by day, and just a bite size for today.

Honoring your intention at the beginning, process what today brings up for you as you think about the "today" part of the verse. What is the hope of today? What hope was not fulfilled? What is the prayer you think God is leading you to about "today"—in retrospect at the end of the day, or at the beginning of a new day? The learning stance of a simple concept such as "today" is what we're after. Today is full of promise or full of disappointment or something in between.

In the "daily bread" that Jesus speaks of, we know that in the Scriptures, God taught the Israelites dependence on him and his sustenance: "Then the LORD said to Moses, 'I will rain down bread from heaven for you. The people are to go out each day and gather enough for that day'" (Ex. 16:4). Contemplating the prayer of "give us today our daily bread" exposes the anxieties we face. When we grasp tightly to outcomes we cannot control, we've given in to the temptation of the anxiety of the day. Remember the impermanence of the daily bread, the fact that the manna will spoil if we hoard it.

The contemplation of "our daily bread" can serve us well, especially when we are tapped into the abundance of God's fullness of love expressed on the cross, rather than into our anxieties. We can ask these questions: Should God always give us what we need? What is the manna that God is calling us to gather into our lives for our nourishment and sustenance? We can help ourselves recognize those things that are finite, the things we need every day to thrive. As we contemplate "today our daily bread," we identify the meaning of the daily bread, the manna, that God calls us to gather for sustenance. Lamott (2018) says it so well: "The desperate drive to own and control in order to fill our psychic holes, relieve anxiety, fix difficulties, and cauterize old wounds takes root at an early age, and is doomed. It is like going to the hardware store for bread. It doesn't sell bread" (p. 36).

What Lamott drives home is the faulty drive to control. To end this exercise, sit in silence again, revisit in your mind what you set out as an intention in the beginning, and now reflect on what you have gained after the contemplation of this verse.

References for Chapter 6

Keating, T. (1992). *Open mind, open heart: The contemplative dimension of the gospel.* Amity House.

Lamott, A. (2018). *Almost everything: Notes on hope.* Riverhead.

Yalom, I. (with Lescz, M.). (2000). *The theory and practice of group psychotherapy* (4th ed.). Basic Books.

CHAPTER 7

Listening and Acceptance

And forgive us our debts,
as we also have forgiven our debtors.
—Matthew 6:12

Gene and Betsy are in their fourth decade of marriage. With Gene newly retired and the kids grown up, they face each other anew. Gone are the days when their kids were the focus of their lives. They are long past building careers and have saved enough to retire with a little left over. His retirement has been good in the sense that they now get to travel and enjoy gobs of time together. However, Betsy is feeling more withdrawn from Gene.

Three years ago, Gene and Betsy were in marital therapy after an affair was uncovered between Gene and Betsy's best friend. The marital therapy was helpful in healing their marriage and protecting Betsy from further betrayal. Betsy chose to stay with Gene because she became convinced that he was sorry for his actions and had conveyed an honest account of all that took place. Gene worked hard in therapy and made proper amends to Betsy, cutting off all contact with Betsy's best friend, and took thorough steps to protect their marriage after the betrayal. Each year when their wedding anniversary comes up, Betsy still struggles with memories of the betrayal and the loss of her best friend.

Betsy has been working on attending to her needs, learning that she is in charge of her own happiness and wellness. She is honest with Gene about his struggles. Thankfully, he is willing to continue to do the work with her and carries her feelings of betrayal with her. Betsy is in individual therapy in order to process the anguish that comes up each anniversary. She is moving forward, step by step.

Betsy and Gene had decades of a loving marriage, a partnership that Betsy felt safe in, and overall, she felt like she was blessed. She had a nice life until the rug was pulled out from under her. All of a sudden, Betsy questioned everything she knew about Gene and the husband she'd thought he was. She was not only floored but felt like a fool. Like Betsy, our clients come to see us because they feel like the rug has been pulled out from under them. They seek our counsel and help because they are confused, angry, in pain, and reeling. What they learn over time and through healing is that life can be unpredictable. The patterns we have set up, the relationships we have built, the way our lives are going are all tenuous. Some things are beyond us. Some things require God's mighty assistance. Forgiving is one of those painful, beyond us sort of things.

Many of our clients struggle with being unforgiven or not being able to forgive. The emotional damage from that unforgiveness can cause havoc. They might reenact abusive relationships, they might self-soothe through addictions, or they might self-isolate, so hurt that loneliness seems a better solution. Unfortunately, the weight of unforgiveness does not get lighter over time. Our clients stand at the precipice of their own undoing, and sometimes we are the only ones who know about this, the only ones they reach for. We are so lucky to be called to this difficult work to help them travel the road of forgiveness.

Sometimes the counseling room is a matter of life and death, metaphorically and literally. How do we help our clients choose the life that God promises, the actions and attitudes that we know will sustain them?

Sometimes our clients choose harm. There is a space, however, between forgiveness, life, and wholeness, and unforgiveness, darkness, and shattered pieces.

As we lead our clients toward wholeness, an essential component of Christian mindfulness that we can use is the practice of listening and, ultimately, acceptance. We'll explore this concept further in this chapter, relying on Matthew 6:12 as our guide: "And forgive us our debts, as we also have forgiven our debtors." For Betsy, forgiveness empowers her to make a choice: to stay in the marriage and focus on repairing her broken heart, or to leave the marriage and focus on repairing her broken heart. Either way, she has to carry the burden of Gene's betrayal. Either way, forgiveness is the ultimate end of acceptance.

The Biblical Basis for Listening and Acceptance

We know that our clients have taken a large step to seek us for counseling or therapy. Most people don't like to ask for help, and consequently, help will not come. James 4:2–3 says, "You do not have because you do not ask God. When you ask, you do not receive, because you ask with wrong motives, that you may spend what you get on your pleasures." Don't get us wrong, this is not a judgment against our clients or counselees. Rather, this verse offers a fair warning from a generous God who is the giver of good gifts—emphasis on good. The goodness we contemplate is about forgiveness—God's best, eternal gift of all. When we support our clients' forgiveness work, we free them to release trauma, pain, hurt, and stress. The daily burden of carrying that weight of unforgiveness becomes lighter.

"And forgive us our debts, as we also have forgiven our debtors." We all pray this portion of the Lord's Prayer, asking God to forgive our debts so that we can become free and clear to give of ourselves to others again. When our clients forgive, they let go of the anger, betrayal, pain, and deep regret that were visited upon them. If our clients have paid a price, they must learn to move their lives forward through forgiveness work. Otherwise they may remain stuck and stunted by pain and bitterness.

The Benefit of the Practice of Listening and Acceptance for Clients

Listening and acceptance, key components of forgiveness work, are no doubt a part of Christian mindfulness. In the following sections, we'll explore some key aspects of the practice of listening and acceptance and how this practice can benefit your clients.

The Necessity and Struggle of Forgiveness

In the space within, down deep, we know that unforgiveness is toxic. If we—our counselees and ourselves, because we are human too—ignore and decide not to pay attention to that knowing, we risk becoming toxic. We must bring the thought into our minds of the event where pain was involved. It is much easier to mindlessly compartmentalize such events, natural to avoid pain. So we must teach our clients to listen and attempt acceptance, repeatedly.

Christian mindfulness practice facilitates the work of forgiveness as identified in the fourth verse of the Lord's Prayer. Yet forgiveness is usually not the first step in healing. Menahem and Love (2013) use two case studies to delineate and then summarize how mindfulness and forgiveness work together. Although they speak from a Buddhist perspective, we can translate their work to a Christian foundation. Essentially, they note that counselors can help clients confront the offense and take perspective. Then they can begin the work of letting go, which is central to forgiveness. Eventually, resentment gives way to mindful awareness and empathy. Christian mindfulness then prepares the way toward forgiveness, makes clear that hard road, and then facilitates the work and ultimately allows the pain of forgiveness to be felt, held, and then, God willing, healed.

Listening and Forgiveness

Listening is a required skill when we need to forgive someone or be forgiven, or both. From a Christian mindfulness perspective, to listen is to take in, hear, and absorb the perspective of the other. Listening is active and aware. Not only that, but listening inside a deep soul space is where we let go of the ties that bind us to our past narratives. When we listen in Christian mindfulness, we promote a searching mind, and God's Word can help us correct any distortion of our value and worth.

Garland et al. (2015) emphasizes the important aspect of cognitive reappraisal that mindfulness in general promotes. When we practice mindfulness, our minds can clear away those schemas and narratives that can contribute to suffering. According to these researchers, when our clients experience high eudaimonic well-being, they are in a state in which they are reappraising, observing, and metacognitively aware. When we practice Christian mindfulness, we listen with our whole being: our thoughts are engaged with our soul values, our bodies are engaged to let go and to be in a calm state in which we can really take in information and observe our reactions to that information. This is what forgiveness work takes: observation of our own reactions.

When our clients are able to listen to their reactions—recoiling, resistance, or on the positive side, receptivity—to forgiveness, they can take a step back. They can enter a new space where they can see and acknowledge what happened, who was wronged, who was the perpetrator, what needs to be done, if anything, to repair, to seek restitution. Some of our clients might need to seek restitution themselves. Perhaps they contributed to the wrong and are the ones who need forgiveness. They might need to ask for restitution for past toxic behaviors, or worse, maybe they have paid a steep price for something done to them. Other clients need simply to choose forgiveness and not have any interaction with their abuser (a healthy and just choice) to loosen the chains of sins that keep them down.

Forgiveness work requires listening. This listening helps our clients calm their minds, decipher what is needed so they can make good judgments as to how to forgive and whether forgiveness means moving on from the past completely. These difficult and complex judgments required for forgiveness work can really only be sorted out in a calm, thinking, and analytical mindset. The Christian mindfulness practice that involves listening helps to calm our counselees' heart rates and decreases fight, flight, or freeze responses. Porges (2017) explains that our nervous system craves reciprocal interaction and that we all, as humans, regulate each other's phys-iological states to help each other feel safe (p. 99). Therefore, deep listening that promotes safety, that provides this calm or peace, occurs in the context of relationship. And so why not with the center of relationship in Christian mindfulness: God in Christ, who regulates us the most, who can calm the roaring waves? Christ is the source of deep listening. He promises to coreg-ulate with our clients, and with us, altogether.

Acceptance of What Is Fleeting

Listening to and leaning on Christ also helps promote acceptance, a key Christian mindfulness aspect. In mindfulness derived from Buddhism, acceptance is about realizing the impermanence of all things. This acceptance is a key change mechanism for clients when intervening in mindfulness-based therapies—in particular, in acceptance and commit-ment therapy, and in dialectical behavioral therapy. The Taoists call this posture of awareness *wu wei*, roughly translated as "nondoing, not forcing, letting things be just as they are" (Watts & Huang, 1975). *Wu wei* is a kind of acceptance that can find an easy path, a calming path, right in the middle of suffering. In mindfulness, generally, the concept of acceptance is rooted in the idea of impermanence.

As Christians, we understand that on this side of heaven, things will not always be what we hope they will be. Even good things are fleeting. And nothing on earth lasts, so life is impermanent. However, there is also permanence in Christ. For the Christian counselor, therapist, and healer, acceptance is undergirded by the way God sees us, and how we can under-stand ourselves in light of that eternal perspective. We are accepted by God, despite our sinfulness. "There is no one righteous, not even one" (Rom. 3:10). There is a permanence to our sinful state in life on earth. Therefore, forgiveness comes when we knowingly accept the frailty and limits of our-selves and our world. Acceptance is not to obfuscate problems, to gaslight people's hurt or pain, but is to understand the role of suffering during life.

Our clients are impacted by their mental health, by their stressors, by their circumstances. These are all hard to accept, understandably so.

However, acceptance is a step toward growth and healing because our clients learn where the starting point is. When our clients cannot or do not accept their emotional states or troubles—when they are in denial—they perpetuate their conditions. In the context of relationship, our clients' lack of acceptance of what is ruptured and of what is needed in forgiveness work continues the ruptures. Repairing those ruptures for our clients means they need to work on accepting where they fall short. Or they must come face to face with past ruptures that are disturbing. Abuse and trauma are all too often many of our counselees' sources of emotional pain and injury, which feel all too permanent to them.

The path toward wholeness and survivorhood from abuse and trauma is still paved in a costly forgiveness that required the death of our savior. Those shipwrecks in their living memories can be hoisted to shore, toward safety, with God's help. Instead of drowning, our clients can swim confidently into the depths of God's grace and love. In forgiveness work, waves of peace will wash them anew.

Therefore, forgiveness is not a subtle and powerless act. When we navigate forgiveness work to assist our clients toward healing, we must comprehend the injustice that was and is the cost. We can help them hold these truths deep in their souls, minds, and bodies for God's healing to emerge. Acceptance is the way to loosen the tightness of the emotional pain that sits deep within the structures of the mind and soul, and where the pain is stored in their bodies. Clients can breathe in acceptance and cry out because of its cost.

To work on acceptance also means that the vicissitudes of our counselees' feelings, emotions, and reactions are anchored in what they think they can accept, right now. For example, a lot of the foundational conceptual work of mindfulness in secular spaces has been because of Dr. Jon Kabat-Zinn's mindfulness-based stress reduction (MBSR) intervention with patients who experience chronic pain. Kabat-Zinn's patients could tolerate their pain better, even experienced it differently, because they were in a mindful state: aware of their bodies, focused in their minds. Their pain tolerance increased, thereby decreasing the experience of pain (Trammel, 2017).

The difference for us Christians is that acceptance is also soul work. It means our clients can tolerate their present sufferings a bit better because they know that God is at work with them. (We want to make it clear here that abuse and trauma should not be tolerated as a normal part of our counselees' lives. Their safety matters. We must follow our professional and lawful responsibilities. Acceptance never means being all right with breaking the law or with placing someone or keeping someone in harm's way. These are violations of our ethical and professional responsibilities.) A healthy acceptance is the beginning. Peter first has to accept that Jesus' walking on water is real, that the crashing waves are nothing to God. So he steps out of the boat in faith, but the winds howl and he becomes unsure (Matt. 14:22–33). For our clients, acceptance is the faith part: yes, there is a threat, the suffering is real, yet that is the beginning; they can learn to walk on water. Our clients practice acceptance within the context of the reality of life. This does not mean they have to lower their expectations or maintain average or mediocre results in therapy. It simply means, that, yes, there are pains in life. We all live anyway. We all can thrive anyway. Awareness is not forced. It emerges in God's presence, even amid the violent waves and howling winds. And those waves and winds of our pain are fleeting. Ultimately, as our clients build acceptance, they see the healing taking place.

Our clients truly are capable of observing, accepting, seeing their feelings, emotions, and reactions change—with help and support, and in the loving, compassionate arms of Christ. When our counselees' reserves are full, because of God's grace and salvation, they are more able to forgive in a way that releases sorrow, pain, and the shame they have suffered. The Christian mindfulness part of acceptance is to help our clients realize they cannot escape his grace, no matter what, because wherever they go, there God is.

Notes for Mental Health Professionals

Listening takes focus and time. However, with practice, listening comes more easily. Building listening space is important throughout the day, because it is a time for us to check in with ourselves and our work. In that time, we can explore how our clients are impacting us mentally, physically, spiritually. So try the practices sprinkled throughout this book, which are meant for you as well so that you can help clients on the Christian mindfulness path. For refreshment and realization, sitting and listening time for you or your clients won't go to waste. We do a lot of listening in our work, which is wonderful. The stories and lives we get to be a part of are valuable and important. As we know, listening is about hearing a different perspective and reflecting empathy and compassion. Many of us are trained well in active listening. However, we need to remember that the skills that come easily to us because of our training are not as accessible to our clients, just because they are not as practiced.

As we hear our clients' stories, we can be impacted. We also can lean on God while our clients lean into the state of knowing Jesus. As God coregulates us, we can then be peaceful listening coregulators for our counselees. God remains present and available to all of us. Even when we are not listening, the Spirit hears what we all really need in the counseling and therapy room. The Spirit understands where our clients are most helpless and hopeless. Sometimes our clients can access their deepest needs when they have spent time listening. Otherwise, only the noisiest needs, like the squeaky wheel, get the attention. Listening more deeply, tuning in to the Spirit of God's leading helps us know where to listen more deeply. When our clients understand that we are listening not just to their present needs but to their deeper ones as well, they feel understood and heard all the more.

Contemplation Exercise

MATTHEW 6:12

This contemplation is geared toward a client who needs forgiveness or needs to forgive someone as part of their therapeutic work.

Begin in a still space, seated, perhaps with eyes closed, hands in your lap, focused on your breathing. Let's start this contemplation with "and forgive us." Notice that there is an "us," that Jesus is asking all of us to pray because we all need forgiveness. So breathe in this truth that you are not alone. Your neediness, your weakness, your sinfulness: acknowledge them in the stillness. Work on accepting this reality. Realize you are not alone in it, even in the emotional weight of having someone to forgive. Breathe in and out three strong breaths. With each breath, accept the need of forgiveness. Feel free to speak it aloud. Ask of God for yourself and for others: "Forgive us."

Meditate for a few more minutes. Picture God's hands reaching down, lifting your face to him. Note any emotions you feel, anything that rises, not forcing anything to lift up that isn't there. Listen either way. Innately, you will know him, the Great Shepherd. Listen internally for his voice of forgiveness, granted by his hard-fought grace.

Move on to the next part of that phrase, "our debts," our sinful behaviors and actions. Note them in your mind now. Observe them and delineate with the Holy Spirit's help whether they are guilt still requiring God's mercy, or absolved sin, absolved guilt. Shame will dissipate when we intellectually grasp with soulful awareness that our guilt is paid for. What mistakes are you ashamed of? Process them, observe them in the stillness of this space.

Last, think about the end of this verse, which is often the hardest: "as we also have forgiven our debtors." For this part of the verse, incorporate some movement. We use our bodies in Christian mindfulness because we believe that as holistic beings, our bodies, minds, and souls are not separate entities but can feed back to each other. Because forgiveness sometimes can be difficult, working through movement can be helpful. Try the following movement along with a slow reading of "as we also have forgiven our debtors" circulating in your mind.

MINDFUL MOVEMENT OF LETTING GO

Try this mindful breath and movement exercise with me: First, stand in a comfortable position with eyes closed, focusing your mind on the last part of the verse: "as we also have forgiven our debtors."

Breathe in—a big, deep inhalation. Breathe that breath into your whole body. Let it travel as you exhale. Breathe in and out again.

Next fold your hands in the prayer position and move them in to the center of your chest, toward your heart. Breathe in while you take into your heart Christ's forgiveness.

Breathe out. On the exhalation, move your hands and sweep them out, palms facing up.

Imagine letting go. Picture all of the emotions of unforgiveness releasing from your hands. It's hard. We want to hold on to past pain, past hurt. People should pay for their wrongs. Of course they should. But why hold on? Breathe in and out again while repeating in your heart three times (or as many times as you need) "as we also have forgiven our debtors." Each time, go deeper into the phrase. Inhale and place your hands in the prayer position. On the exhalation, sweep your hands out while saying "as we also have forgiven our debtors." Breathe in again and think about what else you need to do in this moment in order to forgive. Notice how and when your breath, body, and mind come together. Note where your mind goes, the thoughts that come up as you breathe in and breathe out while moving your hands in this way.

Now sit down. Take another breath and lay your hands on your lap. Sit still and just work now in your mind, with your body symbolizing your work in releasing. If it's helpful, with your hands on your lap, slowly clench your fists while acknowledging any anger or tension you have as you think about this forgiveness work. What is it that you cannot accept about this situation? Clench your hands on this thought. Now unclench your fists, release the anguish you may be carrying. Try it again, as you clench your fists in your lap, acknowledge your hurt or pain. As you unclench, let these intense feelings go, asking God to replace them because they have taken so much space in your mind, body, and soul. Breathe in and out again.

Release it all to him with your body and mind. Release your grip and give God space to reign in your heart, in your spirit, in your mind. Again, from your lap, sweep your hands out from your body, extend your arms, palms up as you exhale. Put your whole mind and body into it. It's a confession to our savior. Say in your mind on the exhalation, "Lord, it's hard to forgive. I'm working on it. I accept that this is where I am." Sweep your hands out, palms up to the heavens. Release all the ick, shame, or trauma of that interaction in your mind or of that situation that you experienced. Let Christ take it.

Now move into listening, acceptance of God's grace. Receive his grace. We bow to his will and his way. It is beautiful when he responds and takes our putrid messes. He cleans us up. He wipes up the ick. He releases his aroma. We can breathe with the words enveloping us again, "forgive us our debts, as we also have forgiven our debtors."

References for Chapter 7

Garland, E. L., Farb, N. A., Goldin, P. R., & Fredrickson, B. L. (2015). Mindfulness broadens awareness and builds eudaimonic meaning: A process model of mindful positive emotion regulation. *Psychological Inquiry, 26*(4), 293–314. https://doi.org/10.1080/1047840X.2015.1064294

Menahem, S., & Love, M. (2013). Forgiveness in psychotherapy: The key to healing. *Journal of Clinical Psychology, 69*(8), 829–835. https://doi.org/10.1002/jclp.22018

Porges, S. W. (2017). *The pocket guide to the polyvagal theory: The transformative power of feeling safe.* Norton.

Trammel, R. C. (2017). Tracing the roots of mindfulness: Transcendence in Buddhism and Christianity. *Journal of Religion & Spirituality in Social Work, 36*(3), 367–383. https://doi.org/10.1080/15426432.2017.1295822

Watts, A., & Huang, A. C. (1975). *Tao: The watercourse way.* Pantheon.

CHAPTER 8

Equanimity and Subtle Temptations

And lead us not into temptation,
but deliver us from the evil one.
—MATTHEW 6:13

Vincent has been serving as a pastor for more than twenty years. Lately, he has been battling insomnia and his schedule has been more demanding, a reflection of the numerical growth of his congregation. He often has back-to-back appointments with his congregants every day of the week. He has been working this kind of schedule for more than a decade now. However, he's noticed that he looks forward to a particular congregant's meetings with him. She comes to him for spiritual direction and care, but he relies on her for an emotional uplift and feels refreshed and called again to his work. It's as if she reminds him of why he keeps pastoring.

Vincent begins to think about her outside of work, which leaves him feeling guilty and ashamed. Aware of his growing fondness toward his congregant, he has wisely sought counsel from a trusted professional outside of his congregation, someone he already has been seeing to help him work through the stresses of his pastoral work. He knows this job is difficult and realizes the toll it takes on his emotional well-being and the impacts of the stresses of pastoral work on his family.

Over the course of counseling, Vincent begins to understand that he is human and that these feelings of attraction are natural, but need to be dealt with. To act on them would be detrimental on all levels: guilt, shame, and betrayal would wreak havoc on both his and her lives and families. In counseling, Vincent names his temptation and the emotional hook that has developed. He is developing the noticing skills he has lacked and has linked his feelings to emotional gaps that come from his family of origin issues. He is able to observe himself without shame or judgment, but with equanimity, so that he can be unhooked from the intensity of his feelings, particularly for this congregant. He learns the skills of curiosity and empathy as antidotes to his feelings of attraction. Instead of seeking a thrilling escape, he tunes in to the subtle shifts of mood and attends them in a self-caring way. He understands that he has built up a fantasy in his head as an escape.

Like Vincent, many of us and our clients face situations in which there are ethical issues and challenges to our values and, ultimately, to our walk with Christ. What is it with our fallen nature's propensity toward sin? So many of us have experienced that seemingly irresistible pull of temptation, or know someone like Vincent who has. It's like the hymnist writes: "Prone to wander, Lord, I feel it, prone to leave the God I love; here's my heart, O take and seal it; seal it for thy courts above." We wander away from our God daily, hourly, every second of every day. Our wandering hearts and minds are embedded in our sin nature. Some days we feel invincible, forgetting that God reigns, believing instead that we are the creators of our own universes. Those temptations that reveal themselves in our deep and hidden intentions are more obvious to spot. We then have a choice—give in or get them out, which can be easier said than done. Acknowledging that we are often willing to trade God's luxurious gifts of a holy and fulfilling life for a shoddy imitation is a fact of our sinful nature.

However, those subtle cues, when emotions follow the thoughts that crisscross our minds, are often hidden and tricky. Behind complicated emotions and attachments are excitement, titillation, pride, or rebellion. These feelings can be intense and can feel so right. They make us human but also make us forget the responsibilities and callings that God has set before us. As therapists, counselors, and healing practitioners, we are folks whom clients lean on to develop insight and awareness. Our clients pay some of us good money to excavate hidden emotions, motives, and behaviors in order to heal.

In the research literature, equanimity is likened to decoupling emotion from hedonic pleasure. It is an emotional state in which acceptance is fostered and emotions are not tied to what we Christians would consider to be temptations (hedonic pleasures) (Hadash et al., 2016). We would argue that the practice of equanimity is an essential part of Christian mindfulness. For the Christian, equanimity means to understand that all states of emotion—high ones and low ones alike—eventually decrease in intensity. Equanimity also means that we can stay in a stable place emotionally and spiritually in the face of challenges with some resolve or intention.

We can equip our clients with strategies to help them gain equanimity. For instance, we can show them how to step back from intensity instead of embracing it. Or we can encourage our counselees to recall when they have faced similar challenges and have been able to maintain equanimity. Perhaps it was during times when they did not feel challenged. Other times, clients may talk about their feelings as being disproportionate to the stressor. In Christian mindfulness, we begin in acceptance of where our clients are and then help them build to a place where they can find glimpses of feeling steady, even amid suffering.

Biblical Basis for Equanimity

In the Bible, Christ personifies equanimity when he faces temptation in the desert (Matt. 4:1–11; Mark 1:12–13; Luke 4:1–13). In the accounts of his temptation, we observe that Satan commands Jesus. Each time, Jesus responds with truth contained in Scripture. In Matthew 4:10, Jesus tells Satan to leave him and quotes the verse, "Worship the Lord your God, and serve him only." There is great strength and resolve in equanimity. The biblical foundation of equanimity in the face of great temptation repudiates a dispassionate, passive, and zenlike detachment.

Christ faces temptation head on, but without giving Satan any wiggle room. Scripture is antidote. Resolve requires a steady faith, and emotions are not necessarily tamed but rather funneled by the truth of God's Word. Equanimity, therefore, is an emotional state that is informed by scriptural truth. We neither have to give in to temptation, as Jesus modeled, nor ignore it. Christ was not in denial of the effects of temptation. In Matthew 4:11, we note that afterward, "the devil left him, and angels came and attended him." Even Christ needed attending to. So must we lean in to Christ to attend to us, to restore us after we have faced temptation, and return to the fifth verse of the Lord's Prayer: "And lead us not into temptation, but deliver us from the evil one" (Matt. 6:13). Part of God's delivery system is for us to look at temptation with scriptural truth. We do not allow our emotions to determine our behaviors in the face of temptation. We steady them. We find equanimity in Christ's wisdom and grace and his words for us. We embrace with equanimity a knowing stance: that if Christ faced temptation, we will too, and our resolve to face temptation means that we move forward through it, not deny or detach or be surprised when it comes.

The Benefits of Equanimity for Clients

As Christians, we know that emotions are part of our normal biology and psyche. Facing challenges with equanimity does not mean that we should help our clients to be in denial, or minimize our clients' troubles or suffering. In Vincent's case, denial would only further keep him blinded, not resolved to face temptation as Jesus did. There is no room for toxic positivity that equates any kind of intense negative feelings—depression, anxiety, and so on—with a lack of faith. Toxic positivity brings more harm, not help, to our clients, who likely already feel shame over not being able to make themselves feel better or finding themselves in tempting situations. Toxic positivity is more a function of denial than of facing the facts of a situation.

If emotions were a choice, who would choose to be depressed, anxious, traumatized? Equanimity, in the context of Christian mindfulness practice, means that we help our clients practice stabilizing their emotions by not putting too much stake in them. We take emotions seriously, but we help them understand that emotions fluctuate naturally. If we can help them get those fluctuations to be more manageable, then our counselees will feel relief. We understand that with equanimity, our clients can make better decisions that will provide a pathway toward acceptance and healing. More stability in mood and the lessening of the intensity of ups and downs amid stressors is to be celebrated. In the following sections, we'll explore further some key ideas on the subject of equanimity.

Empathy and Equanimity

Empathy coincides with the idea of equanimity. As Christians, we often relate temptation to the idea of God's judgment. In Christian mindfulness, we allow God the room to judge our feelings and fluctuations, and embrace that God has made us as emotional beings—that he understands emotions because he created them. Equanimity in practice means that our clients can take a step back from their emotions because they have empathy for themselves. This is important because our clients need to see their thoughts, attitudes, and potential actions through a more objective lens. High emotions, high emotional fluctuations, color that ability to be self-aware.

We, our clients, and all humans are less triggered when we can be honest with ourselves without shame. Empathy is the vehicle to this honesty. Oftentimes, clients who have wild emotional fluctuations are told that they are out of control, and others try to control them because their emotional output is uncomfortable to watch. However, when we can provide a safe, caring space for our clients, and they can tune in to the unconditional acceptance of who they are in Christ, equanimity flows naturally.

We give God the power to speak truth into our clients' intentions while we help them cultivate equanimity.

Equanimity is not the dulling of emotions, either. It is simply zooming out of the high intensity. Equanimity means our clients are driven more toward compassion and can honestly evaluate themselves—their motives, desires, temptations—more accurately. In Christian mindfulness, we encourage our clients to approach God confidently, because he is the creator of emotions. God is much bigger than any human emotion, and awareness of his presence can help shift our counselees' fluctuations, because they do not have to be alone in them.

What can feel paradoxical is that it is not by avoidance that our clients can achieve equanimity. Rather, it is a movement toward the thoughts and feelings that might be triggering the dysregulated emotions. When faced in the moment, what felt so intense may pass. We help our counselees and clients recognize that they are not their feelings and that they can return to center by not putting too much stock in their emotions. Clients who are practicing mindfulness notice, even during a confusing storm of emotions, what parts of their feelings begin to dissipate a little bit and then a little bit more in the next moment, and so on.

However, in Christian mindfulness, we help our counselees face themselves head on, even when it feels intense, but doing it with empathy. We do this by helping our clients acknowledge that their feelings, even the intense ones, are not the whole truth. It is important we do not explain away strong emotions, that we link them to our counselees' stories and histories and help them recognize their pain and frustration. Empathy leads to equanimity.

Likewise, in Christian mindfulness, we offer our clients compassion for their feelings, but we do not take too much stock in them. We help our clients remain skeptical of their emotional ups and downs, helping them to reach into the wisdom of what their emotions are telling them. We help our clients put into words what they are feeling, thinking, believing. We model a nonreactive stance, an equanimity, when asking God for his peace, calming the body's reaction through breath work and helping our clients quiet their minds. All of this engagement can work toward equanimity. A loving, nonjudgmental space fosters this movement out of intensity, decentering the importance our clients have placed on their emotions to tell them the truth.

If we can help our clients name their emotions, help them to sift through them while using breath as an anchoring point, we enhance their resilience to emotional fluctuations. A good visual analogy is of a tall palm tree in gale-force winds. Instead of snapping, the agile trunk of a palm tree bends with the wind. As our clients lean into their emotions, owning them, naming them, and observing them one by one, they bend with each one, instead of breaking.

Tuning In to Subtle Emotions

On the other hand, clients can be so disconnected from their emotions that they might not even be aware of what is happening underneath the surface. Excavating hidden emotions requires our clients to slow down and create the space within that God uses to reveal his help. We, as therapists and counselors, need God's tools so that we can dig deep to assist our clients when dealing with complex situations or relationships, or even complicated feelings and motivations that they are unaware of. These kinds of temptations can be overwhelming and sensitive, so they're easy to avoid. They can also be seductive and make our clients question God's faithfulness and challenge their values and even their very selves. But God knows each one we serve in the counseling room better than that. He knows them better than they know themselves: "Indeed, the very hairs of your head are all numbered. Don't be afraid; you are worth more than many sparrows" (Luke 12:7).

In Christian mindfulness, metacognitive awareness of your clients' thoughts helps them identify patterns and hidden roots of the emotions or motives that trip them up. Hanley, Garland, and Black (2014) describe an important difference between state mindfulness and trait mindfulness. State mindfulness is the action of attentive, nonjudgmental awareness that allows for metacognitive observation of thoughts. Trait mindfulness is the ability to exhibit nonjudgmental awareness and attend to the present moment in everyday experiences. The importance of this distinction is that state mindfulness allows us to broaden our attention to attend to hidden emotions and motives. Though these researchers address this ability as important to understand our own narratives and stories, ultimately we pay attention to state mindfulness while we are in session. The purpose of watching for state mindfulness is to help our clients become aware of what they tell themselves so that they can practice disrupting those internalized scripts. For Christian mindfulness practitioners, that means mindfulness meditation in the Christian stream allows our clients to challenge their temptations, recognizing not only the stories but the motives in their thought lives. This ability to track state mindfulness in session with our clients leads to the development of Christian mindfulness as a practice they can hone outside of session.

Curiosity and Subtlety

Curiosity is the driver of Christian mindfulness and helps our counselees observe their thoughts in the moment with a dispassion and an objectivity that strengthens their ability to find a path away from sin and self-destruction. This time of interior curiosity and searching pulls back the curtain from their inner motives. When the interior of our emotional lives becomes conscious rather than hidden, our illicit cravings dissipate.

Metacognitive awareness, or self-awareness, is the outcome of Christian mindfulness practice. Curiosity about the self is developed. We help our clients to be curious about their reactions, to stop themselves and say, "I'm curious about how I'm reacting," which moves them into an investigative response. Again, Christian mindfulness allows for nonjudgment because they can hold off until they sense God's presence with them. This curious watchfulness is not wasted on judgment but rather is a gentle nudge toward healthier and more holy living, an assent to God's purpose, his lesson, rather than one's own. Whether or not they are Christ followers, our clients will experience benefits in their psyche and soul when they can view themselves objectively, watchfully. To accept that they are both saint and sinner and to take steps toward healthier choices demands watchfulness.

Now they have the tools to forego temptation and understand that when they face temptation, wherever they go, there God is, so they do not have to face it alone.

Notes for Mental Health Professionals

In our work with clients and counselees, the tools of Christian mindfulness can help improve equanimity in their lives. Whether a temptation is subtle or strong, naming the emotion behind it helps our clients find strength in equanimity.

We can empower our clients by utilizing a desensitization technique that focuses attention away from temptation and moves them toward God. In Vincent's case, working with him might go like this: "Vincent, can you imagine for a minute that you are in a situation of being drawn to that congregant? With eyes closed and slowed breathing, let's talk about what it is about that fantasy that is drawing you in. With slow, deep breaths, tell me what you observe about how you feel in those moments. Picture it like a movie scene if you can. Now zoom out a bit as if you are watching yourself like the director of a movie would. As your scene with the congregant plays out, note any strong feelings and note any subtle ones. Put words to your desires in that moment." In this example, having Vincent name the feelings helps point him to his ultimate desire—perhaps, for example, feeling wanted again, feeling alive, feeling desired.

Continuing to work with Vincent in this way helps him understand how normal these feelings are and also how fleeting, especially if he were to lean into them behaviorally. Equanimity in this situation will help Vincent to let go, mourn the fantasy, and equip him for reality, where Christ is at work in and through him.

Having said this, there are certain mental health conditions that drive strong emotions, such as mood disorders, including bipolar disorders as well as Cluster B personality disorders. All of these have symptoms of emotional dysregulation of such an intensity that prevent clients from a curious stance toward their thoughts. Those mental health issues need to be the focus of treatment before you attempt to lead your clients through exercises of equanimity. When your clients are stabilized, then isolating subtle emotions and helping them find balance in their feelings will be more appropriate.

Contemplation Exercise

Matthew 6:13

Our subtle feelings are the most difficult to pinpoint. They are reflections of both subconscious and unconscious longings that psychoanalysts might describe as either our most innate longings or destructive impulses. Begin with sitting and breathing deeply a few times. Work on contemplation of the first part of this verse: "and lead us not into temptation." This is an unusual verse to fold into a mindfulness practice, but try it nonetheless and see what comes up for you.

The verse is an action, but stated as a negative: "and lead us not into temptation." It is a prayer asking God to help us refrain. The "not" part is interesting. Sit for another minute and contemplate "the lead us not" part of the verse. How does God usually lead you?

Take another minute and just sit in this space and contemplate the concept of temptation. Stay curious about your temptations. Step back with empathy and compassion, and in the quiet space, unpack why you think these temptations come up for you. When do they come up the most? What purposes have these temptations served for you? Ask God to help you right now in this quiet time.

What has been the outcome in the past as you have been led into temptation? This is not the time to sit in guilt and shame, but it is a time to sit in equanimity and evenness. In your mind, face the challenge of past temptations and receive God's correction and grace with a sense of control. If this is difficult at this time, that is all right. Move on to the next section and come back to this step. Simply jot down or note in your mind any desire to return to this idea. Identify what you might need to prepare yourself for should you come back to this contemplation.

Now let's move to the present moment, remembering that we are empowered the most to make positive changes in the present. Start with the simple three-breath practice first. Breathe and let your mind attune to your breath. Then with eyes closed and mind focused, name the temptations you are facing. Don't look to the past. Be honest with yourself. Are your temptations in the realm of sexuality, food, work, relationship, addiction, neglect, restriction, control? Inhale the first part of this verse, "and lead us not," and on your exhalation, pray out "into temptation." Do this again so that your rhythm of breath and prayer are aligned. Inhale and exhale. Try doing this at least three times. Relax your muscles as you exhale, and in your mind, commit the whole part of the verse as a prayer to God: "and lead us not into temptation." Embrace any confirmation of this prayer in your soul, heart, or mind, and sit in grace and in gratitude that God hears you.

Next let's take the second part of the verse: "but deliver us from the evil one." Let's acknowledge that evil exists. We do not have to meditate on the evil and pain and suffering that come with acts of evil that we hear about or witness. But it is important to acknowledge that evil exists. However, even more important is the Lord's protection and salvation that are offered because of Christ's death on the cross and his resurrection. We are a redeemed people, and by his blood we are healed.

> But he was pierced for our transgressions,
> he was crushed for our iniquities;
> the punishment that brought us peace was on him,
> and by his wounds we are healed.
>
> —ISAIAH 53:5

Identify any difficult thoughts about temptation or evil. Approach any associated emotions with evenness, equanimity, and the calm presence of Christ, your savior. Observe your thoughts and bring them back to the phrase "and deliver us from the evil one." Again, it is important to identify and name the things that we need deliverance from. Our mental health wellness is tied to mind, body, *and* soul work. Some days we can focus just on the mind part. Some days, the body part. Some days, the soul part. This integration of our full selves is the way we can consider how God might be supporting, speaking to, and delivering us. Sit in awareness of your thoughts and any sensations in your body. Where does our deliverance come from? Christ can soothe those tight places that you might notice in your muscles as a result of the stress of temptations.

The sensorimotor learning of mindfulness is also a place to recognize subtle temptation. Identify in your mind any emotional hooks that lead to unexpected emotional attachments. Perhaps you might be aware of an emotional hook toward someone you find attractive and feel drawn to. Perhaps it's someone or something that has helped you cope in the past, but that relationship should stay in the past. What are red flags that you must not ignore, and that you cannot ignore if you are God's person? When inappropriate emotional hooks or attachments are left to their own devices, down the road, full-blown sin can erupt. These hooks might not be romantic entanglements but other forms of temptation such as ego, pride, and greed. Lord, deliver us. To close out this time, simply breathe again and speak the verse in your heart to God. Inhale "lead us not into temptation," and exhale "but deliver us from the evil one."

References for Chapter 8

Hadash, Y., Segev, N., Tanay, G., Goldstein, P., & Bernstein, A. (2016). The decoupling model of equanimity: Theory, measurement, and test in a mindfulness intervention. *Mindfulness, 7*(5), 1214–1226. https://doi.org/10.1007/s12671-016-0564-2

Hanley, A., Garland, E. L., & Black, D. S. (2014). Use of mindful reappraisal coping among meditation practitioners. *Journal of Clinical Psychology, 70*(3), 294–301. https://doi.org/10.1002/jclp.22023

PART 3

ATTITUDES AND SITUATIONS IN NEED OF CHRISTIAN MINDFULNESS

In part 3, we will focus on ways we can help our clients apply Christian mindfulness to the following important areas of life: relationships, societal issues, work, ministry and leadership, health, and attitudes in general.

We introduce each chapter with a passage of Scripture to contemplate, and follow with contemplation prompts for clients. We then describe and review some basic concepts that will help clients organize their thinking in this important area of their lives.

We also offer exercises in each chapter. These exercises are built for you to use with clients or to adapt as you see fit. Think of them as templates to personalize for the clients you feel will benefit from them.

Finally, each chapter ends with questions for reflection that you can use as prompts for your clients' journal entries or for deeper discussions with you during your next meeting or session.

Again, our hope is that this section can further the Christian mindfulness practice for you and your clients and help prompt reflection and discussion to move your therapeutic interventions along. We know that the practice of Christian mindfulness will set your counselees up for connection with God. As they relate to God, the benefits of that relationship will extend to their interaction with others at home, in the workplace, in their ministries, and so on. We also know that Christian mindfulness practice will enhance client functioning because it promotes inner healing work that comes from Jesus, and that healing will flow outward into their lives. They will learn to self-regulate and to have for themselves and for others a compassion that is grounded in faith.

May God grant you favor in your work with your clients, and may he continue to heal as only he can, to empower our clients to live according to his will and ways, and to give them courage and strength to do so.

CHAPTER 9

Mindfulness in Marriage and Parenting

A new command I give you: Love one another. As I have loved you, so you must love one another. By this everyone will know that you are my disciples, if you love one another.

—JOHN 13:34–35

Contemplation Prompts for Clients

JOHN 13:34–35

- How is this a new command God gives? (What was it before?)
- How has God loved us?
- How has God's love informed you as to how to love others?
- How does your love for others show up in your life?

Marriage and Intimacy

Christian mindfulness practice can enhance the way our clients attend to their marriage partners in conversation, creating better emotional and sexual intimacy. In marriage, clients often neglect the communication skills that help them improve their bond, the quality of marriage, and the quality of life within marriage. Christian mindfulness is about loving well through communication.

A fruitful Christian mindfulness practice begins with listening to God. When we listen, we access our whole capacity for love and can experience more openness to give and to serve others. We are filled with God's love first. When God takes care of us and we are at peace and our emotions are calm, we can love better. And love is the ultimate goal of the Christian life, as stated in John 13:34–35.

We must learn to love better through listening. When we do, we connect with the whole person as well as ourselves.

Conflict and Christian Mindfulness

Sometimes our clients need to understand how their spouses are interpreting and processing conflict. Behind each conflict is disappointment or hope or fear or anger that needs working through. Providing a nonjudgmental talking and thinking space allows both parties to feel supported and also creates an opportunity for the spouses to work together toward solutions, in love. The following is a template for a Christian mindfulness practice you can have your clients use to help them work through arguments, preferably before their next argument.

Christian Mindfulness for Conflict Preparation

To reduce intensity and to help you self-regulate, it is a good practice to ask for time to come back to the argument. Arguments heat up quickly, and our rational side dissipates in favor of our more carnal fight response. At the height of the argument, when the intensity becomes toxic, take a beat and breathe. Make sure your spouse gets to say what they need to at first. Listen, but don't absorb. Try to step back.

Here are a few steps based on Christian mindfulness practices to help you attain emotional regulation when you find yourself in a conflict:

1. Take a deep breath and observe your thoughts as you listen to your loved one. What are you hearing? Tune in, even when the emotion is high, and breathe deeply (without sighing passive-aggressively). Tune out any distractions. Just listen while breathing, noticing your body, noticing your reactions. Stay curious about that.

2. Before you speak, step back in your mind. Pause. It's tempting to talk and overwhelm. Do the opposite. Ask your spouse if you can just sit for a minute and absorb what you are hearing from them. Breathe through this minute, paying attention to your thoughts and feelings. Own your thoughts. Ask God to make his compassion and love tangible. Breathe in God's love for you both.

   a. Assess: Are the judgments you are making honoring your loved one? Do they uphold your loved one's volition? Is making judgments or decisions seeking the best outcome for both of you? Or does your loved one just need you to listen to, accept, and love them?

3. Notice any high emotions, which can look like either anger or withdrawal—both are unhelpful. Help your spouse and yourself by catching any distortions.

   a. Self-soothe by understanding where your mind is, where your thoughts have gone. If they have gone to an angry, defensive position, take time away to process. Ask God to soothe hurt places within. Ask him for peace. Breathe God's peace into your body.

   b. Let your loved one know that you need to take a short break to think and breathe. Estimate how long you will need.

Sometimes you might need to drive to another place, preferably one with nature sounds (take care to make arrangements with your spouse for childcare if needed so you don't abandon your responsibilities during your time-out). Other times, you might need just three to five minutes to pace around. Try this short break first. Ask God to bless that time away and to allow it to minister to your spouse as well.

   c. Come back to your spouse when you're calm, after your anger has died down. Try to reconnect before you both go to bed. Ask God to help you both not to go to bed in anger.

4. Tell your spouse how much you love them and how you are trying to listen and understand, how you are working hard to take deep breaths to calm your internal reactions.

   a. Ask for grace from your spouse before you speak. Accept that you may not hear what you want, but be intentional about noticing when your spouse is listening and give them credit for that. Speak a quick prayer of gratitude to God for bringing your spouse into your life.

   b. Observe any efforts your spouse is making. Notice signs of distress. If you can muster the energy and goodwill, ask for permission to move in for a hug or a kiss even in the midst of the conflict. If possible, pray together and ask God to comfort both of you toward healing and reconciliation.

5. Rehearse your thoughts. Get used to observing your mind and emotions and to finding words that seem to help your spouse understand where you are coming from. In your mind, plan for the resolution of the next conflict, because conflict is inevitable this side of heaven. The goal in Christian mindfulness is to work through conflict with attention to the other person as well as to your own reactions.

Compassion is key—for yourself *and* for your spouse. In the quiet of your mind, remind yourself that God is with you. Take another deep breath. Detach from any reactions, especially anger. Notice the thoughts attached to them. If you feel that your spouse's attack is unfair, reflect on that unfairness. Ask God for wisdom. Come back to the argument. Express what you noticed in that quiet space and communicate your feelings and thoughts, not your reactions or defense. Be quick to listen. Be quick to forgive. (Though threats, abuse, and violence are never okay. Those need to be dealt with differently.)

Christian mindfulness will help you regulate your emotions. Christian mindfulness practice will help you be more emotionally available, resilient, and present in working out resolutions with your spouse. Ignoring things is not mindfulness.

Tuning In to Intimacy

Perel (2017), an infidelity expert, talks about the differences between how men and women are socialized in matters of sexual intimacy in the broader culture: "Men are socialized to boast, exaggerate, and overrepresent their sexual exploits, while women minimize, deny, and underrepresent theirs.... Sexual honesty is inseparable from sexual politics" (p. 55).

The social aspects of sex and intimacy in marriage are often different between the genders. Christian mindfulness practice within the context of sexual intimacy incorporates the body and attunes to sensations in order to build intimacy. Christian mindfulness is therefore an equalizer, where intimacy outflows the attention and awareness that connect both spouses.

Sensate Focus with Christian Mindfulness Exercise

Yarhouse and Tan (2014) detail the basic steps of sensate focus exercises as they relate to treatment for various sexual issues. You and your clients can learn about it in more detail by taking a look at that book. What we provide here are some exercises to build intimacy through spouses' paying attention to each other as an aspect of intimacy. This leads to feelings of safety, of a sense that the walls between them are coming down and they can be available to each other.

Set a timer for five minutes the first time you practice this exercise, and build up to ten minutes after a few days of the exercise.

1. Sit facing each other and look into each other's eyes. You can hold hands or place your hands in your laps.
2. Breathe deeply together at least five times, with the goal of regulating your inhalations and exhalations together.
3. Hold and caress each other's hands. Continue to look deeply into each other's eyes. Pay attention to when you might feel uncomfortable or your mind is distracted. Help each other stay focused in each other's presence. Giggle if you must, but then return to each other's gaze. Say to each other, "I thank God for bringing you into my life." Follow that with other statements of gratitude for another minute.
4. Move into any other physical touch that feels nice and safe and meaningful until the timer is up. How you use the rest of the time is up to you.

Though it's not exhaustive, the foundation of a mindful sensate-focused exercise is rooted in listening and presence. It is remarkably helpful to give couples time and space to sit with each other. In our busy world, couples often are distracted in each other's presence.

Using the five senses, each person reconnects with their body individually and then intentionally notices their spouse. As the therapist and counselor, you can build on this practice by helping the spouses discuss what this exercise brings up for them. Oftentimes there may be baggage from past sexual sin or fear from past sexual encounters or traumatic experiences.

Sometimes clients have distorted expectations because sexual intimacy was considered dirty and was not grounded in a biblical theology that includes the Song of Solomon and teachings about intimacy and sex. So many issues can come up, so it is important for you, the therapist and counselor, also not to be afraid but to use Christian mindfulness to help soothe or self-regulate even your own reactions as clients bring things up. Because Christian sex therapy is a specific expertise that is beyond the scope of this book and exercise, it's a good idea to support your work with further training and reading, especially if this is a new area of therapeutic counseling for you.

Parenting with Christian Mindfulness

The challenge for parents of kids young or old is finding time to focus on themselves outside of their various roles, including as parents. Mindful parenting is not just tuning in to a child's needs but also balancing parenting duties with time to just connect with the child (Danaan, 2015). Often, parents are distracted by other responsibilities, and it is easy to zone out with electronic devices or other distractions as a break.

Dedicating time to read to and snuggle with younger children and to talk with and listen to older children takes focused effort. It is easy to be inconsistent in these ways of connecting, bonding, and loving.

At the same time, it is easy for clients to care so much for their children that they neglect themselves. They can be overcome by good intentions to provide the best education and activities for their children, driving and pushing themselves and their kids toward activity rather than connection. The exercises in the rest of this book can be used as Christian mindfulness practices for parents' own self-care.

Parental Rest as Antidote to Burnout

Many of our clients who are parents experience exhaustion and overstimulation because of a number of factors, including poor sleep, lack of self-care, routine, work stress, trauma, and loss. Koslowitz (2019) provides a short summary of parental burnout as including feeling overwhelmed, ineffective, detached, or emotionally or physically exhausted.

The problem with parental burnout is that exhaustion and numbness compound each other when left unaddressed. Encouraging our clients to practice Christian mindfulness can provide them with tools to stay healthy mentally and physically. For instance, resting in between parenting duties—playtime, homework, or even feeding, bathing, and napping schedules—prevents the compounding effects of stressor upon stressor. Helping our clients to find that rest in our offices or in their times between our meetings will provide them a much needed reprieve.

Our clients can shift from task-parenting to opening up heart space for their children for better bonding and nurture. Here is a short Christian mindfulness practice you can do with your clients at the beginning or end of your sessions to give them some respite and to help them reconnect with themselves as people, as children of God themselves. Feeling the warmth of God's love and nurturing will be an embracing corrective for them and an antidote to the hurriedness of modern parenting.

In-Session Parental Rest Exercise

First, close your eyes and let's acknowledge that this time is a gift from God to give you some respite from everyday parental duties.

- Set an intention for this five-minute rest as being with God as his daughter or son.
- Breathe this intention in and out. On the inhalation, ask God to prepare you for this time and to meet you. On the exhalation, ask God to help you focus your thoughts and your heart toward him.
- After your breaths, recall that God is your heavenly Father and that you are to him a precious child. Meditate on any verse or thought that reminds you of his care for you.
- Simply focus on an image of rest while being with God, Abba, Lord, here in this place.
- Is God holding you in his arms? Are you kneeling at his feet in a restful pose?
- Determine what feels accepting and warm. Where are you resting within God's presence?

- Use your breathing to help you maintain your focus on being in God's presence, with Christ nurturing and giving you comfort.
- Just focus on the image. There is no sound. There is no duty. Just simply rest in God's presence, allowing God to be the comforter.
- To close, breathe in and out again. Allow this time to sink into your mind and dig deep into your soul. Receive the comfort, rest, peace, presence, or whatever you experienced in this quiet moment. Seal it in as a sacred rest that you can return to because God is always with us.

Parental Presence

Your clients' parent-child bonds are worth discussing and nurturing. Helping them enjoy their times with their children provides benefits to the family overall. Helping them navigate other issues in your counseling or therapeutic sessions is buttressed by the work of helping them to be in a state of calm, rest, and peace.

The next exercise is for your clients' everyday challenge of acceptance and staying in a calm place, especially during conflict. When something is happening with a client's child or when the child is saying or doing something inconsistent with the family's values, a client often withdraws or becomes aggressive. Your clients must find and practice an assertive and authoritative, but not authoritarian, way of relating as they develop their parenting skills.

When it comes to raising children, whether they're toddlers or teens, our capacity to be present, to listen, to accept, to love, and to encourage them (setting limits included) and to spend quality time together gets squeezed out by other priorities: activities, chores, tasks. Helping your clients set priorities, depending on their schedules, is an ongoing goal. Christian mindfulness practice can help ensure your clients' proper cultivation of that relationship. Part of bonding is helping a parent feel like a safe space for a child to go. Encourage your clients to try the following exercise.

Mindfulness Exercise for Parents

- When your child is doing or saying something upsetting, first identify why you're upset. Take a beat to rest. Do not talk to your child until you work through these steps.
- In a quiet space, with eyes closed, sitting, take in three deep breaths and just name your child's upsetting behavior or action. Is it disrespect? Is it poor behavior or choices? Just name what it is during these three breaths.
- Keep contemplating and decide to stay calm and speak calmly to your child. Breathe in again and focus your thought on this intention: "I'm going to stay calm and speak calmly." Notice your breathing and notice that your mind will jump around trying to justify your anger. Self-soothe by focusing your mind.
- Stay in mindfulness and identify at least one good outcome of your remaining calm. Imagine the benefits.
- Access your faith in mindfulness. Ask the Holy Spirit for wisdom. Rehearse in your mind what you will say, what you will do to bring peace and calm even if you must correct your child. Rehearse how you will react when your child responds to your words and presence.
- Notice your child's reactions as you talk and engage. Look at your child with compassion and love no matter their level of anger. Care for any hurts and pains, said and unsaid. Access your warmth for your child. Breathe and learn from what they say. Stay curious and caring. Make asks, not demands. Hold the space for healing and reconciliation.
- After your interaction, return to your breathing again. Take another three deep breaths and seal in what you learned and thought in this moment.
- Reflect on the interaction. Evaluate in your mind in a quiet space, even for a minute: How did it go? Were you able to be calm? What were the challenges of staying calm?

Summary and Reflection

The goal for our clients who apply Christian mindfulness to their familial relationships is love. To love and be loved requires attentive presence. When our clients practice mindfulness, they extend their capacity to stay in this state. The slow process of connection, bonding, loving, listening, and reflecting, especially during times of conflict in their closest relationships, is countercultural. The tendencies to zone out, to multitask, to be busy and distracted are constant pulls in a culture that elevates busyness and productivity. With faith, all clients are capable of establishing and then living out this mindful bonding process. The encouragement comes from you, the Christian healer. May these exercises also remind us of our need as counselors and therapists to meet our clients in Christ's love as God calls us to do so in service to his kingdom.

Questions for Reflection

1. In relationships, we often talk about love and bonding. In your mindfulness practice, what came up for you initially when you needed to slow down?
2. What did you notice in your loved one as you took space away and then came back?
3. What choices did you make internally—in your thoughts or in ways you sought God for a calm space? What was one choice? What was the other choice?

References for Chapter 9

Danaan, C. (2015). *Zen and the path of mindful parenting: Meditations on raising children*. Leaping Hare Press.

Koslowitz, R. (2019). The burnout we can't talk about: Parent burnout. *Psychology Today*. https://www.psychologytoday.com/us/blog

/targeted-parenting/201909/the-burnout-we-cant-talk-about
-parent-burnout

Perel, E. (2017). *The state of affairs: Rethinking infidelity.* Harper Collins.

Yarhouse, M. A., & Tan, E. S. N. (2014). *Sexuality and sex therapy: A comprehensive Christian appraisal.* InterVarsity Press.

CHAPTER 10

Mindfulness in Friendships and Deepening Bonds

For where two or three gather in my name, there am I with them.

—MATTHEW 18:20

Contemplation Prompts for Clients

MATTHEW 18:20

- Who are the two or three you gather with? Why?
- How has gathering been a source of support for you? In what way?
- How does God show he is with you in your connections and social supports?

Belonging Matters

Our society is experiencing an epidemic of loneliness. At the time of this writing, many cities all over the country have closed schools, restaurants, churches, and other businesses and institutions because of the COVID-19 pandemic. We have never seen this kind of shutdown and widespread living under quarantine. Our access to community and our ability to see and meet with friends are much diminished. In response, churches are trying to reestablish safely distanced gatherings. The pandemic has reminded many of us that the life-giving and spiritual gifts of meeting with one another in community are priceless treasures.

Belonging matters. Our social supports lift and carry us through troubling times. The role of community is paramount in a responsible society. We cannot overemphasize the importance of our relationships with others and with God. Trammel, Park, and Karlsson (2021) argue that one of the biggest differences between a mindfulness practice that is centered in faith or religion versus a secular one is the connection we have with God. When our clients practice Christian mindfulness, they keep in mind that they are acknowledging that God is with them—no one is alone in Christ.

As counselors, therapists, and healing practitioners, we must remind our clients of the importance of their social supports and the power of the community that belongs in Christ. Unaddressed social and emotional loneliness inevitably leads to consequences for our society and for our individual health and life expectancy for years to come (Charles & Wolfer, 2018). Even when we lead our clients into a mindful presence with us and with God, our clients sense the balm of community. Their loneliness is lessened. The healing presence of another goes deep, while the loneliness becomes shallower and light filled.

Hard Question for Us

Do your clients feel like they belong anywhere? Most of our clients have faced abandonment, rejection, and even trauma, all of which have contributed to their being in your office or counseling space. Evaluate how you feel about them. Do your clients belong to you? Why or why not? This is a gentle reminder that sometimes, we as healing professionals face our own sense of abandonment. These issues are important to deal with because they so easily create barriers within the therapeutic space.

Belonging Reminder

To improve your clients' sense of belonging, read again Matthew 18:20 and help them home in on the truth that they belong. Belonging and social isolation are two different things. We help our counselees and clients gain social connections when they can cultivate a true understanding of themselves, which is that they belong to God. In chapter 21, we talk about how the Blessing can be a powerful healing tool for clients, especially as they incorporate Christian mindfulness skills as they receive it. You might want to speak over them blessing-like "you belong" statements and have them learn to receive those words of belonging. Here are some helpful truths about belonging that you may want to read to your clients or counselees before you begin the meditation that follows:

- You belong: to a God who sees and cares.
- You belong: to a community that lives out empathy, compassion, grace, and acceptance. If you don't feel that, we will figure that out together. It is out there!
- You belong: to a higher purpose, a kingdom unseen.
- You belong: Christ died on the cross so you can be embraced by an eternal, unfailing holy love.

You Belong Mindfulness Meditation

- Begin with breathing. Inhale for four counts, hold for four counts, exhale for four counts. Do this at least three times to calm your body and your mind.
- Think about the word belonging. What feels positive about that word? Name the people, including friends (past or present), who help you feel like you belong.
- Stay in this space of noticing what comes up for you as you contemplate the word belonging, and bring your breathing back to the thought of belonging.

- Take three deep breaths again to prepare to move into the idea that you belong to God.
- Be aware of God's presence with you, that God created you, that your true belonging is with Christ. Everything about you belongs to Christ because he saved and redeemed you.
- Take another deep breath. Inhale with the words "I belong" and exhale with the words "to Christ and his community." Do this several times until these words sink deeper.
- Contemplate: What does Christ's community look like for you? Where have you found it? Or what must you do to find it? What must happen for you to feel like you belong to God's community? How will you include others in that belonging?
- Confess your intentions to God moving forward into belonging to him and his community.

Acceptance and Bonding

Smith (2010), author of *The Good and Beautiful Community*, references Richard Foster's observation that readers were using his book *Celebration of Discipline* in isolation. Smith reminds us that spiritual growth best happens in a community where there is unity. Even when we are bound to have disagreements, we need each other. Conflict and disagreements are better had and better endured when the bonds of friendship are rich and plowed. When neglected, disagreements more easily turn into arguments, which turn into broken bonds.

Christian mindfulness helps us all acquire the perspective of others through radical acceptance. Our clients may need to gain that perspective for their healing. They may lack a sense of belonging. They may hurt and lash out or step into social situations awkwardly because they are still learning what it means to belong and bond. Maybe they have never had this experience of belonging in any social relationship. Perhaps they have lost the only ones they have ever trusted.

The practice of Christian mindfulness will expand your clients' ability to regulate their emotions, which opens them up to experience more empathy for others. As they develop and value their connections with others, we can walk with them in this path so they can hold others while others hold on to them. Relational bonds truly do not return void. Through friendship, our clients survive and sustain through whatever causes their suffering. Ramsey (2020), a licensed counselor and author of *This Too Shall Last: Finding Grace When Suffering Lingers*, reminds us, "I reject the notion that I am an individual being, built by the bulk of my successes, suffering in the wake of my failures. . . . We are not sole trees standing stalwart in an open field, rooted only as deep or wide as our effortful faith will grind into the ground. We are more aspen than oak, reaching skyward in hope, glorious in waving gold, both our beauty and survival formed and sustained in interdependence" (p. 77).

Ramsey (2020) reminds us that, ultimately, our interdependence is built into us—our psyches and our souls—and acts as a corrective for our scrutiny of the self. Taking time to be with others, our clients build a healthier view of themselves, nurtured and corrected in community and belonging.

We might remind our clients that healthy mindful friendships include time to talk, doing activities together with intention and purpose, evaluating and sharing life goals, focusing on God rather than impressing others, honoring the other while listening and attending and minimizing distractions. As our clients dive deep into their need for connection, or feel the corrective emotional response of the work you have done with them, they in turn can give others the gift of friendship bonds developed in the open heart space of mindfulness.

Radical Acceptance: Deepening Bonds of Grace

For some of our clients, diving into friendships and deepening bonds is risky. Their hearts have been hurt before. Perhaps they do not want to open up again. Such clients will have to risk radical acceptance of themselves and their friends in order to deepen friendship bonds. Dr. Marsha

Linehan, creator of dialectical behavioral therapy (DBT), writes about the concept of radical acceptance "of what each of us has to accept; our past, the present, and realistic limitations on the future and skills to tolerate distress without impulsively or destructively reducing it" (Linehan & Wilks, 2015, p. 98). Being available to others in friendships means that clients need to accept their limitations as well as the limitations of their friends. Expecting perfection out of imperfect people seems a foolish cause, and to encourage our clients into the messiness of radical acceptance with others who recognize their own flaws is the perfect answer for building bonds.

Radical acceptance differs for Christians in the sense that although we accept that suffering exists and that letting go is important, we still move toward a hope that includes God. Rather than just relinquishing control, we relinquish control to God. Our clients then radically accept other people with a biblical framework that recalls Matthew 18:20, that where they gather with others, God is there.

Acceptance, however, does not mean approval. We can disapprove of our friends' behaviors, especially if we know and understand how harmful sinful behaviors can be within a friendship. For instance, all of us as professionals know that any kind of abuse should not be tolerated. Radical acceptance does not include approval or minimization of such behavior. Radical acceptance does, however, help one to move on from a toxic friendship, and to do so in a way that honors our clients' personhood, worth, and value as God-created beings.

There is room, therefore, to accept and not to judge when a client struggles in the ups and downs of normal friendships. There is room for their friendships to exist just as they are, in the present moment. However, God is also present in all of those relationships. Our clients can exhibit grace in their friendships because Christ and the Holy Spirit are within those bonds to secure, strengthen, redeem, and renew.

The following exercise infuses a faith focus into Linehan's dialectical behavioral therapy. It will deepen clients' bonds of grace so they can gather with two or three, where God is present with them.

Christian Radical Acceptance Exercise

- Christian radical acceptance begins with a mindful and faithful outlook. Begin with a breathing exercise. Close your eyes. Breathe in and out deeply a few times until you feel comfortable with the rhythm of your breathing.
- Observe what you are resisting in the other person. Is it something that you need space from? For what reason? Does this resistance honor God? Why or why not?
- Pray for your time with God in this space to surface your emotions about this relationship.
- Ask God for help as you sort out what the reality is in this friendship.
- Notice your body, breathe, and observe the emotions attached to this friendship. Note any negative feelings or memories that cause you to resist it. Stay curious about those feelings.
- Identify and pray about your part in this friendship. Acknowledge to God what you have contributed to it. Confess anything you feel burdened by.
- Ask God for help in accepting what you think and feel about this friendship. Ask him to direct your steps in it and for help to be a good friend in general—whether in this friendship or in a healthier one.
- Acknowledge the gift of friendship and the deep bonds that can come out of healthy friendships. Practice acceptance that all friends are flawed and sinful, just as you are flawed and sinful.
- Contemplate Matthew 18:20 and practice acceptance of the both/and: God is present in *both* the friendship *and* in the sinful and flawed nature of our human relationships.

Our clients' feelings of vulnerability in their friendships masks their longing to belong and for deep bonds. We all want to belong. We all want deep bonds. Getting there is the hard part. What we, as therapists, counselors, and healing professionals, can provide is a safe harbor for the ups and downs of human friendship. We can help our clients acknowledge that they already belong—to God, to a community, to us. They simply need the time and mindful space to explore the meanings of their friendships. We need to celebrate their wins each time they take a step toward belonging in healthy friendships and any effort they make to deepen those bonds.

Questions for Reflection

1. Evaluate your sense of belonging in friendships. Who can you openly share your concerns with? What is it about that person that helps you open up?
2. How has God been present in your friendships?
3. What do you need to accept about your friends in Christian radical acceptance?

References for Chapter 10

Charles, V. A., & Wolfer, T. A. (2018). Loneliness and congregational social work. *Social Work & Christianity, 45*(1), 8–23.

Linehan, M. M., & Wilks, C. R. (2015). The course and evolution of dialectical behavior therapy. *American Journal of Psychotherapy, 69*(2), 97–110. https://doi.org/10.1176/appi.psychotherapy.2015.69.2.97

Ramsey, K. J. (2020). *This too shall last: Finding grace when suffering lingers.* Zondervan.

Smith, J. B. (2010). *The good and beautiful community: Following the Spirit, extending grace, demonstrating love.* InterVarsity Press.

Trammel, R. C., Park, G., & Karlsson, I. (2021). Religiously oriented mindfulness for social workers: Effects on mindfulness, heart rate variability, and personal burnout. *Journal of Religion & Spirituality in Social Work: Social Thought, 40*(1), 19–38. https://doi.org/10.1080/15426432.2020.1818358

CHAPTER 11

Mindfulness and Work

*This is a trustworthy saying. And I want you to stress
these things, so that those who have trusted in God
may be careful to devote themselves to doing what
is good. These things are excellent and profitable for
everyone.*

—TITUS 3:8

Contemplation Prompts for Clients

TITUS 3:8

- Do you count yourself as one who trusts in God at work? Why or why not?
- What does it mean to be careful to devote yourself to doing what is good at work?
- How often can you honestly say that you have led decision making or made a decision at work that is "excellent and profitable for everyone"?

Everyday Work Stress

Work stress can be a constant hum that sends our clients' ability to find peace far outfield. When they are able to catch moments of grace within their workdays, they can sustain their workflows. However, do our clients care about their work beyond just being productive? Do they feel that they've made a home run in their jobs or career choices? As followers of Christ, our clients need to understand their value, which is a challenge when they feel like they've hit foul balls.

For our clients to be able to perform at work and do so with a sense of purpose, Warren (2012), pastor and author of the bestselling book *The Purpose Driven Life*, states, "Your mission has eternal significance. It will impact the eternal destiny of other people, so it's more important than any job, achievement, or goal you will reach during your life on earth. The consequences of your mission will last forever; the consequences of your job will not. Nothing else you do will ever matter as much as helping people establish an eternal relationship with God" (p. 9).

Part of being purpose driven at work is for our clients to sense that they are on a mission with God, that their jobs are part of that mission. They must sense that who they were created to be is affirmed by God, that peace at work evolves from a sense that God is in their jobs with them. His presence is near them every step of the way. Christian mindfulness practice is a sacred pathway to peace and comfort for clients who are disconnected and want to have a sense of purpose at work or are experiencing work stress. Whether they are overwhelmed, hopeless, angry, or confused, our clients are going to be impacted by their employment. If they have faced job losses recently, then the impact of stress cannot be overstated. A general Christian mindfulness break throughout a workday can be profoundly helpful for our clients—to gain strength, for greater bandwidth, and to refocus.

As work stress takes its toll on our clients, we can encourage them to take a daily mindfulness break at work to recenter themselves in Christ, wherever they are, whatever they are doing. This is possible, we know. For example, Wolever et al. (2012) conducted a randomized controlled study at a workplace where the intervention was a twelve-week one-hour mindfulness class either online or in person during the workers' lunch breaks. The researchers found significant results for those workers in decreased perceived stress, improved sleep, and improved heart rate variability (a sign of less stress-related reactivity in the body). Though their intervention was a secular one, the awareness, present-moment noticing, and adaptability skills gained in a Christian mindfulness practice provide similar benefits to prevent burnout (Trammel, Park, & Karlsson, 2021).

How can we help our clients apply mindfulness during their workdays? The following Christian mindfulness exercise is to help clients take a brain pause, a brief respite that can be done during a task but preferably is done in a quiet space, even if it is just for a few minutes.

Work Stress Mindfulness Break

- Find at your workplace a quiet space to sit that feels comforting. Maybe it's outside in the shade of a tree or in a small corner near your workspace. If you normally are moving about in your job, take a moment to sit still in a comfortable yet dignified position.
- Start with your palms placed on your lap.
- Sweep your hands up so that your arms are stretched out and your palms are facing each other over your head. Touch your palms together. Sweep them back down onto your lap.
- Do this again and incorporate your breathing: inhale, sweep arms up, touch palms together. Exhale, sweep them back down, place your palms on your lap. Try doing this movement three times, with eyes closed, concentrating on your breath and movement.
- On the fourth time, now incorporate a prayer: while sweeping your arms up, inhale and pray, "Lord, I give to you my work. Multiply it. Strengthen my body, mind, and soul for my workday."
- While sweeping your arms back down, exhale and pray, "Be with me here at work for the tasks and relationships you have set before me. Go ahead of me. Help me follow your wisdom and direction."

Mindful Purpose over People Pleasing

Amanda Jaggard, an associate partner with the executive coaching firm Novus Global, and cofounder of Novus Global's Meta Performance Institute for Coaching, asks, "What if work could be holy?" She explains that we can help our clients transform work into a holy space and place. We do this by helping our clients shift to their purposes and priorities. This shifting means that our clients need to learn how to lead themselves and show up for work in a way that is meaningful and growth oriented (A. Jaggard, personal communication, August 20, 2020). Sometimes our clients' sense of purpose is rocked by adversity, barriers, or shifts at work. Other times, clients are disconnected from a sense of purpose at work. Having a work life that feels purposeful is a universal need. It is one of God's greatest blessings (Gen. 2:15).

As Christians, we are called to be peacemakers with a kingdom-focused purpose. Clients who are struggling with work stress may be interested in people pleasing or may have tapped out of their purpose, becoming less effective and less engaged with work tasks. We know also that part of the foundation of strong mental-health recovery is our clients' ability to work and to maintain an occupation.

Office politics and interpersonal dynamics can be distractions for many of us. For our clients, they can be sources of emotional injury. The reenactment of rejection or scapegoating or neglect that many of our clients experienced in their childhoods plays out at work. Dealing with conflict can be a focus of your work in the counseling office. But for our part, as Christians who practice mindfulness, we are called to stay in the lane of peace. Thus, we can support our counselees' advocating for a healthy workplace for themselves and for others. Our clients need tools to navigate the tricky dynamics that might come up at work, and Christian mindfulness provides a tool for discernment and reflection that will help them be successful. Not only that, but we are all called toward excellence (Titus 3:8). Keeping the peace while pursuing excellence at work can be difficult to balance. When our clients are starting a project or have a decision to make,

Christian mindfulness practice can keep them in pursuit of excellence and not just people pleasing.

The following exercise can help your clients maintain a Christian mindfulness practice oriented toward their work lives.

Walking-in-Purpose Mindfulness Practice

You can maintain a Christian mindfulness practice oriented toward your work life in this way:

- First, practice mentally accepting that we cannot expect perfection of ourselves or others, as Paul reminds us in Romans 3:23: "For all have sinned and fall short of the glory of God." Practice acceptance by acknowledging this truth and saying an ancient prayer from the Eastern Orthodox Church called the Jesus Prayer: "Lord Jesus Christ, have mercy on me, a sinner." Pray this prayer in earnest several times in a row, and I promise, the truth of your frailty and God's grace will take root. Every day, take a minute to read Romans 3:23 and pray the Jesus Prayer, and humility will become your mindset at work.
- Second, take a deep breath and size up your situation internally. What emotions are coming up for you in this moment? You can do this with eyes open: walk around the office for a few seconds, but do so slowly and intentionally, exploring each step in your gait. It's better if you can get outside and be alone. While walking, take a step and say this quick prayer: "Lord, I step into your grace. Help me understand my internal reactions. With each step, help me understand that you have put these feet on the grounds of this workplace. With each step, enable me to walk in peace. Make my steps move toward you. Direct my steps as you prepare me for [insert situation, e.g., a meeting, a decision that needs to be made]. Thank you, Lord. I take these steps toward you and ask that you work through my brokenness toward excellence in you."
- Third, after you have finished your meeting or work for the day, close your eyes for a minute, take a deep breath, and ask God to lead and

direct you for the next step. Ask him to make a way for you and your workplace and your leaders. No matter how much judgment you have against them, practice nonjudgment and acceptance, allowing God's grace to fill your steps. In your Christian mindfulness practice, it might sound like this: "My intention in this time, God, is to let go and accept what is happening now, the good, bad, and ugly." Breathe in this prayer. Breathe out consent to it.

Mindful Leadership

Christian mindfulness practice is about standing in the truth of God's presence while noticing how we miss out on him in our lives, especially at work. Mindfulness supports leadership development because it develops awareness of self and the impact of the self on others. Acknowledging how our clients navigate workplace realities is good information for our sessions with them. Mindfulness is supportive of their leadership development, and the Christian aspect of that practice supports the deeper healing or knowing that you and your client are working on together in the counseling or therapy space.

Through Christian mindfulness practices applied to work situations, our clients can learn how to notice and observe themselves with the filter of nonjudgment, which is essential for hearing God's prodding. Some of our clients lead others formally in their workplaces or informally in their roles as parents or caregivers, church lay leaders, Little League coaches, PTA organizers, and so on. Each role in leadership is full of decision making and influencing that leads to others' good. Fostering the good often means that our client-leaders need to repair their understanding of themselves and how their historical or family of origin issues (attachment style, defenses, unconscious biases, etc.) trip them up.

Dr. Devin Singh, founder and president of Leadership Kinetics and associate professor of religion at Dartmouth College, expands on the idea of leadership: "Leadership is about influence but also about service, such as the concept of servant leadership that is partly derived from Scripture." As a leadership coach, Singh describes how mindfulness engages with leaders in their self-growth. He says, "The client is the expert. However, when coaching leaders, there are prophetic moments where we [as coaches] guide and even confront." Singh is also an expert on emotional intelligence (EQ) and explains that our client-leaders need to own and understand their emotional landscapes, harnessing all emotions, which he identifies as powerful tools for leadership skills that are for the good of all. The individualistic models of leadership in the past must be balanced with responsibility to the community and the organization, whereby the benefits within the workplace are accessible by all (Singh, D., personal communication, August 24, 2020).

Therefore, mindful leadership is about our clients' being aware and tuned in at all levels—noticing where they are influencing, where they are more effective as servant leaders, and even when harnessing their anger in the face of injustice can lead to a Titus 3:8 type of change. Especially for this latter point, there is a holy truth to this emotional ownership that begins with mindfulness. All who are under a mindful leader can harness for their work lives the good that flows from this kind of leader.

Mindful leadership also means our client-leaders are able to see their work and move in the world with a both/and stance, not an either/or reaction. The gift we can provide in the therapeutic space is to foster that space for them to perceive work situations and notice their impacts emotionally: within themselves, within their relationships, within their organizational environments. We can help them make ties from their perceptions to their family of origin issues, their defenses, their attachments, and their faith (among other ideas drawn from your theoretical approach).

If our client-leaders cannot perceive themselves in this way, it is time for more practice in mindfulness-based skills. The gifts of mindfulness relate to cognitive and emotional shifts that are more powerful than we may realize. Noticing, paying attention, understanding those internal narratives without judgment are, according to both Jaggard and Singh, transformative tools for higher impact and higher outcomes in leadership. Leaders can respond instead of react. They can manage internal conflicts and work-based tensions maintaining a dialectic with intentional mindfulness practice. Moving forward in mindful leadership means that decisions are based on an inner knowing, fostered in a knowing that is not self-serving but in service to others.

Mindfulness for Inclusive Workplaces

The secular version of mindfulness practiced in myriad workplaces is a sanitized corporatization of an ancient spiritual practice. The results of this diffusion of mindfulness away from Christian or Buddhist practice (we have to acknowledge the Buddhist foundation; see chaps. 1–2 for more on the origin of mindfulness) toward workplace productivity has been challenged, especially in Buddhist journals. Particularly, Sun (2014) questions mindfulness stripped of its religious meaning to foster an emphasis on workplace efficiency, productivity, and profit. Mindfulness ripped from its Christian or Buddhist roots commodifies and manualizes the practice for self-focus and workplace productivity, rather than compassion and inclusivity.

Because hyperindividualism is toxic to mindful presence, we as Christian healers must counter a mindfulness practice that is oriented toward productivity and commodity in a space clear of ethics or not grounded in Christian values. We must help our client-leaders and workers look outward, not just inward. Though mindfulness practice is an awareness and attentional space in our minds, bodies, and souls, the fruit of mindfulness practice should bear out in service and cultivation of others. In the best sense, mindfulness supports, even enhances:

- A collective sense of self
- An abundance mindset rather than a scarcity mindset
- Humility and a learning stance
- Responsibility
- Love of neighbor
- Weeping with those who weep
- Acknowledging, not gaslighting, suffering

- Maintaining joy (not happiness or naivete) in adversity
- The church as the body of Christ, with all parts important

Self-focused mindfulness is just for the self. There are plenty of ways mindfulness can serve only the self rather than lead to a stance of serving others. In addition, mindfulness from a Christian perspective means that we see the weak and vulnerable. Clients who struggle at work can be brave to step up to doors that perhaps are closed to them. Clients who are door openers can break down doors to let others in. Christian mindfulness is to help open up heart space to those who are often ignored, invisible, or disenfranchised from the earthly blessings of work.

Let's pursue mindfulness for self-care that ultimately serves others. Let's continue to orient our clients toward an outward-looking stance in their interactions at work and in their self-care mindfulness practice. The following exercise is a gratitude practice to orient them to gratitude and inclusion of others in the workplace.

Workplace Gratitude Exercise

- Begin by getting into a quiet place in your mind, using your breath as an anchor to still your thoughts, still your soul.
- On your inhalation: thank God for breath, for another day of life.
- On your exhalation: thank God for the ability to work (mind, body, and soul).
- Inhale: thank God for your workplace (the good, the bad, the ugly).
- Exhale: thank God for your work colleagues (the ones who are easy to love, the ones who are hard to love).
- Sit in silence for another minute, concentrating only on your breath, paying attention and observing what comes to mind.
- Ask God to place in your mind someone you think might be deprived of the blessings of influence at your workplace today.
- Pray for that person: for their welfare, for their sustenance, for their full inclusion in your workplace.

- Sit in silence for another minute, observe your thoughts, your emotional reactions, and your body. Note any significant thing.
- Inhale: thank God for this time.
- Exhale: ask God how you can practice gratitude and serve the person he placed in your mind.

Questions for Reflection

1. Acknowledge the work stresses you face regularly. Determine the roots of those stresses.
2. Identify your work's purpose in a mission statement for yourself, and include in your statement how you will mindfully work on behalf of others you have leadership influence over.
3. What does gratitude look like for you at work?
4. Who is left out at work? How can you include them?

References for Chapter 11

Sun, J. (2014). Mindfulness in context: A historical discourse analysis. *Contemporary Buddhism*, *15*(2), 394–415. https://doi.org/10.1080/14639947.2014.978088

Trammel, R. C., Park, G., & Karlsson, I. (2021). Religiously oriented mindfulness for social workers: Effects on mindfulness, heart rate variability, and personal burnout. *Journal of Religion & Spirituality in Social Work: Social Thought*, *40*(1), 19–38. https://doi.org/10.1080/15426432.2020.1818358

Warren, R. (2012). *The purpose driven life: What on earth am I here for?* (expanded edition). Zondervan.

Wolever, R. Q., Bobinet, K. J., McCabe, K., Mackenzie, E. R., Fekete, E., Kusnick, C. A., & Baime, M. (2012). Effective and viable mind-body stress reduction in the workplace: A randomized controlled trial. *Journal of Occupational Health Psychology*, *17*(2), 246–258. https://doi.org/10.1037/a0027278

CHAPTER 12

Mindfulness for Ministry

For my yoke is easy and my burden is light.
—MATTHEW 11:30

Contemplation Prompts for Clients

MATTHEW 11:30

- How would you describe the yoke of ministry to someone else?
- How often do you feel depleted in your ministry? Why and how?
- Imagine a burden being lifted. What does that feel like in your mind? How about in your body? How would a lifted burden change your emotions?

Pastors and Burnout

The stress and blurry boundaries of pastoral life can tax the body and soul. Periods of rest and refreshment are often interrupted by congregants' needs. Clients who are pastors also desire to be wanted and needed in their congregations. In postmodernity, the cult of personality is ubiquitous and has led to some disastrous results. (Look at Christian news stories within the past year.) Many godly pastors or lay ministers did not come into the pastorate lightly. They understood the sacrifices and rewards that come with leading people to Christ and to a deeper walk with him. However, left unchecked, the burdens of the pastorate can lead to burnout. Like many healthcare providers, our ministry clients are healers also—providing spiritual direction, teaching, and comfort. So how does a healer become healed when their energy tank is low?

Our clients must acknowledge that they are in a high-stress profession. Burnout is a real and studied phenomenon that leads to dullness of emotions, health problems, and detachment from relationship. Hester (2017) defines pastor burnout as unaddressed stress attributed to ministry that without proper management evolves into chronic emotional fatigue, isolation, apathy, and an inability to recognize one's own accomplishments. Burnout increases the risk of exodus from ministry, as well as mental health issues and ethical violations that create fractures within the church.

Results of a study by Moceri and Cox (2019) demonstrated a statistically significant reduction in blood pressure readings and self-reported stress levels of Christian clergy who participated in regular mindfulness interventions, indicating that mindfulness-based stress reduction helped them manage their stress better and prevented burnout. Anecdotally, we know that mindfulness is a meaningful stress-relief intervention. Its practice is born of tuning in to God. The spiritual formation of the practice is simply lifegiving, life nurturing, and life affirming. From recent news of pastors who have attempted or completed suicide, we know how important care and support for our ministers can be. For pastors who struggle with depression or anxiety and are seeking help, mindfulness is an appropriate practice that has proven effective in treating these conditions. A Christian mindfulness practice can bring some comfort especially for ministers who are skeptical about therapy, counseling, and other healing-based interventions.

Social workers, mental-health practitioners, public servants, and medical professionals all are trained to identify the signs of burnout, and mindfulness is a well-researched useful tool to prevent and treat it. Christian mindfulness provides pastors the chance to unplug and get back to the basics of ministry. As writer Anne Lamott says, "Almost everything will work again if you unplug it for a few minutes. That includes you."

Clients who are in ministry often struggle with getting into a space where we, as counselors, therapists, and healers, are necessary for restoration. Our clients can stand up, preach, lead, counsel, spark a vision, and communicate well, but the weight on their shoulders will result in aches and pains as if they have misaligned spines, leading to a skewed message and long-term implications for their ministry. Sometimes the misalignment doesn't show up until it has thrown everyone off balance—pastor, minister, and congregation. Let's support our ministry clients by helping them spend time with God in which the adrenaline in their bodies can wear off and they can really take stock, listening to what God is saying to them and through them. Realigning clients' ministry work with the work of God's mission on earth requires some time for thinking and a place where their souls are at rest, where their roots are replenished by good soil so they can once again bear good fruit.

One thing we can encourage our client-pastors to do is to get away from their congregations for a bit. They might need us in the counseling space to give them permission to take a break, to cajole or even prod them into it. Sometimes pastors and ministers are afraid that all will fall apart if they are not present in the congregation. We can use a solution-focused approach to help them get away, even for a little bit, to tune in to the whispers of their souls that they might not hear otherwise.

Encourage your client-pastors to go on a silent retreat, one where they don't know anyone and where there is no obligation to connect. Numerous biblically based spiritual directors provide such retreats. Have your client-pastors report back to you what they heard, what they learned, what they need to do to enrich the soil of their lives for the refreshment and nourishment required to get them through the heat and droughts inherent in ministry.

Staying Emotionally Present

Clients who minister to others often neglect their emotional and mental-health needs for the sake of their flocks. This is easy for them to do because they often view their congregations as sheep they are responsible for shepherding. Stepping out of that caretaker role can be challenging for them. Some like being needed. Others believe their congregations will descend into chaos without them.

Whatever the case, pastoral leaders might resist your counsel as they wrestle through the push and pull of congregational leadership with you. You are there to guide, to listen, to encourage them to be present with God and with themselves. Christian mindfulness breaks down their resistance because in the quiet, they know that God's yoke is easy and his burden is light.

Clients who hold ministry positions may not have been held (emotionally speaking) by anyone for a while—or ever! We know, through attachment theory, that lack of or inconsistent nurturing can lead to greater anxiety and feelings of insecurity. Pastors, generally speaking, are a hearty community, leading with great aplomb. But they are not immune to depression and anxiety. Holding them in a present-moment way of thinking, feeling, and being will provide a less cognitive-centered experience for them, which makes way for new skills to be built, new emotional territory to be traversed, new baggage to be unpacked with someone. You, as the professional counselor or therapist, act much like the Sherpas of the Himalayas. You have skills, equipment, and wisdom that lead to the success of the expedition, but often you go unnoticed, staying in the background. Your ability to negotiate emotional terrain will help your clients who are ministers survive the grueling path ahead. This work will take oxygen and endurance, because these mountains are not easy to climb. However, with God's help, with his steady and gracious hand, you will reach the other side.

Pastors need your wisdom and skill. Rohrer (2012) recognizes and summarizes nonanxious presence this way: "But in order to be that nonanxious presence, I was going to need to remove myself from my chosen place of believing that I was at the center of the solution. What I keep learning in the practice of ministry is that the way I make ready a people prepared for God is simply to invite people to wake up to God.... I need to be asking, 'How is God revealing himself to us, and what difference does that make in how we will live our lives?' A passionate dedication to the singularity of this question can transform our ministry as pastors—and make us nonanxious" (pp. 58–59).

The anxiety and heaviness of ministry can be a burden to our clients that many congregants are not privy to. Our clients often suffer in silence, berating themselves for their neediness, because they are often the "center of solution," as Rohrer states, to their congregants' issues. To be keepers of God's call in many people's lives means our clients in ministry may not even recognize their need for quiet rest in God's presence beyond just a study or message-preparation time. They may be able to preach the need to be in God's presence, they may be good at counseling others toward the easy yoke of Christ, yet they may remain alienated from the peace of Christ that transcends all understanding to guard them (maybe even from themselves).

It is good to remind our clients in the pastorate of their humanness. Being put on a spiritual pedestal means that their humanity suffers. They may not have tumbled outwardly, but let's be wary of their tumbling internally. Your presence matters to your clients. Your clients matter to their congregations. A virtuous path that flows through the kingdom might even be in that space between your chair and your client's.

Part of preventing pastoral burnout or exhaustion is for your pastoral counselees to have a regular time to evaluate and be aware of their emotions. Burnout can look like irritability, exhaustion, numbness, or, worse, depression, and/or suicidal ideation. Assessment is an important step in the work.

Sometimes your pastoral counselees are exhausted, and talking through their emotions can feel like another burden, instead of an unburdening. As a way to move beyond language and into creativity, a mindfulness journal can incorporate expression through language, art, and creativity. The way to our clients' hearts might not be through their heads. We might need a different outlet to assist them in finding their souls' work. A nonspeaking, nonverbal way of being with you can provide space and relief for clients who are exhausted or who work primarily with their voices. A mindfulness-based journaling exercise, such as the following, can build in reflection time and support the process of self-care and of clarifying needed areas of support.

Mindful Ministry Journal Prompts

- If you were to pick a word for or draw a picture of how you are feeling in the ministry at this moment, what would it be, and why?
- Journal about your congregation's most pressing needs.
- Journal about your role in meeting those needs.
- How good are you at meeting your spiritual, mental, emotional, and physical needs? What needs are you neglecting? What needs are you meeting?
- How would you describe (in words or a drawing) your sense of God's presence in your life?
- Name three ways you feel God's presence working through you.
- In mindful attention, be aware of where your focus and thoughts go. Name three of the things taking up mental space.
- Name at least three people in your life you are thankful for, and maybe another three you need to lean on more.
- Draw a picture, put some color on paper, or find a poem that speaks to the heart of your ministry or purpose.

If your clients are willing to share this mindfulness journal as a regular part of their therapy or counseling, continue to help them go deeper, with intentionality, in the writing and sharing of it. It can be rote otherwise. We don't want our counselees to lose focus and stay in a cognitive-only space. Help them mine for emotional content that may be latent and need repair. Add to these prompts by finding creative art outlets to assist them. Other ideas may be listening together to a song that your client has brought that expresses who they are. Another might be to ask them to bring in a photograph they took of the week as a way to give voice to their struggles or gratitude. Get creative and help your clients in ministry get out of their heads or whatever spaces they go to most often. This applies also to other clients who are similarly in positions of leadership, ministry, or intellectual endeavor in which it can be difficult to process their emotions and avoidance takes the form of using a lot of words without saying much.

Retreating to Relinquish

Getting away from the day-to-day can be a refreshing break, a place where a change of scenery and location signals to our clients' brains and bodies that it's time to retreat. The invitation to retreat with God on a regular basis is a delightful ritual. Some pastors or ministers are able to do this and have the resources to do so. Others are living on shoestring budgets. Give them free or low-cost options. Luckily, a retreat can simply be a place of pondering and silence during a respite day. It could be a visit to a park bench under a shady tree. It could be a retreat center outfitted with all the wandering paths and spaces that spark creative rest. In any case, the idea of a retreat is important.

Our counselee-pastors will benefit from a time of retreat to relinquish their daily burdens, take stock emotionally, mentally, spiritually, and even care for themselves physically. It is a time and place to build new connections with God, to listen to the groans that only the Holy Spirit can enable to bubble up from beneath the surface. Our clients might not be able to put into words the meaning of this time, but the refreshment they find is like the sound of a bubbling brook. Whether monthly or yearly, a simple practice of silence is all that is needed.

You can remind your clients to practice the art of silence. Recollect that many biblical persons were called and refreshed when alone and in a silent place. Moses noticed the burning bush. Ezekiel was a lonely prophet but had a powerful message from God. And so many others display this truth. Your clients can take the time to sit in silence and stillness, using

Christian mindfulness practice, to shed the cares of this world and reconnect with their humanity rather than their roles, with their personhood rather than their duties, with their emotions and connection with God rather than their tasks. The following is a short retreat exercise that your pastoral counselee can do anytime.

Self-Care Mindful Retreat

- Find a quiet spot, preferably in nature, or in a favorite coffee shop or library or wherever. It should be a third place: not home, not your office, not a usual spot. However, it should be comfortable and relaxing.
- Take a look around in this third place. Breathe in and say in your mind, "This space and time is just for me."
- Set an intention for this time to be just about you. It may feel indulgent, but this time for you will be good. It's time to reconnect with who you are, your interests, what you think, what you feel. Just sit in the nondoing so that you can attend more fully to who God created you to be.
- Remind yourself that you have no obligation to do anything or be anyone. Simply start this time with a prayer of thanksgiving: "God, thank you for this time for me simply to be me, who you created me to be, and for a time of having no tasks. Help me center my thoughts on just living in the present and fill me with your peace and joy."
- Catch yourself if your mind wanders to work or home life, and go back to your intention for this time.
- At the end of this retreat time, commit in your mind when you will do this again. Close out your time with God: "Thank you, Lord, for this time to think, feel, live, and be me. Thank you for creating me with the gifts and talents you have developed in me. Please bless the work of my hands, guide me, and nudge me to care for myself, because you have created me as precious in your sight. Thank you."

Questions for Reflection

1. As you look through some of your journal entries, what do you notice is a theme of your emotional experience in ministry? What feeling words come up?
2. What are the barriers to your scheduling a regular retreat from work?
3. How have you used the retreat? What have you discovered about yourself and who you are—what you think, believe, and feel?

References for Chapter 12

Hester, J. A. (2017). *Stress and longevity in pastoral ministry: A phenomenological study* [Unpublished doctoral dissertation]. The Southern Baptist Theological Seminary.

Moceri, J., & Cox, P. H. (2019). Mindfulness-based practice to reduce blood pressure and stress in priests. *Journal for Nurse Practitioners, 15*(6), e115–e117. https://doi.org/10.1016/j.nurpra.2019.01.001

Rohrer, D. (2012). *The sacred wilderness of pastoral ministry: Preparing a people for the presence of the Lord.* InterVarsity Press.

CHAPTER 13

Eating Mindfully

"Then compare our appearance with that of the young men who eat the royal food, and treat your servants in accordance with what you see." So he agreed to this and tested them for ten days. At the end of the ten days they looked healthier and better nourished than any of the young men who ate the royal food.
—DANIEL 1:13–15

Contemplation Prompts for Clients

DANIEL 1:13–15

- Daniel's friends, Shadrach, Meshach, and Abed-nego, all stood apart spiritually, and also in how they treated their bodies while in exile in Babylon. In what ways might you feel that your body is in exile?
- How can you better treat your body, like Daniel's friends, while in exile?
- What does "healthier and better nourished" mean to you for your health and for your body?

It is so easy to choose our salty or sweet snacks when we're anxious, stressed, depressed, or depleted of energy. Our modern lifestyle offers many quick and easy food options that can be delivered to our doorsteps within minutes. Unfortunately, for many of our clients, mental health issues can exacerbate appetite or dietary issues. When clients are anxious or depressed, appetite suppression or overeating patterns can compound their need for nutrients that affect their mental health. Recent studies have shown that certain diets and even nutritional supplements can improve mental well-being, and that diet and exercise can complement traditional treatments of psychotropic medication and therapy (Frazier et al., 2012; Melnyk et al., 2013; Vicinanza et al., 2020). Hence, healthy eating can contribute to mental wellness.

When I (Regina) was in private practice in the Chicago area, I often worked with young women who suffered from eating disorders, both binge eating and restricting. I partnered closely with a nutritionist to help our clients incorporate healthy meals. My office was located on a medical campus, and part of the therapy was to walk through a hospital's cafeteria. What I learned from these brave client-warriors about mindfulness and their relationship with food is how mindless our culture can be when it comes to choosing, preparing, and consuming meals. Even as they prepared to walk through the cafeteria, I learned about expectations for beauty and unrealistic and toxic weight standards.

We've used part of the story of Shadrach, Meshach, and Abednego in Daniel 1 as the contemplation verses for this chapter not only as a reminder of wonderful men of God who are standing apart in a land where God is not worshiped but also because of the biblical truth inherent within: God can be honored through our bodies, and that can be a spiritual and countercultural act. In Western society, our food is fast. Our lifestyles are busy. Mindful eating and healthy practices can do wonders, as they did for Shadrach, Meshach, and Abednego. These Babylonian exiles' diet was so different that the officials noticed. They were scrutinized, perhaps ostracized, and yet they made mindful dietary choices.

In addition, these three provide a fine example of how mindful eating can be countercultural. Our Western culture values thin bodies but doesn't emphasize mindful eating in order to get there. Our clients' social media feeds present to them distorted standards of beauty. Our modern culture highlights misshapen figures via Photoshop and sculptured designs by plastic surgeons that lead our clients to disdain their own bodies and features, which God so lovingly created for them.

We know, as professional practitioners, that body images connect to our spirits and minds. Thus, when our clients struggle with eating disorders or devalue persons, including themselves, for not having able bodies, we should understand these distortions' impacts on emotional, mental, and spiritual health, and that the body, mind, and soul are a system.

Choosing Foods Mindfully

Part of eating mindfully is being intentional about the way we eat. Even choosing which foods we eat can be a ritual of self-care. You may recall that Shadrach, Meshach, and Abednego set themselves apart from others in the royal Babylonian court by consuming vegetables and water instead of the rich foods and wine served regularly. They asked the guard of the court to test their health after ten days to compare it with the health of other members of the royal court.

These three believers knew that their diet not only was healthier for them but also was a demonstration of their identity as followers of Yahweh, the God of Abraham, Isaac, and Jacob. And God blessed their choice. They looked healthier and better nourished than the others.

The same can be said of our clients. We can encourage them to adopt a healthier diet and teach them how to be intentional in their eating choices. Dietary advice is beyond the scope of this chapter, and we are not dieticians. However, mindful eating and the mindful care of the body as a temple can buttress therapeutic work even beyond the treatment of eating disorders. And we can partner with our dietician and nutritionist friends to assist clients with healthy dietary plans. Such a partnership is even more important when we are treating folks who have chronic health conditions where diet is important, such as diabetes and eating disorders. I (Regina) have observed great success in the recovery of my clients when I have partnered with a licensed dietician during the treatment process.

Getting back to our scope of practice, mindful eating can slow down our clients' process of eating and help them engage it differently by noticing, observing, savoring, and reframing.

A mindfulness exercise that is popular in secular mindfulness circles is the raisin-eating exercise, popularized by Dr. Jon Kabat-Zinn. We like to integrate Christian imagery and Scripture into this exercise to connect body, mind, and spirit in the counseling room. The following instructions are written for you to use with clients, but please adapt them to yourself if you want to practice on your own.

In-Session Mindful Eating Exercise

- Have your client bring to the session a nutritious and delicious food item. It should be simple and not need refrigeration. A raisin, a grape, a small tomato, a small mandarin orange—something small and easy to transport. In session, you can start this exercise by first reading Daniel 1:1–17 out loud together. Then have the client take a deep breath in and out, and read it to themselves one more time. Solicit their thoughts about this chapter. Affirm their responses. Help them understand the choice Shadrach, Meshach, and Abednego made and contemplate why they made it.
- Next ask your client to hold the food in their hands and contemplate it. Prompt them to think about where this item originated and how it got to their hand. You can guide them in a visualization

of how it grew on the tree—the sunshine, air, soil, and water that fed it and the nutrients it contains.

- Have them slowly take a bite. Guide them by saying, "Now take a bite and savor it. Close your eyes if it's helpful. Chew slowly, focus on what is happening as you chew."
- If your client wants to integrate faith into this exercise, you can guide them in a short prayer: "God, we thank you for the journey of this [name the food item] to the hand of [client's name]. We thank you for the nourishment it provides, and thank you for nourishing our bodies through the act of eating. Thank you also for the people who brought this [item] here to us. Teach us how to receive your gifts of faith, which are nourishment for our souls. Meet [client's name] in this act of eating with intention."
- Instruct your client to savor each bite, chewing slowly, redirecting their thoughts to the taste, the smell, and the sensation of eating. Then take some time to process with your client their experience. You can ask, "How was the exercise? Was it a strange exercise? How so? What sensations did you notice as you ate? What was new to you as you slowed your eating down? Did anything change?"

You can use this exercise to help your client develop a plan of mindful eating to support any changes in diet that their medical doctor has already advised. It is important that we do not treat beyond our scope of practice. Our role is to support the client and to provide space for them to discuss issues or successes they have experienced with diet choices that their physician and allied health colleagues have addressed with them.

Eating as Gratitude

Eating mindfully is a practice to slow down the experience and help our clients not to have an additional to-do list but to incorporate mindfulness into a daily habit of nourishment. We can remind our clients that as they care for their bodies through nourishment, they are caring for the gift that God has provided them and for the dwelling of the Holy Spirit: "Do you not know that your bodies are temples of the Holy Spirit, who is in you, whom you have received from God? You are not your own; you were bought at a price. Therefore honor God with your bodies" (1 Cor. 6:19–20). We honor our bodies when we sense and take pleasure in the taste and texture of our food. In our modern fast-paced lifestyle, it is almost as though we inhale rather than savor our food. We can re-elevate the eating experience even at our modern dining tables.

Consider the English Benedictines, who ate at a communal table three times a day and devoted themselves to eating as ritual with prayer and contemplation (Albala et al., 2011). What is unique about the monastic journey around eating is not only that it is a practice of prayer and listening but also that it emphasizes service and community. Eating in its fullness is a ritual of love. Gathering around the dining table is a celebration of unity, of oneness in humanity and vulnerability. Because we depend on food for nourishment, the food that is gathered and prepared for us can be sources of gratitude for our clients and ourselves.

Oftentimes, our clients struggle with isolation in the midst of their emotional pain. Encourage their engagement with others through "the breaking of bread." Whether or not it's around a formal dinner table, connecting with family and friends during a meal can nourish the soul. Preparing a meal is an opportunity to redirect one's attention to others. Reflecting on what it means to gather, prepare, serve, and then enjoy a meal enhances our ability to appreciate eating as a practice of caring and sharing, understanding that each meal takes many hands to make. From the farmers and field workers who plant and pick the foods we enjoy, to the delivery truck drivers who transport them, to the grocery workers who stock our neighborhood stores with fresh ingredients, to those at home who labor to put a nutritious meal on the table, many hands contribute to our enjoyment of meals, and sharing their gifts with others can be a delight and a practice of mindful gratitude.

Eating with Gratitude Exercise

For homework, instruct your client to prepare a simple meal for themselves and to invite at least one other person to share it with them for the purpose of expressing gratitude. Ask your client to prepare the food mindfully by finding a simple recipe, shopping for its ingredients, and preparing it while practicing the following mindfulness steps. Encourage them to work through this list in their journal. Have them journal their experience and report the results of this exercise to reinforce the neat step your client took to connect and practice gratitude.

Prompts for the exercise and for mindful journaling:

1. Think of a person to invite (a supportive friend or family member, or an acquaintance who is a positive person in your life). **Write down answers to these questions:** Why is this person a good choice? What has this person said or done that has encouraged you? How has this person impacted you?

2. As you hunt for a simple recipe, notice what meals feel comforting to you. If relevant, does this meal bring up a memory for you? **Jot your memory down.**

3. Shop for the ingredients for the meal you will prepare. When you come home, think about each item as you unpack it and put it away. Where did it come from? Who planted it, picked it, delivered it to your community, and stocked it in a store? Say a short prayer of gratitude for each person involved in this chain of events. **Write a short reflection** about what this short prayer has stirred inside of you.

4. Prepare the meal. As you labor, focus on each step. Breathe as you

stir the sauce or boil the water or heat the pan. Note the aromas in your kitchen. Thank God for the meal you are preparing and say a short prayer of blessing for the time to come with the person you will be sharing the meal with. Pray for their safe travel to your home. **Journal about your short prayer experience: What did you notice as you labored? What came to mind as you prayed for your guest's trip to your home?**

5. As you sit with your guest, thank them for coming. Tell them why you chose them for this gratitude meal. As you serve them the meal, note their reaction. Take in any positive feedback. Receive your guest into your mind, into your heart, and acknowledge the gift of their presence silently. Focus on the conversation. In moments of silence between the two of you, focus on eating and gratitude. If your guest is open to praying, give thanks to God for their role in your life and for the meal God has provided. **After your guest has left, write a short reflection on this experience.** Note any words of gratitude that you recall bubbled up inside of you. Note any words of gratitude that you received from your guest. Note any conflicting feelings or negative thoughts. In your journal, identify the source of those thoughts. What are you learning about yourself and your comfort with inviting others to eat with you in your personal space?

6. **Last, journal about the whole experience with a perspective of nonjudgment.** What did you learn about yourself? What made you capable of this exercise? What were some barriers? Did you identify any negative thoughts? If so, what are they, and why do you think they came about? Did you receive any feelings of joy, warmth, connectedness, comfort, acceptance, or love? What brought these wonderful feelings up for you? Write a sentence in your journal that reflects gratitude for this exercise and the learning you gained.

After this exercise, review with your client what worked, what went well, what did not go so well, what they had hoped to gain from it, what they did gain. Assist your client by providing positive feedback for their efforts, no matter the outcome. If they feel comfortable, ask them to share with you and reflect on some of the thoughts from their journal. Reflect with your client on how their preparing a meal and eating it with a supportive person fed their soul.

As the Benedictines demonstrate, fellowship within relationship grows stronger through eating with others. Help your client unpack how they view the impact of their simple acts of shopping, preparing, and sharing a meal with a supportive person. Develop within them a sense of their capability as they provide an opportunity for gratitude through eating. In *Liturgy of the Ordinary*, Harrison Warren (2016) writes beautifully that "eating itself reminds us that none of us can stay alive on our own.... We are born hungry and completely dependent on others to meet our needs. In this way, the act of eating reorients us from an atomistic, independent existence toward one that is interdependent" (p. 71).

Eating mindfully contributes to our own well-being and our clients' well-being. There is a lot of excellent, newer research on how a healthy diet is a catalyst for decreasing duration and intensity of depressive episodes and in buttressing mental-health wellness (Frazier et al., 2012; Hutchison et al., 2016; Melnyk et al., 2013; Vicinanza et al., 2020).

We increase our knowledge about ourselves around eating habits. To be mindful is to be grateful. As we ponder our thoughts and judgments about food and how we eat, we are able to consider the chain of labor and care that goes into a meal. Each one. The benefit to our clients of eating mindfully comes to fruition as we allow a simple process that we often take for granted to become a sacred ritual or even duty. Eating mindfully with another opens up the world again, reminds us and them of the enjoyment and warmth we all receive when we can break bread together. Our internal worlds shift by including supportive people on our life's journey. Gratitude becomes the outgrowth of this bigger world. Eating mindfully is the vehicle to wider vistas.

Through mindful eating and caring for the body, we recognize that we are holistic beings, and we experience emotional and spiritual benefits. For some of our clients, this is hopeful news: their daily habits toward health can build a tangible result. For other clients, this is bad news, because a mindful approach to health through eating, exercise, sleep (all the things that are challenged during bouts of depression, anxiety, and other disorders) is difficult while they are still building skills of noticing and observing. However, we, as therapists, counselors, psychologists, pastoral counselors, and other healing professionals, know that good mental health needs to be resourced in the body as well.

Eating Mindfully as a Blessing

Mindful eating is an intervention toward a more God-honoring view of one's body. In addition, mental health is a key aspect of overall health, and mindfulness helps foster good mental health by helping us develop coping strategies as well as metacognitive awareness of destructive thoughts. There is an inherent feedback loop when we support our health in all aspects of our lives: body, mind, and spirit. In addition, our clients' ability to care well for their bodies can be challenged when they soothe their emotions with food or detachment from life.

Christian mindfulness brings to mind scriptural examples of healthy eating and other physical choices. Christian mindfulness means that we are aware of what we eat. We ingest food and drink for nourishment, and that nourishment is not only physical. Nutrition comes from healthy foods, but so does a clearer thought process unhampered by the conveniences and chemicals of our modern lives. Food is a symbol of God's provision throughout the Bible and is tempered with boundaries. Manna, for example, could not be kept until morning: "No one is to keep any of it until morning" (Ex. 16:19). Also, some manna was to be saved as a living testimony of God's provision for the Israelites after their escape from Egypt. It was to be stored in a jar for later generations to remember (Ex. 16:33).

For Christians, eating mindfully means to look to food as a way toward a health-oriented blessing—physically and spiritually. When our clients who are Christ followers can be mindful in their eating and in their health habits, they are like Israelites keeping manna stores to remind them of God's provision for them. Similarly, our overall approach to health and a healthy lifestyle can be thought clearing and give us the energy to follow God in new ways. Christian mindfulness can extend our capacities and give us strength in any undertaking we are called to. We can confidently remind our clients to focus on the present moment, to attend and attune, to take, eat, and be nourished, and to be still because there is enough manna for today.

Have your clients try the following mindful eating practice as a step toward a Christian mindfulness lifestyle.

A Mindful Blessing for Meals

- Before a meal, say grace. Give thanks for the food and lean into the Lord's Prayer: "Give us today our daily bread." Then pause before eating. Pray a blessing over the food: "Lord, bless this food, bless the preparer, and bless me, the eater, to enjoy this gift of a meal with you."
- Take the first bite. Chew slowly and notice the flavor and texture of the food. In this exercise, it helps to eat something that is tasty to you. No judgment whether it's a bite of vegetable or a rich, yummy morsel. But do pick something tasty.
- Notice the smell and the flavor as you taste and ingest the food. Is it sweet, pleasantly salty, have bitter notes or a fresh green flavor? Savor the morsel bit by bit.
- Tune your mind and senses: take it all in and let the flavors settle in your mouth. Swallow the morsel. Notice and feel its weight in your stomach after it goes down.
- Say another prayer: "Thank you, Lord, for this food you have provided."
- Do this throughout the meal, and especially after an exhausting or emotional day.

- Slow your meal down as a Christian practice of gratitude and mindful eating. Let your body and mindful eating be the only things you think of. Over time, this practice will transform the way you feel and how you eat and approach health, because it allows God his rightful place as the provider of your health.

Eating mindfully is about our clients' building their capacity to enjoy food, to practice gratitude, and to choose, prepare, and savor meals as part of their daily practice. The enfolding of a Christian mindfulness skill while eating is also an easier and more accessible way to get into the practice. Our clients' experience of taste is more robust, the meal itself can perhaps be less anxiety producing, and, with a mindful approach, the awareness of the eating habit itself is built in. In addition, integrate the practices in this chapter with other therapeutic interventions around eating: food diaries, mindfulness exercises from other parts of this book to manage anxiety or reactivity around food, and so on.

References for Chapter 13

Albala, K., & Eden, T. (Eds.). (2011). *Food and faith in Christian culture.* Columbia University Press.

Frazier, E. A., Fristad, M. A., & Arnold, L. E. (2012). Feasibility of a nutritional supplement as treatment for pediatric bipolar spectrum disorders. *Journal of Alternative & Complementary Medicine, 18*(7), 678–685. https://doi.org/10.1089/acm.2011.0270

Harrison Warren, T. (2016). *Liturgy of the ordinary: Sacred practices in everyday life.* InterVarsity Press.

Hutchison, S. L., Terhorst, L., Murtaugh, S., Gross, S., Kogan, J. N., & Shaffer, S. L. (2016). Effectiveness of a staff promoted wellness program to improve health in residents of a mental health long-term care facility. *Issues in Mental Health Nursing, 37*(4), 257.

Melnyk, B. M., Jacobson, D., Kelly, S., Belyea, M., Shaibi, G., Small, L., O'Haver, J., & Marsiglia, F. F. (2013). Promoting healthy lifestyles in high school adolescents: A randomized controlled trial. *American Journal of Preventive Medicine, 45*(4), 407–415. https://doi.org /10.1016/j.amepre.2013.05.013

Vicinanza, R., Bersani, F. S., D'Ottavio, E., Murphy, M., Bernardini, S., Crisciotti, F., Frizza, A., Mazza, V., Biondi, M., Troisi, G., & Cacciafesta, M. (2020). Adherence to Mediterranean diet moderates the association between multimorbidity and depressive symptoms in older adults. *Archives of Gerontology and Geriatrics, 88*. https://doi .org/10.1016/j.archger.2020.104022

CHAPTER 14

Healthy Lifestyle and Mindfulness

*Do you not know that your bodies are temples of the
Holy Spirit, who is in you, whom you have received
from God? You are not your own; you were bought at
a price. Therefore honor God with your bodies.*
—1 CORINTHIANS 6:19–20

Contemplation Prompts for Clients

1 CORINTHIANS 6:19–20

- What does it mean to be a temple of the Holy Spirit?
- Why is there a price for you?
- How can you honor God with your body?

The wellness trend of late—as exhibited by the growth of wellness products, alternative medicine options, and even wellness influencers—seems to be less fad and more established as a way to keep one's self healthy. When most people think of wellness, they often think about preventive health, better nutrition, clarity of mind, increased energy, freedom from disease. Today, wellness practitioners abound. Spa experiences including botanical skin care and herbal teas along with the latest healing practices—the best your money can buy—are marketed and sold. I (Regina) grew up around family members who often sought preventive wellness instead of disease management approaches. As a Chinese American raised in California, I drank ginseng and herbal soups to maintain health. I was taught that eating tendons and ligaments built up my body's own connective tissue, that cupping would reduce my po po's (grandma's) aching back, and that acupuncture regulated menstruation cycles and effectively addressed pain in place of heavy drugs.

This wellness trend is all for the good, but there is more to wellness than fancy supplements and expensive experiences. Wellness as a philosophy assumes a mind-body connection that those of the spiritual persuasion already know about. For the Christian who meditates and practices mindfulness, Scripture provides the tincture that produces healing. How does Scripture offer health and wellness, especially for clients who might be interested in this mind-body connection? The Bible is grace filled and advocates moderation in all things, particularly in what we consider to be vices. For instance, on drinking alcohol, the goal is not abstinence but moderation—to be mindful of how much alcohol is consumed and to enjoy it for the purposes it serves, as part of an offering of harvest (Num. 18:12), as a symbol of abundance and God's blessing (Deut. 7:13), and as part of a celebratory experience (John 2:3). Excess drink and drunkenness always lead to the worst of human depravity (Gen. 9:18–28; 19:30–36; Hab. 2:4–6, 15).

Our wellness is affected by the stimuli and challenges of each day—our clients' sufferings or our daily workloads. Financial stressors, family conflicts, and spiritual dry spells alter us and can impact the way we feel in our bodies. Our physical, mental, and emotional health are gifts that need upkeep. When we or our clients neglect our bodies' systems, there is bound to be an effect.

Our bodies are also systems: a combination of electrical signals, connective tissue, fat stores, muscles, and more than enough parts to fill an anatomy encyclopedia. As counselors, therapists, and healing professionals, our bias in our work is toward the psyche and mind. However, part of the healing work we do with our clients requires them to build their bodily health as well. Though we are not medical experts, we work in concert with such experts through assessment and advocacy of wellness practices recommended to our clients by their physicians.

Not only that, our embodied presence in the therapeutic space creates a model for how our clients view their own bodies. We must make our health a priority to keep strong and sharp the tool of our work, which is us, contained in our bodies.

Viewing Health Holistically

Mindfulness practices in our daily lives can be a resource for both clients and practitioners. These practices help us become more aware of how we treat and care for our bodies. If we truly believe that we are made up of body, mind, and spirit, as the Scriptures say, then when we care for the body, the mind will be affected, and therefore so will the spirit. Our clients often come in with patterns of disruption in their appetite and sleep, and other health issues that compound the mental health issue that we are treating. And our own nutrition, sleep, diet, and exercise patterns set the stage for how present and attuned to our clients we will be.

We hope what has emerged for you as a therapist, counselor, psychologist, pastoral counselor, or healing practitioner is that Christian mindfulness practice is a lifestyle and not just another set of practical steps. Christian mindfulness interventions are as much science as a reflection of truths in Scripture: acceptance of our sinful nature and understanding that God is active in our lives and is present with us. God will direct our clients as they call on him and his promises of everlasting peace. When we live out Christian interventions, we nourish our spirits and minds. In addition, we must treat our bodies mindfully if we are to continue living out the fullness of God. He has given us one body—our one bag of bones—as his temple (1 Cor. 6:19).

Mindful Habits: Sleep and Exercise

The core of a Christian mindfulness approach toward health is the connection of the practice to the aim or goal. In the previous chapter, we used mindfulness to build awareness around eating. There are so many ways to combine mindfulness with other healthy patterns of living, and research continues to support the benefits of mindfulness-based interventions geared toward health issues.

Mindfulness and Sleep

We undervalue sleep as a society, because it is counterintuitive to our emphasis on productivity and finding our value and worth in our abilities and work. However, sleep's function is restoration. Lack of sleep shows up in our energy levels, our appearance of health, and our ability to think clearly and critically and to find rest in God.

Another challenge for many of our clients, especially when their treatment is geared toward mental health issues, is sleep. Fostering good sleep habits and the practice of good sleep hygiene are foundational treatment goals for many of our clients, especially those who suffer from depression and anxiety where the presenting symptoms include interrupted sleep or too much sleep. Most of our clients who suffer from depression, anxiety, or stress have difficulty sleeping. Sleep hygiene refers to the habits and skills we can train our clients to acquire to improve the quality and quantity of their sleep. Christian mindfulness can be a huge asset for improving sleep hygiene because it features truth from God's Word that may be a soothing balm to our clients in their patterns of stressful thoughts.

Research supports the idea that mindfulness practice is restorative and supports good sleep (Kim et al., 2016). In fact, Greeson et al. (2018) demonstrates that mindfulness-based stress reduction reduces sleep disturbance and cuts across multiple symptoms to reduce stress, leading to improved health.

It is fascinating and worth noting that the Bible contains many instances of God's speaking to people during dreams. For instance, in the Old Testament, God talks directly to Joseph, promising that Joseph will rule over his family. God speaks to him even before he is under duress. Joseph's brothers are jealous of his dreams: "'Here comes that dreamer!' they said to each other. 'Come now, let's kill him and throw him into one of these cisterns and say that a ferocious animal devoured him. Then we'll see what comes of his dreams'" (Gen. 37:19–20).

Another example is God's providing comfort in a dream to the other Joseph in the Bible: "Do not be afraid to take Mary home as your wife" (Matt. 1:20).

Thus, it might be safe to say that when we help our clients establish healthy sleep patterns using a Christian mindfulness framework, we may be helping them to hear from God as well.

According to Carl Jung, dreams are symbols of deeper psychological meaning. Many of you understand this integration of dreams and Christian symbolism better than we do. We simply offer a reminder that sleep is not just a physical state but can include spiritual health as well. If we define health holistically to include spiritual health, Christian mindfulness practice becomes even more robust for clients who suffer sleep issues. Physical and emotional health concerns emerge when sleep is a struggle. Therefore, it is more important than we might surmise to assess sleeping habits regularly, as well as to foster good sleep hygiene through Christian mindfulness practice. The following exercise is written to buttress your clients' efforts toward better sleep.

A Mindful Blessing for Sleep

Begin in the evening, before you are ready to sleep but after you have prepared for sleep through your evening routine (dressing, hygiene, etc.).

- Lie in your bed with your hands by your sides or placed gently over your heart. Inhale deeply, picturing your lungs filling with air. Exhale slowly, picturing air emptying from your lungs. Do this at least three times until you find a good rhythm for your breathing. Notice your breaths, notice your heartbeat, feel the bed beneath your body. Prepare your thoughts for prayer.

- Pray something like this: "Lord, thank you for these moments of rest. I savor this period of restoration. I ask for your blessing over this night. Please restore my body, my mind, my emotions, and my spirit through sleep. Thank you for caring for me, even for my sleep. Rest my thoughts, Lord. Please bring me peace and comfort. Amen."
- Breathe deeply again as before, picturing the air entering and leaving your lungs.
- Try this breath meditation:

  - As you inhale, say an affirmation in your mind: "I am able to sleep."
  - Exhale: "God, please grant me the ability to sleep."
  - Inhale: "Thank you for this moment to rest, Lord."
  - Exhale: "Lord, please bless this moment of rest."
  - Inhale: "Thank you for this blessing of night, Lord."
  - Exhale: "Lord, please bless this night."

Exercising Mindfully

It may seem counterintuitive to pair exercise—especially vigorous exercise—with mindfulness. However, there has been a growing trend, especially among runners, to use mindfulness while running to enhance both performance and the experience of running (Mateo, 2020). For us as counselors and therapists, the important aspect of this pairing is that exercise can boost mental health wellness. On top of that, practicing mindfulness while exercising makes that mind-body connection more apparent.

Moving our bodies, pushing them toward exercise, has myriad physical health benefits for all parts of our bodies. Effects can be found in the cardio-vascular, muscular, and even neurological systems. Dementia, depression, and anxiety are all mitigated by exercise, for instance. We would even posit that there are spiritual benefits as well: clearer thoughts, time to commune with God, time to reflect and be in awe of our bodies as crafted by the Creator.

We tend to shy away from discussing physical exertion with our clients, but perhaps we should address it more explicitly in session or in meetings, being careful not to frame it in a shameful way but to promote it as one tool in the therapeutic toolbox. First Timothy 4:8 puts it this way: "For physical training is of some value, but godliness has value for all things, holding promise for both the present life and the life to come." Though exercise will not be necessary for eternity, it is necessary for the functioning and well-being of our clients who will benefit from it. A Christian mindfulness practice for exercise includes the idea that all that we strive for in our bodies is useful for the kingdom. As the verse in Timothy explains, it has some value. Not for all things, but some. And in our clients' cases, a mindful exercise practice can improve their exercise experience and expand their abilities in both soul and body.

Physical activity can be a source of shame for our clients. Some clients underexercise or overexercise to the point of bodily risk. Many clients find it difficult to adhere to physical exercise. This is where a Christian mindfulness practice can support our clients' efforts to use exercise as a tool for their well-being. Schneider et al. (2019) found that the most effective mindfulness-based interventions for this promotion included physical activity aspects. Many of the studies these researchers reviewed included movement-oriented interventions, the most frequent being yoga.

This makes a lot of sense because yoga as a form of exercise syncs body with thoughts, movement with breath. As Christians who want to improve our clients' lives and play a role in their using all of the tools that will benefit them physically, emotionally, and spiritually, we can promote a pattern of exercise as a way for our clients to incorporate mindfulness into their regular movement schedule as well as to support and encourage physical activity. Again, as therapists, counselors, psychologists, and other practitioners, our role is to support, not to provide medical or health advice. We can simply train our clients toward accessing their motivation and self-care in physical exercise through Christian mindfulness.

Mindful Exercise Prompts

As you undertake a specific physical activity, reflect on the following prompts before, during, and after your activity.

- Before your exercise:
  - What do you notice about your body? Is it tense, stiff, flexible, ready to move?
  - What do you notice and observe about your attitude toward or reaction to embarking on exercise? Do you feel dread, excitement, responsibility, obligation? Do you look forward to this exercise?
  - What do you think you will feel at the end of the exercise? Accomplished, happy, relieved, in pain?
- During your exercise:
  - Notice your body's capacity. What surprises you about what it can do? What surprises you about what it cannot do?
  - Observe your thoughts and self-talk. Are your thoughts positive, encouraging? Are they focused on other things that are more negative?
  - Notice any emotions, positive or negative. Do you feel frustration, self-satisfaction, lifting of mood and stress, hopelessness?
- After your exercise:
  - What do you notice about your body after you exercise?
  - What do you notice about your emotional state after you have exercised?
  - What do you notice about your thoughts about this exercise?

Walking Mindfully

Every year, I (Regina) have the privilege of attending a writer's retreat sponsored by my university at Serra Center, a Catholic retreat center in Malibu, California. I look forward to it because the setting is beautiful and it is a productive time for me. More than that, my time in Malibu is punctuated by sacred moments when I walk the grounds. I exercise my body and look at the lush trees, native flora, and majestic scenery. I take in the sounds of the waves. I relish the gentle breeze and notice how the air moves around while I walk up and down the paths. I feel the grass on my bare feet, the damp soil, and the way the curves of my feet settle on the earth.

While walking the grounds, I break free from confined space not only to take in the nature around me—clean air, sounds of birds, cobalt blue ocean—but to take steps in my writing journey. Each step is a metaphor for the work I do in my mind. I move forward and envision the progress I make, with God by my side, to do God's kingdom work. Exercising mindfully, whether walking, running, swimming, shooting hoops—whatever your pleasure—expands the benefits and the experience. Moving our bodies can help us connect internally with God's presence and subsequent stirrings of our souls.

Walking is the easiest and most accessible type of healthy exercise that our clients can engage in. It is not costly, and if our clients are able bodied or if accommodations can be made for their limitations, then taking a walk mindfully can help them get out of their heads, their usual spaces, and provide a lift in their moods. Not only that, walking can signify a journey of contemplation and the beginning of a new adventure.

The retreat center has a large labyrinth made of rocks that beckons visitors through a granite gravel path. Overlooking a hillside vista with ocean views, it is perfectly situated. The ancient idea of the labyrinth, which dates to the fourth century, is to take a journey with God. To walk in the labyrinth is to walk toward God. The path leads to the center. One must prepare with reflection, prayer, and intention. Mindfulness during such a walk focuses the mind on God's presence. Having journeyed to the center, one leaves something behind or refocuses before journeying out of the labyrinth. Many mementos are left at the center of the labyrinth. Often they are mementos of loved ones who have passed. The labyrinth walker intends to heal from their grief, and their outward journey is beautifully and heartbreakingly shared with others who walk after them. A communal grief can be felt as well as a communal hope in the risen Christ, especially when walking out from the center, back toward the beginning. When the labyrinth is finished, the journey with God is complete. One is never alone, as we know as Christ followers. God is always with us wherever we go. We are never alone in Christ.

As Christian counselors, therapists, social workers, psychologists, and other healing practitioners, walking mindfully is a journey inward as well. When we can be more self-aware, we can be more present with our clients. In your own mindfulness practice, see if walking gives you a different perspective. Walking mindfully can be a dedicated time of devotion, or it can be simply a time to walk—not to think, not to worry, not to plan, just to walk. For therapeutic purposes, if possible, invite your client to take a mindful walk outside your therapeutic space, ensuring confidentiality and privacy. If that is not possible, share with your client the following instructions for a mindful journey walk so they can complete it between sessions and report how it went later.

Mindful Journey Walk Exercise

- Plan at least a ten- to fifteen-minute walk. Find a private space to walk, preferably with some grass or a nice path near trees and where you can hear the birds or the breeze. Before you walk, set an intention for this time. Perhaps you want to walk with God or release your anxiety to him. Perhaps you want to use this walk as a symbolic journey toward a goal, perhaps a mental-health wellness goal. Use this time to focus on God's presence, understanding that you do not walk alone.

- Begin the walk by breathing. Take three deep breaths and one slow step. Tell God your intention for this walk. Say to him, "God, I want to walk with you," or, "I want to take this journey with you." Ask God to teach you something about where you begin this walk and where you might want him to take you. Submit your thoughts and agenda to God now.

- Next walk very slowly. Rosenbaum (2017) suggests inhaling while lifting your foot, and exhaling while placing your foot down. The point is to keep your attention on your feet and on the ground and on the sensation of movement in your body.
- Notice your thoughts and identify whether you can focus on just breathing and walking. If your mind wanders, don't judge yourself; that is normal. Let the change of scenery be an anchoring point for your mind to focus. Take slow steps, not gentle or hard, and take each step very slowly. Feel the way your heels and toes touch the ground. Notice where your mind goes as you walk slowly just like this, step by step and slowly. Simply note your thoughts and bring your mind back to walking. Walk at a pace that is slower than your normal walking pace.
- Become aware of your body while you walk. Feel your heartbeat. Take a few deep breaths. Breathe in the goodness of nature around you. Smell the aromas—hopefully grassy, green, clean. If they are not, just simply breathe in with gratitude and acknowledge your body's ability to take in oxygen and use it to give you what you need for this walk.
- As you come to the middle of your walk, evaluate how far you have come. This is a short journey, but a journey nonetheless. Acknowledge that you gave yourself this space to be with God, to sense his presence with you. Picture that he is walking beside you. Notice any feelings that come up about God's presence. Tell God about them.
- Focus your attention on this relationship between you and God. Take a few deep breaths again, saying a short prayer asking God to stay with you on this walk until the very end.
- As you come to the end of your walk, look around again. Take stock of where your thoughts are. If they are on to something else, bring them back to this spot, where you are, grounded by your feet on this path. You can remind yourself if you've wandered off by praying, "Thank you for this time to meet with me, God. Help me to sense your presence again." Receive any word from him. If you don't

receive any word from him, that is all right. Be aware again that you kept this time and made this walk as a way to slow down, to be mindful and to have this journey. After you have finished your walk, give yourself kudos for this effort and for any lessons or insights you have gained.

When our clients can take noticeable steps toward a healthy lifestyle, and apply Christian mindfulness to support, motivate, or initiate those steps, we can be confident that they are being nourished in all senses of the word. In Christian mindfulness that addresses healthy eating, sleep, and exercise habits, our clients are taking care of their bodies. They are living as exiles in a culture that is not necessarily health oriented. Physical nourishment brings returns on your clients' ability to think more clearly, feel better, and sit in God's presence, as it did for Shadrach, Meshach, and Abednego. May your clients in exile know that their homes are not on earth and that God's kingdom is their inheritance, where they will sit healthy and nourished forevermore.

Questions for Reflection

1. How can you think rightly and biblically if you are undernourished (body, mind, and spirit)?
2. What health practices mentioned in this chapter (eating, sleeping, exercising) most appeal to you? Why? What other health practices appeal to you?
3. Name the benefits you will be mindful of as you make efforts to eat, sleep, and exercise in ways that support a healthy and nourished lifestyle.

References for Chapter 14

Greeson, J. M., Zarrin, H., Smoski, M. J., Brantley, J. G., Lynch, T. R., Webber, D. M., Hall, M. H., Suarez, E. C., & Wolever, R. Q. (2018). Mindfulness meditation targets transdiagnostic symptoms

implicated in stress-related disorders: Understanding relationships between changes in mindfulness, sleep quality, and physical
symptoms. *Evidence-Based Complementary & Alternative Medicine
(ECAM)*, 1–10. https://doi.org/10.1155/2018/4505191

Mateo, A. (2020).What actually is mindful running and how do you do
it? *Runner's World*. Retrieved from https://www.runnersworld.com
/training/a22160937/mindfulness-in-running/

Rosenbaum, E. (2017). *The heart of mindfulness-based stress reduction: A
MBSR guide for clinicians and clients*. PESI Publishing and Media.

Schneider, J., Malinowski, P., Watson, P. M., & Lattimore, P. (2019). The
role of mindfulness in physical activity: A systematic review. *Obesity
Reviews, 20*(3), 448–463. https://doi.org/10.1111/obr.12795

Kim, S. M., Park, J. M., & Seo, H. J. (2016). Effects of mindfulness-based
stress reduction for adults with sleep disturbance: A protocol for an
update of a systematic review and meta-analysis. *Systematic Reviews,
5*, 1–6. https://doi.org/10.1186/s13643-016-0228-2

PART 4

THERAPEUTIC EXERCISES COMBINED WITH MINDFULNESS

In part 4, we focus on the integration of therapeutic exercises with Christian mindfulness. The chapters that follow are practical and cover mindfulness with remembering, guided imagery, progressive muscle relaxation, boundaries, cognitive behavioral therapy, centering prayer, and *Lectio Divina*, ending with a beautiful integration of the practice of the Blessing with mindfulness. Many of these interventions are useful in mindfulness-based therapies, and you might be familiar with some because they originate in secular-based mindfulness interventions. We have added a Christian twist to them so that you can use them more fluidly in therapy or counseling situations. A few of them are drawn from the work we have trained others to do inside and outside of the classroom, and we hope you will find them useful in your work as well. The details of the exercises are included to give you a good template to work from, as well as Christian principles and biblical support for their use.

The chapters in part 4 include scripts that you can integrate into your counseling or therapy work. We often find that it is helpful to try them yourself a few times before using them with your clients, to become familiar with the practices and find your own language and style for your counseling or therapeutic work. We have found that scripts are easy to adapt, especially at first. Thus, we hope this part of the book becomes a resource you turn to as needed for different clients' needs and situations.

CHAPTER 15

Remembering as a Way to Develop Mindfulness

There is a popular video circulating around social media of a former ballerina who is ravaged by Alzheimer's disease. She is listening to music through earphones. We see her move, first with her arms, then with her head tilting and turning with the music. Her movements seem strange but magnificent. The screen splits. One half stays with this ninety-year-old woman as she moves with the music. The other half shows a young ballerina: arms sweeping overhead, head tilting and turning. We come to understand that this ballerina is the old woman when she was young. The young ballerina is much more fluid in her movements, and yet we watch with awe as the old woman remembers every single part of that complex dance. All she needed was the music to jolt her memory of who she was and still is—an elegant ballerina.

Remembering can do the same thing for our clients. Using concepts from positive psychology and Martin Seligman's work, we expand on the idea of remembering as a practice of gratitude and affirmation. In mindfulness, we remember the past not to stay in the past but to acknowledge gratitude for the present moment. In this chapter, you will find a script we created that draws from Gestalt therapy and the work of Fritz and Laura Perls, using the empty chair technique to help your clients deal with unfinished business about themselves, with God's help. The script provides a mindfulness approach to gratitude and affirmation practices. Later in this chapter, we also discuss how the present moment is full of narratives of what God has done in the past that impacts our clients' present-moment experience. From the ancient Israelites to our day, the story of God's faithfulness hearkens back while calling to us today.

Recapturing the True Story

Our memories play a powerful role in the narratives we choose, consciously or unconsciously. As our clients live moment to moment, they carry narratives about their past, especially about themselves and their capabilities. As Christ followers, can our clients acknowledge God's hand in their lives? Is their locus of control within or external? Is their internal story and their sense of the past grounded within a strong internal locus of control, or do our clients externalize and blame?

Even though in Christian mindfulness we discuss and practice the present moment, this past-to-present orientation is important to acknowledge. The way our clients remember is fluid. There is opportunity for them to deal with the past so they can live more fully into the present moment with the confidence that comes with a relationship with God.

Remembering is an important part of living out what God calls us to as flawed beings in need of salvation and grace. In the Old Testament, God remembers his covenant with Abraham. In Exodus 6:5, God remembers the Israelites, descendants of Abraham, as they are enslaved in Egypt. They suffer and are put on a path out of Egypt as they cry to God to remember them. Our clients often cry out from the ways they feel destroyed by circumstances. As they express, grieve, and mourn, as they ask for help, we know our God remembers.

Remembering is a step toward building attention and forces us to slow down so we can flourish. The meaning of our lives is past and present intertwined right now, in this present moment, which is a moment to mindfully remember. As we sit in awareness of the present moment, our minds may flit to thoughts in the past before they settle down. In our work with our clients we can leverage such moments to draw them into a space that is grace filled and bubbling with gratitude for the gift of God's presence in the now.

Our clients often come with stories about why they are in therapy or counseling with us. Sometimes those stories do not jibe with their histories. The memories they share are sometimes flooded with inaccuracies. That is okay. That is what makes them human: flawed, in need of grace.

A Remembering Script

Through mindfulness, we help our clients remember who they were, who they are, and not only who they are becoming but also what they stand for, how they stand for their values and why they do so. Here is a script for helping your clients be mindfully aware of their past proud moments while acknowledging who they are now.

Remembering and being mindfully aware of the present moment seem like opposite things, but in practice you can think of both. Our minds' concept of time is fluid, but God is outside of time. So imagine that your life is to God not just a moment in time but moments upon moments when he is there. He is present with you in the past and now.

Sort out what memory you want to ponder in this present moment. Close your eyes and take four deep breaths, slowing the rhythm of your breathing down. Focus just on your breath and try not to judge how you are breathing. There is no right way to breathe. Just breathe, slowly and deliberately.

Now I ask you to focus on a memory of something you did that you are proud of. It could be as simple as taking a shower when you didn't feel like it, or something big like asking for a promotion or making a healthy decision. Identify the moment, and then think about the time and place it occurred. Relive this memory in your mind, and breathe as a way to take this memory into the present moment.

Note in your mind whatever you can see, hear, touch, or smell in this memory. Breathe those things in. Now bring this memory into the present moment, here, with me in this space. What do you notice about how you feel now, as you come into this memory? Are your emotions the same as or different from before this memory? Is your breathing the same as or different from before this memory? Is your body feeling the same as or different from in the memory? Note any differences or similarities in your emotions, in your breathing, or in your body.

With your eyes still closed and keeping this memory in the present moment, observe how you feel when you contemplate that the you in the memory is the same you today. Assess this knowledge within yourself: you in this memory is still the same you right here and right now.

As you keep your eyes closed, I would like you to come up with a few words that describe this person to yourself. What are a few adjectives you would use now to describe the person who did this hard thing in the past? How would someone else describe this person to you now? Are there skills or strengths you can see that you have developed from the past to now? What are they?

Now let's notice where you feel God has been in this memory. Where is God in that point in time? What do you feel God is saying about that person who did that hard thing in the past? What adjectives would God use to speak about you? What skills or strengths did Christ assist you with in that moment? How do you feel about Christ's strength in you? If it's helpful, say a prayer of gratitude to God for being there in that memory. If it fits, say another prayer of gratitude for the kind words you are taking in about yourself, that acknowledge how cherished you are as God's child. Say a prayer of thanks for the strengths he has given you.

Next let's just sit here in this space, breathing together. Let's notice any affirmations you have received from this exercise. Keep your eyes closed and your mind focused on the work here and now, because God is here with us to help you understand who you are in this moment and how he has carried you from the past into this point in time.

What insight about who you were then and who you are now comes up for you? If you cannot articulate it through words, what feeling or picture describes this person in the past becoming this person now? Hang on to these affirmations. Write them down right now if you can, or journal about them tonight or sometime before we meet again. At least once a day before we meet again, I would like you to meditate on the affirmations you heard from God and the prayers of gratitude you prayed. Is that all right with you?

After using this script, it is important, as you know, to debrief the experience with your client. This script provides a good opportunity to continue to explore in the safety and skill of your professional training negative or traumatic memories, as integrated with an exposure or EMDR based treatment. Again, all this depends of course on your client's stability and readiness, which it's important for you to assess using your best clinical judgment.

An Empty-Chair Recollection Script

The next script utilizes the empty chair technique with a Christian mindfulness approach. This script can be used or adapted to confront specific issues that a client is struggling with, such as a poor boundary or low self-esteem, or simply to explore how they feel about themselves in the present. The point of the exercise is to help your client deal with some unfinished business in the past.

Your client's ability to enact this type of role play will help you understand more about the narratives about the past that they hold on to. Our clients often have harsh internal critics, according to Fritz Perls, that keep them from working out of their cognitive schemas. Working in the present with your clients through this Gestalt based technique presents an opportunity for you to infuse faith where it is usually missing. Helping clients decode their motivations and intentions, or just acquire general self-awareness about how they hold inaccurate stories about themselves (or perhaps stories that are accurate and telling!) can be a powerful way to break through toward healthier, healing-oriented views of themselves. You might have to help them identify times in their lives that have some unfinished business based on your assessment and what you know about your clients. Either way, you can use the following script to lead them through this period to help them. Adapt it to the circumstances that best suit a particular client.

As you use the script, pay attention to your client's nonverbal cues. Observe your client, doing so with a warm, supportive presence. This is a moment not to analyze but simply to observe. If they are struggling, you can prompt them: "Hey, I'm here with you. It's okay." Or, "I know this is going to feel awkward, but give it a try. Tell your past self that you feel awkward." Or even inject a little humor to help normalize the exercise: "You can even tell your younger self that your counselor is making you do this."

Before you use this script, you may want to study this technique and practice it a few times so you know how to guide your client, watch for verbal cues, and be prepared for intense emotions during the exercise. Use your best judgment, of course, as a trained professional. It might not be suitable for trauma work, so please be aware of that before you embark on it with your client.

This exercise is to help you recollect a time in your life and to acknowledge all the ways you have evolved to where you are today. In mindfulness, we practice honoring the awareness of ourselves so that we can be more fit for God's use.

To begin, think of yourself during your middle- or high-school years, or even as a young adult. Pick a period in your life that stands out to you. Think about yourself at the time—your insecurities, the way you dressed or looked, the relationships you had, your home life. Just acknowledge all of that. Try not to put a label on it, judging it as a good or bad time in your life. Just let the memory be what it is.

There is an empty chair in front of you. I'm going to ask you to do a little role playing and pretend you are talking to your past self at the age you have pinpointed. In your role play, I would like for you to acknowledge who you were at that age, what you struggled with, and how you were coping, but with the wisdom of now, in this moment. To prepare for this chat, let's reflect together on what you remember about your-self at that time and all the things I mentioned: age, struggles, coping.

Now please face the chair and picture your past self there. Imagine that you are encouraging the person sitting there, helping your young-er self along. I will be quiet just to support you in the room. I am not judging you, there are no rights or wrongs in how you approach this exercise. As you feel emotions and form thoughts and words, breathe deeply and experience both your younger self and your older self. Take them in so you can more fully immerse yourself into both roles.

Reflect on these prompts as you begin your talk: What would God say to this young person about your circumstance? What do you think or feel about God at that time? How can you help your younger self embrace who God made you, how he is fashioning you into the person you are today? Speak kindly and gently to your younger self, observe the emotions that come up for you, both from the standpoint of your younger self and your self now.

The strength of this scripted exercise is in your clients' building aware-ness of their hopes, wishes, and desires as they look back on their younger selves. They begin to notice unfinished business or rigid cognitive schemas. They also build awareness of their emotions, paying attention to them in the moment and doing the hard work of identifying them and perhaps even confronting themselves in this moment.

Debrief this exercise with your clients to help them come out of that experience and be grounded in the present moment with you in your ses-sion or meeting. We do not want your counselees to feel stuck emotionally or cognitively in the past. Debriefing helps bring them back to center.

In the debriefing, you might notice a conflict between what you observed that they experienced and how they talk about it with you. Be sensitive and gentle regarding any shame they might be experiencing. They might feel vulnerable and want to go back into hiding. Gently nudge them and focus on their positive engagement with this exercise. Applaud their effort. It is hard work!

Work through with them any intense emotions or memories that come up, being gentle in your questioning, while providing the warm, stable support to help them come back to equanimity. Again, congratulate them for their hard work. If it's helpful, lead them through a mindfulness exercise to bring relaxation back, to thank God for his presence and his faithfulness throughout. Close the time in prayer, if your client desires.

Conclusion

Hearkening to the past while staying aware of the present can be a powerful way to incorporate Christian mindfulness into a therapeutic practice. Remembering is tied to who clients feel they are now. They cannot know the present without remembering the past. Lessons from their history will help them write the next chapter in their lives and begin a new season. Remembering is the song that our clients will carry with them in order to dance elegantly in the present moment with God as their greatest dance partner.

CHAPTER 16

Christian Imagination
Paired with Mindfulness

What do you picture when you think of God? This is one of the questions I (Regina) have been asking pastors for a study on pastors and their definitions of mindfulness. I receive many answers that captured the imagination: The wind. A large body of water. "I see him in the swaying of the palm trees," one pastor told me. Stimulating the visual field of the mind is a way to help our clients anchor into God. If we think about attachment theory and how secure attachment can play a role in our clients' healing work, God is our permanent object. He is greater than an object—much greater! We Christ followers know that, but we can more effectively help our clients live and breathe his permanent presence in their lives when God is a part of their Christian imagination.

Think for a moment about your first experience seeing the Grand Canyon or of a different memorable time when you witnessed the vibrant purples, oranges, and yellows of a gorgeous sunset, or heard the gurgles of flowing water when walking along a riverbed, or stared out over the vastness of an ocean, breathing in the briny air. If you can recall what that experience was like—seeing the colors, hearing the calls of the birds—you are utilizing both your imagination and your memory to transport yourself to a place in your mind.

Now imagine medieval painters or stained-glass craftsmen who read the Scriptures and brought an illiterate community to a saving truth through art and iconography. These images were powerful and still are. Walk into a cathedral made during this period and you will feel the soaring heights of God, see the beauty of the Savior through the stained glass, understand the holiness of God that words cannot quite convey. We see and experience because, as human creatures on earth, we rely on our senses to tell us about reality and about God.

Incorporating Images into Therapy

We live in a visual culture where we're bombarded with images on television, social media, and the internet. The sheer amount of what we see can make our eyes weary. And though the quality of the images we see multiple times a day does not render a soaring, holy, transcendent experience, we are transfixed nonetheless.

The visual arts are a respite for our weary eyes and a resource as we seek to provide our clients with tools for healing. Our clients' images of God, Jesus, and the Holy Spirit are personal and may draw from representations they have gained from their churches or pop culture. We can stimulate our clients' Christian imagination as a resource for soothing, to quiet the anxieties they are working out so that they can grasp a permanent object of love and grace in the midst of treatment.

If your counselees are willing and able, ask them to find a piece of artwork that they admire or enjoy. This can be a good tool for therapy because it allows for discussion about what appeals to them about an image and about what the artwork teaches them. In Christian mindfulness, we can help draw our clients to images of art or nature and encourage them to bring those images with them to counseling or therapy to share with us. Oftentimes, the process of picking out that image and reflecting on it is a form of mindfulness. Our counselees who are drawn to the arts or images may find them soothing and good focal points for subsequent mindfulness practice.

Another positive trend in psychotherapy that lends itself to an experiential and visual practice of Christian mindfulness is "walk and talk therapy."

In this type of therapy, you meet your client on a hiking trail. Choose a trail that aligns with your client's physical abilities. An alternative to a hiking trail is a labyrinth at a nearby retreat center. Pick a place where you can put into practice more saliently in real time the guided-imagery script given later in this chapter. For the session, you can have your client use this script *in vivo*, live and in person, with your guidance and help. This will allow your client to have a memory they can return to, with your guidance.

Guided Imagery in Christian Mindfulness

The power of guided-imagery techniques is that they create a transcendent experience. Our clients can transcend their worries and find respite using their internal senses. The Christian mindfulness aspect is intended to help them build awareness of the present moment by noticing when they are stressed in their bodies—tight, clenched, uncomfortable—and then find ways to release that pressure to find a looseness and flexibility of body, mind, and soul.

As Christian mindfulness practitioners, we can utilize guided-imagery techniques infused with God's presence as a way to teach and minister to our clients to bring peace to their anxious thoughts. With practice, our clients may go to imagery whenever they experience panic, worry, or stress. In addition, guided imagery that rests on God's presence teaches our clients more about themselves—their worth, the arc of God's enduring love and justice, the salvation and acceptance that they can attach their self-worth to. The image that they go to is built in their imagination. It is not truth, per se, but an emotional truth of God's omnipotence and omnipresence in their lives. Christian guided imagery is the result of scripturally sound truth and is embedded in a mindfulness practice that serves the therapeutic goals you have identified together.

Christian guided imagery has been used throughout Christian history and hails from both Western Catholic Christian practice and the Eastern Orthodox Christian tradition. We understand that God granted those believers throughout history the ability to be grounded in the presence of

God. In Christian history, we see the use of images in statues, icons, and stained glass as a way to help believers learn more about God and the truths found in Scripture. Further, many Eastern Orthodox icons are meant to be used as a way to transcend their earthly focus to ascend into the holy places. The Christian imagination is subject to the truths displayed in the icons, teaching believers who could not read the Scriptures.

Most of us in the fields of social work, counseling, and psychology recognize that guided imagery is a good grounding technique because it can help dissipate fear, anxiety, and trauma reactions with skilled support. Our clients can benefit from finding an image to work on to help improve a mindfulness state, one in which the present moment resides in a nonjudgmental way, and in which they can sense God's presence.

Attachment Theory and Guided Imagery

It is in God's presence that our clients can find a secure attachment. Often, we work with clients who have attachment issues, and if we understand the work of British psychoanalyst Donald Winnicott, then we know that our counseling and therapeutic presence is a "holding environment" where clients come to see us as reliable, trustworthy persons in their lives. Even better is that God provides our clients the truest, securest permanent holding environment possible. The Christian mindfulness practice we presented in chapter 4 was on the first part of the Lord's Prayer, starting with "our Father." We can draw from that image of God as our Father as an anchoring image. If your client has not done that exercise yet, we encourage you to revisit that chapter, especially if your client wants to incorporate God into the guided image as described in this chapter.

It is helpful to understand that our clients' attachment to God for a sense of security might be connected to family of origin issues, so we must tease those issues out. For God to be a permanent sense of comfort in our clients' lives, we may need to help our clients confront distortions they are projecting onto God based on their real (and perhaps undistorted) experiences with parents or parental figures. A guided-imagery practice can be an anchoring point and place where clients can go through thick and thin. Anchoring points offer a valuable permanence, especially for clients who need someone stable in their lives.

A Guided Imagery Script

With these points in mind, you can use the following guided-imagery script to help bring God the Father, Christ the Son, and the Holy Spirit into your client's picture.

> Take three deep breaths in and out. With your eyes closed, I would like you to follow along with me, concentrating on my words while adapting this scene in your mind's eye to what feels comforting, safe, and beautiful for you. Set an intention for this time. Maybe it's a prayer or just a thought: "I would like to _____ during this time." Name in your mind the intention for this restful time.
>
> In your mind, pick a place that is soothing to you. It could be a place you have been or a place you plan to go. It should be in nature and vast enough that there is space for you to take in the scenery. Picture yourself in that place. Perhaps you are on a relaxing beach, walking a trail in a lush forest, sinking your feet into a fragrant garden, or taking in the sight of a red-orange desert.
>
> Find the scene and picture yourself in it. Notice the colors of this place. Notice, perhaps, how the sunlight hits the waves of the sea, glistening on the top of a crest of the water, or how the light casts shadows through the trees, or makes the flowers or the desert sky pop with multiple colors. Take in the colors, breathe in as you see them and the light, and breathe out.
>
> Now notice how big this scene is. You are standing or sitting in a big place. Scan with your mind's eye from the left of the horizon to the front and now to the right. Maybe there are sailboats off in the distance or a pier on one side. Perhaps you see trees and mountains that never seem to end or a vast field of flowers. Notice how big this place is and

how you get to roam in it. Capture the scene in your mind and fill it with look points and landmarks for a few more seconds.

Next take in the sounds of this place. Perhaps you hear birds chirping, a brook bubbling, palm trees swaying, the tall trees' leaves or pine needles rustling in a steady breeze, or the cool of a gentle desert wind. Take those sounds in while I'm quiet for a few seconds.

Then identify the smells of this scene: the smell of suntan lotion, if you are on the beach; or the earthy smells of wood or pine in a forest; or wondrous floral scents wafting through the air; or the clay and cacti of the desertscape.

Afterward, take into your mind the taste of the air. Is it like sea salt? Is it loamy? Is it like the forest surround, green and crisp like the fields, or a bit like the sand?

Use each sense as a foundation for your exploration of this scenery. Just take another beat here to breathe in these things deeply, staying in your scene through your senses.

Next let's focus on your sense of touch. Imagine that you are barefoot. Focus on what you feel underneath your feet: sand, moist soil, or firm ground. Now ground your feet in it. Notice the strength of the earth beneath you.

Imagine now that as you are in this scene, God's light is shining on you. You are in this scene with God. Just you and Christ. Remember that when Moses came down from the mountain after meeting with God, his face shone brightly. This is the same God, the Ancient of Days, who cares for you. Because he knows how many hairs are on your head, this God knows what you need. Envelop yourself in the warmth of unconditional grace. Hold on to the truth of his holiness, which is good and right.

Imagine for a moment that God's great, bright light shines on you softly. Maybe it warms you, starting from the top of your head, and it envelops you with peace. This light melts from the top of your head, travels down to your shoulders, down your stomach, down to your feet, and seeps into the ground below. Settle on this image in your surroundings right now while I'm quiet for a bit more. Absorb and receive.

Reflect now on the intention you set for this time. What did you discover, if anything? What did Christ's light reveal or expose to you emotionally or spiritually? Take another three deep breaths in and out, and slowly open your eyes. Now let's talk through what you experienced.

The questions at the end of this script are intended for you to help debrief this Christian guided-imagery experience. When clients delve into their imagination, with God present, they are working their minds and psyches into a pattern where they can turn to him when they need him. Guided imagery serves both to soothe and to help clients connect to their ability to relax their bodies through their minds. When we utilize guided imagery with our clients, we are activating both the visual centers and calming centers of their nervous systems. Combined, they can provoke a calming effect, bringing down the heart rate, helping clients transcend their anxious thoughts and feelings of despair with noticeably joyful images in their minds.

With God present in their minds, our clients can sense that God is active, alive. If we use the Scriptures along with this guided imagery—such as the tree planted by streams of water in Psalm 1, or the birds of the air that God sees and cares for—we help our clients not just imagine but live out the truth of God's desire to have a deeper relationship with them. If you and your clients are comfortable with it, build in verses that remind them of the truth that God is for them, that God is walking with them, that he created these beautiful places on earth the same way he created them.

Guided imagery becomes more salient as it's practiced. When we work with our clients' Christian imagination, incorporating images of soothing places, we help them access anytime the beauty of the earth, with God present.

Conclusion

We can all picture it: God is in the wind, in the trees, in large bodies of water. Sometimes our clients simply need a rest where it seems there is no rest. They need to feel a peace where peace is lacking. It is in Christian imagination that God can be most real on this side of heaven. Helping our clients step into the present moment in their minds provides a freedom that no one can take away from them. Helping our clients utilize their Christian imagination with Scripture and biblical teaching sets their minds on higher things. Amid pain, suffering, and mental health issues, our clients can transcend, for even a brief moment. And this transcendent experience, where Christ is present, offers them a taste of what is true in heaven, where every tear will be wiped away and there will be no gnashing of teeth.

CHAPTER 17

Progressive Muscle Relaxation with Christian Mindfulness

The popularity of yoga pants as acceptable clothing to wear anywhere from the grocery store to school drop-offs is evidence of the fact that yoga, once seen as a practice for celebrities, has gone mainstream. Part of its appeal is that yoga is a series of movements that provides exercise as well as stress relief, especially for busy professionals, whom yoga studios cater to in nearly every major city around the globe.

Yogis understand that the various poses require a tightening of muscles along with breathing and mindful awareness. As poses are held and released, it may feel like tension is flowing out of the body and the mind. In this chapter, we will practice a similar process of tightening and release through progressive muscle relaxation, with a Christian twist. Progressive muscle relaxation infused with God's presence sanctions our bodies to experience his soothing, holy touch. Sometimes our clients feel stress as pain or tightness in their bodies before they even become aware they are stressed or hurting emotionally. Clients may also feel other issues, such as trauma or depression, through physical symptoms. They may even be more comfortable exploring their bodily symptoms—headaches, digestive issues, tight and sore muscles—before they feel comfortable processing their emotions. When clients experience pain or discomfort of the body and not of the emotions or spirit, psychosomatic issues are at play. Engaging the body with the mind and spirit can be a powerful way of bringing awareness to the body as a gateway to dealing with mental health or emotional issues.

Stress and the Body

At times in our Christian communities, we hear messages that reflect a focus on right thinking rather than on knowing wisdom through the spirit and the body. We might pick up on ways of thinking that relegate stressors to a positivity mindset and an overcoming attitude. Have you or someone you know ever experienced a church service focused on healing during which there were exuberant calls for prayers "filled with faith"? What if one prays with enough faith but healing does not come? Unfortunately, oftentimes the person who is suffering is judged for not having enough faith if they leave the service in the same condition they came in. We have often witnessed a "pray it away" attitude in some Christian circles. The error of these healing services is that the denial of suffering can alienate folks who want to experience the power of faith even when they are not healed from their bodily pain in this lifetime.

As therapists, counselors, and other healing professionals, we are familiar with how this denial of suffering delays the constructive outcomes our clients need and desire. Sometimes mental health issues won't be healed completely. Not yet. However, denying these issues leads to more suffering. An example of this is when Christian leaders tell our clients to have more faith and get off of their psychotropic medications. This can create great harm. Again, sometimes the body has to be addressed so that the mind and spirit can function properly. Prioritizing thoughts and emotions over paying attention to the signals our bodies give makes us dualists. Duality of mind versus body or spirit versus body bifurcates the healing process. In Christian mindfulness practice, the body can put out the loudest signal that our clients are suffering even when they are unable to articulate the pain. Sometimes emotions, negative thoughts, or spiritual disenfranchisement may show up in sleep issues, negative eating habits, or digestive problems before they show up in other ways.

When we lose our mind-body-soul awareness, feeling stress or being stressed out is often treated as a sign of a lack of faith rather than what it is—a signal that something needs tending to. Part of that tending is in helping our clients recognize early on how stress might feel in their bodies. Tightness, muscle stiffness, or more severe pains like constant headaches can be symptoms of stress. It's best to identify stress before it crescendos into full blown panic or exacerbates mental health issues.

The Value of Body Work

As Christ followers, we know that God has a purpose for the time and place he has determined for us. Therefore, we are naturally bound on earth by our bodies. The practice of Christian mindfulness allows us to breathe, to make space for God, and to understand that as we soothe our fight-flight-freeze responses in our bodies, we can more easily cope with the stressors of this world. We live into the growth and kingdom progress that this present moment provides us individually and corporately as we honor our bodies and the bodies of others.

In chapters 13 and 14, we addressed how to equip our clients to eat mindfully and maintain a healthy lifestyle through Christian mindfulness. In this chapter, we provide a script to help our clients detect how their bodies react to stress. Progressive muscle relaxation is a well-documented stress-management technique (Ditto et al., 2017; Lebovits, 2007; Healthwise staff, n.d.), and it can be easily integrated into Christian mindfulness practice. When we address the tightness our clients are experiencing in their bodies and help them relieve stressors in light of the peace of God, the release they experience becomes less exercise and more devotional practice.

This kind of body work is chronicled in the Scriptures. As we see in the ministry of Jesus and his disciples, healing came through touch, through a word of faith, or through an action that was a show of faith in God's healing of the body. The woman who bled profusely in Matthew 9:20–22, for instance, simply touched Jesus' cloak, and Christ made her well. In John 9:1–7, we read about Jesus healing a blind man through anointing his eyes with mud created from dirt and spit and then directing him to wash the mud away in a nearby pool of water. Jesus' ministry included healing of the body.

We do not seek direct healing as we lead our clients through a progressive muscle relaxation exercise, but we do invite Jesus to direct our clients' attention to him, because time spent with Christ is all we need for him to be at work. What comes up for our clients in their bodies may be a surprise to them, or they might resist our directing their attention to parts of their bodies. Jesus is in both the surprise and the miracle, and he is in the past and present pain of their bodies.

A Script for Progressive Muscle Relaxation with Christian Mindfulness

An important step before using this script with a client is to help them understand the importance of not striving. Progressive muscle relaxation isn't goal oriented. Often, our clients want to complete these exercises well. Even in their skepticism they are tempted to please us. Or they have internalized an idea of the self that is predicated on achievement, attached to external rewards for accomplishing tasks. This exercise is not a task to accomplish. We want to set up a time when our clients can focus on just being in their bodies, awake and aware of the gift that God has given them in their bodies.

On the other hand, many of our clients struggle with body image issues, perhaps because of an eating disorder or body dysmorphia or because of ongoing memories and flashbacks associated with past trauma. Many clients therefore reject their bodies and have to learn how to engage them in a healthy way. You may need to modify the following script so that it focuses on one area for one session or meeting, and on another area for the next one. Please adapt it as you see fit. In addition, with clients who experience rejection toward their bodies, use this script over and over to focus on bringing awareness to their bodies. It will be an important process of growth for your clients to step into the safety and wonder of their createdness.

Today I will lead you through a progressive muscle relaxation exercise designed to help you just be in your body. I hope it will help you to notice and honor your body with God's presence and peace. This is a time not to strive but simply to honor and notice your body. So I will ask you to focus on each part of your body. As you focus, register what comes up for you in your mind and even emotions and listen to it. For instance, is there pain, tightness, looseness, or flexibility in that area? What do those sensations tell you? I will also ask you to breathe to engage the calming centers of your body. We can also invite God through prayer to place his healing touch on those parts of your body that hold emotion and tension. Please let me know if you want to stop at any point. We will have some time to process your experience afterward.

Let's start by sitting in a straight but flexible position, with both feet firmly but not rigidly planted on the ground and hands gently on your lap. Close your eyes so you can focus on your thoughts and notice your body from the inside.

Start by noticing your feet on the ground. Observe, with your eyes closed, any tightness or flexibility in the joints of your toes and in your ankles, and on your heels. Observe any feelings in your heels: pain, tenderness, or neutral. Now move your toes and feet up and down off the floor or just with heels resting on the floor. Breathe in as you move your feet upward, toes pointed toward the sky, and then exhale as they return to the floor. Do that one more time noticing any sensation, and pray something like this: "God, thank you for grounding me as my feet are planted on the ground. May your presence release any stress preventing me from being grounded in you."

Next engage your calf muscles by squeezing them tight, inhaling, and holding the squeeze. Release your muscles while exhaling. Also, swing your legs up and tighten so your quadriceps muscles are engaged. Inhale, and then exhale and release. Notice any difference between the tightness versus when your muscles relax. Take a few seconds to notice and observe any thoughts related to your legs. Pray for a healing touch or simply notice how your muscles feel.

Progressive Muscle Relaxation with Christian Mindfulness | 195

Now I ask you to focus your mind on your pelvic region and your hip joints. If this area is uncomfortable for you to think about, just try to observe in your mind why that is. Stay curious about any discomfort by asking yourself why you might be feeling uncomfortable. Identify any feelings associated with those thoughts. Simply breathe in and out to close out that focused time. If you are comfortable—tastefully and in a dignified manner—staying seated, slowly wiggle your hip joints left to right, right to left. Ask God to heal any pain in this region, whether physical or emotional. Breathe in and out, and then still your body.

Next inhale while clenching your abdominal muscles, and then release. Observe how your intestinal region and your abdominal muscles react. Pray for God's peace and warmth to infiltrate this area of your body, which can often be upset by stress. Ask God to calm any sensations as you become aware of any stressful thoughts. Breathe in and out once again, and release.

Now shift your focus to your spine and your back muscles. Note any aches or pains. Perhaps this is a painful region for you. Simply be aware of any thoughts that may flood you about this area. If you won't experience any pain by doing so, breathe in and correct your posture by sitting rigidly straight, and then relax while you exhale.

Now bend your arms up and engage your arm muscles. Tighten your biceps muscles and clench your hands as you inhale. Release and exhale, bringing your hands back down to your lap. Again, note any thoughts about this area of your body, your arms, or your hands. Ask God to wrap his arms and hands around you during this time.

Now roll your shoulders back in a circle a couple of times, and then, inhaling, squeeze your shoulders up, and then, exhaling, slowly bring your shoulders back down. Bring to your awareness any tightness of your muscles. Invite God, in prayer, to soothe these clenched shoulder muscles and ask him to lift the stresses you carry, to lift the burdens from your shoulders, which house the worries or stresses of the day. Acknowledge his goodness as you do so.

We are almost done, great job. Next focus on your neck and its muscles. Slowly roll your head in a circle, as big or as small as you want. Stretch your neck muscles. Inhale as you roll your head in one direction, exhale as you roll it in the other direction. Notice and then release any tension in this area, observing your thoughts, asking God to infuse this area of your body with his healing touch.

Last focus your mind on your head and then the top of your head—where your crown is, where your brain is housed, your skull, and the muscles on the tip-top of it. Take a few deep breaths in and out and, as strange as it may sound, try to breathe through the top of your skull, picturing oxygen flowing out as you exhale and oxygen flowing in as you inhale. Now notice any tightness of the muscles around your skull, and release. Inhale and ask God to fill your head with his goodness, mercy, and peace. Exhale and release to him all pressure from your head.

If you feel led to, you can end this time in prayer to connect with God, or sit in gratitude, or observe any thoughts that you have.

You can end this time in silent prayer or, with your client's permission, lead your client in prayer. After you end this portion of your session or meeting, debrief this experience. During debriefing, if your client notices any pain or need for medical attention, acknowledge their need to follow up with a physician.

Your client might report that they feel much more relaxed in their bodies or report a sensation of peace. Use appendix 1 as a tool to help your client visualize and communicate any changes felt from this exercise. We can help our clients to connect how they feel in their bodies and in God's presence with their experiencing clearer and more relaxed thoughts. Unpack that connection to further their learning about themselves, about how their bodies work in concert with their minds and souls. In Christian mindfulness, we want to acknowledge with our clients that their bodies are going to react differently according to their struggles—that as they work on a particular issue, they may feel the emotional effects in their bodies, especially if they internalize their feelings.

Conclusion

Because life is full of twists and turns, our clients might sometimes clench their way through it. As they incorporate progressive muscle relaxation with Christian intention, they will work out stress and emotions from their bodies, giving them to Christ. With each contraction, they will squeeze out the emotion contained in that part of their bodies, providing some recognition of the work being done. As you direct them to relax, you will witness your clients' pain (emotional, spiritual, and even physical) melting with God's healing touch.

References for Chapter 17

Ditto, B., Eclache, M., & Goldman, N. (2017). Short-term autonomic and cardiovascular effects of mindfulness body scan meditation. In B. A. Gaudiano (Ed.), *Mindfulness: Vol. IV. Nonclinical applications of mindfulness: Adaptations for school, work, sports, health, and general well-being.* (2017–55495–020; pp. 341–357). Routledge/Taylor & Francis Group.

Healthwise staff. (n.d.). Stress management: Doing progressive muscle relaxation. Michigan Medicine. Retrieved September 30, 2020, from https://www.uofmhealth.org/health-library/uz2225

Lebovits, A. (2007). Cognitive-behavioral approaches to chronic pain. *Primary Psychiatry, 14*(9), 48–54.

CHAPTER 18

Boundary Keeping
and Mindfulness

Many of our clients struggle with maintaining boundaries because they have not learned to let go, fearful of the gap that setting boundaries can create. In 2007, many of us heard the news of astronaut Lisa Nowak's arrest. The former astronaut had driven nine hundred miles to harm her ex-boyfriend's lover (Kettler, 2020). The details are salacious, but Lisa, prior to her arrest for attempted kidnapping, was an unusually successful person who had undergone rigorous training but, for some reason, could not train herself to let go of a broken relationship. The process of letting go, whether of a relationship or a past wrong, is difficult, to say the least. Yet hanging on requires energy and concentration and causes depletion. Though Lisa's example is extreme, it showcases how a lack of boundaries can cause anguish and a world of trouble.

Christian mindfulness helps our counselees recognize what things, people, or situations are not for them. The practice assists in good boundary keeping. In mindfulness centered on Christ, our clients can experience mental freedom and less anxiety so that they can more easily let go of toxic patterns. When they do, they make space for all that is good and lovely in God's presence. As a result, our counselees transform.

When we let go, we recognize how God has moved and shaped us through past relationships or situations, but we also recognize that for growth to occur, change is inevitable. As we step into a closer relationship with Christ, we leave behind the stumbling blocks that keep us in sin, that keep us from paths of flourishing in Christ. The boundaries we keep are not so rigid that they prevent forgiveness and reconciliation. They are our commitment to growth in Christ and our commitment not to be stumbling blocks to others.

In the classic book *Boundaries* (a foundational source of this chapter), Cloud and Townsend (2017) help us understand what boundary keeping looks like. They explain that part of the "laws of boundaries" is recognizing that we do not have the power to overcome problematic boundary problems alone. However, we do have the power to confess, submit to God, and ask him to reveal what we must turn away from. We have the power to humble ourselves and turn away from problematic boundaries, to make amends, and to change how we deal with others (p. 13). All of these things require God's wisdom, the psychologists explain. And God is faithful to answer our calls for wisdom.

Cloud and Townsend's (2017) principles of boundary keeping are especially useful to help our clients recognize that nothing is stagnant, that healing and growth can occur even as the pain of letting go is present and sharp. Keeping a boundary is the launching pad to our clients' growth and healing. Letting go in order to keep a boundary may mean leaving behind a person, place, or sense of identity. That doesn't mean our clients can't cherish the gifts of people or situations in their past. But when they let go, they move toward a fullness and joy that can be found only in God's unyielding love and grace.

Brokenness in Boundaries

Christ's abundance is not devoid of the knowledge and experience of suffering. Even Christ's ministry on earth was finite. As finite beings, we yearn for what is eternal because that is the reality of life in the Lord—eternity with him. We can support our clients' movement toward a holiness in their relationships that honors others' holy boundaries and honors themselves.

Our clients often seek our help because of broken boundaries in their relationships. God is our only constant. People fail because we are all fallen, sinful creatures. But our faith is not rocked when we witness Christian leaders' failures playing out in the media, because we understand that no one is righteous, no one is holy like our Lord. We learn from the boundaryless nature of tainted relationships. In Christian mindfulness, we understand that Christ's intimacy is built on his grace, holiness, and justice. We cherish those people who build on scriptural truth. Forgiveness, reconciliation, and the repair of broken relationships are found in God.

In Christian mindfulness, we see the humanity of others—the image of God, the *imago Dei*, that is stamped on all people. Sometimes our clients have been so hurt that they no longer recognize the *imago Dei* in themselves, and they are fearful of reaching out to healthy people. Their coming to us to work on their issues is a brave step. As we assist our clients in their sacred work, we can help them reattach to loving-kindness, mercy, and perfection in Christ. Their wounds are a sacred opening for God to perform his surgery. His sutures of assurance and acceptance bring healing like none other.

Christian mindfulness provides the mental space where normally defended thoughts are brought to awareness. When this happens, detachment takes place. Our clients can see clearly the truth of another person's intentions. They are more available to listen to the warning signs that the Holy Spirit has provided and therefore to find strength in his voice.

The risks that must be taken to maintain boundaries can keep our clients from growth. That's where our supportive, steady presence in the therapy and counseling room comes in. There our clients can absorb the belief that they are worthy of having their boundaries be honored. We can provide the belief that they are valued, that they are God's creations, and our clients can slowly move toward our words, our care, and our belief that they can be good boundary keepers.

A Boundary Keeping Mindfulness Script

This boundary keeping mindfulness script is an example of how we can bring our clients to God so they can recognize what is in need of suturing— what needs to be tied together—and what needs to be loosed in their relationships. When our clients can identify how they are shaped by, and how they shape, others, they can allow people into their lives who bring a balm to their open wounds, not folks who rip apart the seams where there is fresh healing. They can own the responsibility that God has given to all who know him: that we are to build others up in Christ, to become colaborers in community, useful for the kingdom of heaven.

> This time is for you to be mindful of the wounds that you carry from your relationships. The silence in your mind is to allow God, through the Holy Spirit, to help you find release from any tie that you need to let go of, that he may be calling you to let go of. It might also be a time to hear from God in his wisdom to direct your steps in a certain relationship. It is a time to contemplate and find God's peace about a relationship that you are struggling with, so you can be a boundary keeper honoring yourself as you honor others, ultimately bringing honor to God in your relationships.
>
> So let's breathe together to set our minds in a quiet peace. Inhale deeply for four counts, 1-2-3-4, and exhale for four, 1-2-3-4. Let's do this again: inhale, 1-2-3-4; exhale, 1-2-3-4. Now quietly breathe deeply on your own while I stay quiet for a couple of minutes. Just focus on your breath and the act of breathing.
>
> As we transition, stay in this quiet place. Quiet your mind. If you feel led, invite God to dwell in your mind right now. Ask him to quiet your thoughts, your body, and your spirit so you hear from him. You can pray, "Lord, I invite you now to be present with me. I ask that you help me face the truth. Help me to see clearly where I need to let go. Whom do I need to move toward, and whom do I need to take a step back from to grow in you?"
>
> In the stillness of your mind, as you breathe, simply pick out a thought as I move you through some prompts. It is normal if a lot of thoughts come and go during this time. Don't judge those thoughts. Instead, simply treat them just as thoughts. Good thoughts, bad thoughts—they come and go. But I would like you to pick out one

thought to work on with God. It should be about a relationship in which you feel an inkling that maybe a boundary needs to be reset.

So let's begin with breathing and being still. Identify in your mind a relationship that you want to work on during this time. Perhaps a person comes to mind whom you find yourself struggling to keep a boundary with. Or perhaps you have overstepped your boundary with a person and you want to repair that somehow.

Use this quiet time simply to observe what comes up in your mind and identify your thoughts about this person for a minute in stillness. Breathe in and out. Slowly observe what comes and what goes in your mind. Now notice what thought comes up again. Turn over in your mind the thought that seems to land now. Invite God to reveal the truth about this thought and about this person. Make space for him right now in your mind and soul. I'll be quiet for minute while you do this.

Notice any reaction in your body—any tightness. There might not be. Again, there is no judgment in this space, and I remind you not to force anything. Simply see what comes up. Take another big inhalation and exhale.

Now as you sit, I would like you to symbolically place your palms on your lap facing up as a way to acknowledge in your body that you are letting go.

Work on letting go of control in this relationship. Work on letting go of the hurt in the relationship. Work on letting go of any desire to grasp on to this person. Notice your hands, which are face up. Use that as a symbol of your intent to let go. Breathe in and out as you work on letting go. Try not to force things. This is a gentle letting go that you can return to later if needed.

Next, with palms still facing up, receive God's wisdom as you ask in what ways you need to step back in your behavior with this person. In what ways do you need to step forward with this person? Or perhaps God is calling you to step toward someone else to establish or maintain good boundaries. Notice any reactions in your spirit and in your body.

As we close this time out, use these last few minutes simply to soak in the quiet. Note any feelings of assurance, any amplified truths from this time. Acknowledge God's insights, his help, and his presence and speak a prayer of gratitude for them. Soak in all these things. Allow them to root within you. Use these few minutes of quiet to go deeper.

To close, inhale the truths you received during this boundary keeping contemplation. Exhale an assent to God that you have heard him, that you will listen. Inhale, "Lord, commit my way to you." Exhale, "Lord, I commit my way to your way." Inhale, "Lord, make a way." Exhale, "Lord, make me walk in your way." Inhale, "Lord, help me with boundary keeping." Exhale, "Lord, be with me as I keep my boundaries."

To debrief this boundary keeping exercise, and if you deem it appropriate for your counselee, we suggest you use the Boundary Keeping Circle worksheet in appendix 2. The goal of this worksheet is for your client to identify boundaries around the relationship that was the focus of this exercise. You can have your client write inside the circle the feelings, values, or promises they want to keep, and then have them write outside the circle the feelings they experience when they are not keeping boundaries in that relationship.

Have your client draw symbols, pictures, or figurative representations for those feeling words both on the inside and on the outside of the circle. This may be easier for some clients because it is less language based, which might help them access their feelings more readily.

As we encourage our clients to lean into the inward understanding of God's wisdom for boundary keeping, we empower them to express authentically who they are created to be. Instead of being on a nine-hundred-mile boundaryless chase, our clients create a healthy fence for their lives and plant their feet firmly on the ground. As they draw lines for themselves and others, they acknowledge that they are worthy of the dignity and value that have already been assigned to them in the heavenly realms. As they step into the good feelings, value, and self-respect inside the circle, they experience growth. To honor and keep boundaries in a relationship in which they sense they need to step back or from which they need to move toward other folks who can treat them with respect is great learning. And when our clients reap the rewards of that boundary keeping, they grow in the confidence that they can be trusted and that they can make good judgments. In your debriefing, help them identify the good rewards that they can reap in this process.

Conclusion

Boundary keeping is a rigorous training process. When our clients look inward with mindfulness, they can look at themselves honestly and ask who they are latching on to and how badly enmeshed they are with unhealthy people. Helping them to detach for the sake of a healthy attachment to the permanent presence of God is the first step. Then they can gain insight into whom they should choose to keep in their orbit.

The truth comes out when clients practice boundary keeping that is informed by the Spirit. The truth of who they are in the image of God, the truth of how they expect to be treated, and the truth of how they treat others are revealed in their hearts and minds in stillness and contemplation. We are to love our neighbors as ourselves, and make sure that we are not consumed by or enmeshed with one another (Gal. 5:13–15). A client's goal is to grow in boundary keeping in this way: not devouring others and not being devoured by another. This is the essence of being mindful in Christ in our relationships with one another. For we are called to freedom as brothers and sisters in Christ, and we are to use our freedom wisely, not toward the self alone but through love, which flourishes with boundaries.

References for Chapter 18

Cloud, H., & Townsend, J. (2017). *Boundaries: When to say yes, how to say no to take control of your life* (2nd ed.). Zondervan.

Kettler, S. (2020). Lisa Nowak: Why the astronaut drove 900 miles to attack her ex's girlfriend. *Biography.* https://www.biography.com /news/lisa-nowak-lucy-in-the-sky#:~:text=Subscribe%20to%20

Newsletter-,Lisa%20Nowak%3A%20Why%20the%20Astronaut%20
Drove%20900%20Miles%20to%20Attack,movie%20'Lucy%20in%20
the%20Sky

CHAPTER 19

Taking Thoughts Captive and Mindful Transformation

René Descartes' philosophical argument "I think therefore I am" is a declaration of the power of our thoughts. A gentleman named Wim Hof testifies to that power with his almost superhuman abilities to stay in frigid water for hours and to climb Mount Everest in just running shorts and a T-shirt. He was featured in a popular 2010 TED talk during which he was immersed in a container of ice while a scientist spoke of his ability to control his body with his thoughts. Hof describes his scientifically documented technique as simple and applicable to the everyday by way of channeling thoughts to influence the body, including the immune system (VICE Asia, 2020).

Wim Hof's videos are compelling and convincing. However, as Christ followers who support those who are suffering, we also know that it's more than thoughts alone that makes us who we are. As counselors, social workers, therapists, psychologists, and other healing agents, many of us are trained to evaluate change, in the therapeutic sense, by the principles of cognitive behavioral therapy (CBT). In CBT, we build awareness of cognitions and how the reframing of cognitions can lead to symptom reduction in depression and anxiety disorders, among others. The mental health issues our clients struggle with can be tackled by change in thought patterns, according to CBT. The evidence basis for these positive outcomes is well documented in both the clinical and research literature.

Secular mindfulness-based strategies within the CBT framework utilize a strong awareness process to move toward healthier cognitive constructs by observing, noticing, and detaching from thoughts about oneself, especially those that are destructive.

In the light of God's presence, however, all of this is rather reductionist. Jones (2018) provides a biblical basis for this view of the transformation of the self. In Romans 6:6, we are to put off our old self, which is already corrupted, to put on the new self. Therefore, in Christian mindfulness, we seek God's thoughts and an understanding of the limits of our own thoughts.

It is easy to hold our thoughts in a dispassionate way when we know that they are already imperfect. Our thoughts are not simply cognitions but also reflect the state of our souls. Our clients' minds and souls long for hope when they are struggling. Hope is rooted in Christ, who transforms not only our thoughts but our whole being: body, mind, spirit. Therefore, when we think of mindful transformation, we also are counting on Christ's transformation of our hearts, our souls, our instincts, and our view of life, others, and the self.

The transformation that occurs in Christian mindfulness is expansive. It is not reduced simply to thoughts, though they are quite important. The true test of a transformed life is character, the essence of who we are. When we are transformed to the new self, new thoughts also flow more naturally. "I think therefore I am" is good and true, but for a healthy transformation to take place, our thoughts need to be built on a stable foundation of values, character, and fruitfulness.

Transformed Beliefs

Our clients have many faulty core beliefs. Many of them suffer from a low self-concept that feels hopeless and helpless and denies their identity as bearers of God's image. These core beliefs or judgments about themselves come from all sorts of places, such as abandonment, family of origin, attachments, trauma, and destructive patterns of sin. As we walk our clients through steps in Christian mindfulness, we try to help them get to the essence of who they are—that they are unconditionally loved. No one can do this on their own. So when we challenge distorted thoughts that are tied to core beliefs, we invite God's assistance.

Thus, when we use Christian mindfulness to help our clients work with thoughts, they are influenced by the Holy Spirit and Scripture. They exhibit transformation when they can test their thoughts against the standard of Christ's holiness and mercy. As our clients sit in mindfulness, they at least begin to hear themselves and identify their core beliefs, which manifest in their thought patterns. For instance, our counselees become aware of how harsh their judgments are toward others or themselves. Our clients can also sift through judgments that are so distorted they are difficult to correct. Maybe they learn in the time spent in Christian mindfulness that they cannot even hear God's corrective voice because they have bought into that judgment—they believe those harsh words and they are ingrained as core beliefs.

This is the work of therapy. Through the use of Christian mindfulness in this transformational process, thought patterns and core beliefs emerge. Afterward, we deconstruct core beliefs or judgments and construct a new self transformed by Christ's truth and love. Thus, our clients come away with more cognitive flexibility—the ability to incorporate new, healthier thought patterns.

Our clients transform their beliefs about themselves when they become aware of how distorted their thinking is. They are not unworthy, unwelcome, devalued—no way! Our counselees see that we, their counselors or therapists, value them as people, and that God sees them as his beloveds. Grace is freely given. Our goal is the reconstruction of the self into a solid core based on their view of themselves in Christ, who is their cornerstone. This solid self-transformation is both internal and influenced by a community of believers. In our roles as their counselors, therapists, and other healers, we provide that faithful community to assist in their transformation. What a privilege to be in this role. May God use us!

A Transforming Thoughts Script

The following script is intended to help our clients take their destructive thoughts captive and to work on mindful transformation. The goal is to help them put on the new self in Christ.

In this contemplation, I would like you to work on a persistent negative judgment about yourself. We will use this time in Christian mindfulness to be curious about this judgment and to practice how to recognize thoughts related to it.

So let's start in a place of stillness in your mind. Take a few deep breaths, inhaling for four counts and exhaling for four counts. Breathe for another minute, quieting your body and your mind. Your thoughts may jump around at first. Watch them do that and notice when they settle down just a bit. When you notice that your thoughts have settled, identify the worst judgment you hold against yourself. It could sound like, "I wish I was not like ..." or, "I am way too ..." or, "I am the worst because ..."

Maybe you have a flood of thoughts related to this judgment. I would like you to slow your body down by breathing and say to your thoughts, "Slow down, let me hear you one at a time." Breathe again to help manage each thought. Slow any rush or slew of thoughts by taking them one by one. Observe and listen to the sound of your thoughts. Can you find one that sounds like a frequent judgment? Does one you keep coming back to seem to sum up who you are to yourself? How do you think about yourself?

Notice any memories that come up for you about this judgment. Can you locate where you picked it up? Was it a feeling of shame or sadness or anger? Maybe none of those? Is there someone who said this to you, who laid this foundation of how you think about yourself? Our thoughts are portions of what we have learned and what we have absorbed from our experiences. Listen for the origin of this judgment and identify it. I'll be quiet for a couple of minutes while you work on this.

Let's switch gears. Now that you have picked out a judgment, I would like you to work on transformation. I would like you to listen for a minute for God's voice. Maybe there is a soft voice that is correcting, gentle, and able to help you see your strengths. Take a minute to listen for this voice, even in this judgment and the thoughts associated with it. Keep toggling your mind back to listening to God's soft voice. How does he edit this judgment? What does his loving voice say to you?

As you settle into this space, notice in your body any resistance to the correction of your judgments about yourself. Where does this resistance reside in your body? For instance, is it a knotted stomach or a clenched jaw? Maybe there is no resistance or correction.

Finally, observe what comes to your mind in this space now, even if it's unpleasant or you are struggling with focus. What is your mind avoiding, if anything? If it's helpful, I would like you to envision yourself and your judgments as a hollowed-out core. Maybe you see an apple hollowed out by an apple corer. Or maybe you envision a bamboo stalk, standing straight, but hollow inside. Contemplate these pictures and notice how any distorted judgments of yourself eat away at your core. On the outside, folks don't notice, but you do. What does God want to fill that core with? What thoughts come to mind? What feelings flood in, like cement, to strengthen that core?

We are not trying to find what isn't there, but we want to identify, notice, observe. I'll be quiet for a few more minutes as you continue this work. Keep breathing, noticing, observing your judgments, using that picture in your imagination to help.

Finally, I would like you to find a new thought. Maybe it clearly comes from God, or maybe you need to work on self-correction. Formulate it in your mind. See it as a sentence. What is that core judgment? What is the corrective? What does it sound like? Say that corrective belief and thought that God gave you or that you were able to correct on your own. Say it over and over in your mind. Picture the thought or the feeling of peace, relief, acceptance, filling those hollow spots. As Joel 2:25 says, remember that God will restore what the locusts have eaten. Again, work in the silence to fill yourself up with that most true thought about yourself, that correct belief. I'll be quiet for a few more minutes as you do this.

To end this time, breathe in deeply, acknowledging the work you have done. Breathe out, committing to this new belief, this new thought. You can inhale, "I did a hard thing. I did a good job." And exhale, "I commit to this new thought. Help me, God, in this commitment."

As you debrief this exercise with your client, you can reinforce the value of this work. This contemplation is not a relaxing experience. It may be helpful to shift your client to one that is. To help them stay in the present moment and ground them back into their body, rather than their head, you can lead your client through the Progressive Muscle Relaxation with Christian Mindfulness Script found in chapter 17.

As you are talking through this Transforming Thoughts Script, explore with your client any feeling or thought that came from God that felt like a reframing. Sometimes clients will not hear from God. Instead they may experience a flood of thoughts related to judgment and cannot pull themselves out of that overflow of negativity. The pack of lies that they have been sold about themselves may have come from people in the past or in the present. It will be important to unpack those connections—any and all that were made—so you can continue working with them on healing and separating from that toxic identity or person.

Continue to explore the reframing. For instance, many of our clients come with a broken sense of self that keeps them feeling small and ashamed. Help them identify those parts of themselves which cause them shame. What keeps them from taking up space, from trying out those parts that they keep hidden? Those distorted thoughts need to be challenged. We can assist our clients toward healthier, transformed beliefs through Christian mindfulness practice. As they meditate on the reframing, the truth sinks deeper. Perhaps that reframed statement is something like, "My worth is from God. He says I am a child of the Most High, and I'm more than accepted. I'm a king/queen in his kingdom." The reframing for our clients is a cognitive transformation. However, their transformed thoughts are grounded in new beliefs, not just new sentences.

As our clients meditate on and hold new thoughts and beliefs exclusively, we know that neuronal networks are being constructed around those beliefs. We also posit that these truths are soul filling. Even though we cannot see or record that transformation biologically or biochemically, we as Christ followers know when clients exhibit that soul transformation as well.

As our clients acknowledge any transformation happening in the quiet spaces of their minds and believe them to be truthful stories of themselves in their hearts and souls, God is honored. Our clients are worthy of transformation and of the neuronal and soul-filled work they have done. This transformation, over time, can be profound. As we encourage them to sit still and be open to transformation, we honor their work. As we continue to help our clients journey with Christ toward cognitive healing, we understand that the twisted thoughts they were hanging on to did not serve them, so we hold them accountable. Hopefully, our clients walk farther and farther away from those wrong judgments and, as they do so, their cores fill up. The hollow strength that brought them to get help in therapy or counseling just needed reinforcement.

Conclusion

Like a tall stalk of bamboo that sways in typhoon winds, our clients have survived much. We, as their partners in healing, honor that history. However, it may be time for them to stand tall with a core that is filled with the Holy Spirit and sealed with the truth of God. In that thought-transforming work, the beliefs and judgments they hold about themselves are of great importance. We leverage the practice of Christian mindfulness so they can hear those thoughts and core beliefs clearly. Being aware of our thoughts is the first step. The second is to identify when those thoughts are judgments that are simply unfair, harsh, and untrue. The third is to look for truth. We do that in Christian mindfulness so we can hear God's voice. We can meditate on Scripture. We are moved by the Holy Spirit. The fourth is to transform those thoughts, to eschew those judgments that are not rooted in the truth that we are all created in God's image. Our thoughts need to catch up to those truths. As we practice mindfulness, our Christian truths bear fruit. The fruit of that transformative mindfulness practice is the sweet corrective voice of our creator, who is the lifter of our heads. Our thoughts and judgments about ourselves are raised higher in light of the worth he bestows on us as his creations.

References for Chapter 19

Jones, I. F. (2018). Christian formation of the self strategies. In John C. Thomas (Ed.), *Counseling techniques: A comprehensive resource for Christian counselors* (pp. 197–220). Zondervan.

VICE Asia. (2020, March 9). Meet the superhuman Wim Hof: The iceman. Retrieved from https://www.youtube.com/watch?v=soHwRkIkTHA

CHAPTER 20

Centering Prayer and *Lectio Divina* as Mindful Devotion

D o you struggle to sit in the quiet, and find it hard to focus when you read Scripture? Do your thoughts wander off in the middle of prayer? Or how about when listening to a sermon? Does your mind go to your to-do list, the score of the football game, or some other distraction?

It is natural to experience dry, dull, and muted moments when we feel we are supposed to be engaged in being filled with God's Word. When we turn to God in Christian mindfulness, we set up a devotional practice that also addresses our anxieties, worries, and fears. As we step into God's presence every day, we learn from him, and his teachings hit us in a fresh way. Parts of even familiar passages of Scripture magically stand out.

A daily Christian-mindfulness practice as a way of devotion shapes our clients' outlook on their days, themselves, and their worlds. *Devotion* is defined by the *Merriam-Webster Dictionary* as "a religious exercise or practice for private use" (Devotion, 2016). Time spent in devotion is rich. It's a bookmark in the day, a point when we can be filled with the knowledge and presence of God. Part spiritual formation, part therapeutic exercise, the exercises in the rest of this chapter aim to help your clients work with their minds in a softer way. Instead of trying, grasping, our clients will learn to let go and let God's abiding voice meet them each day of the week. The exercises are meant to foster awareness of God to support the therapeutic work you are doing with them.

The Benefits of Devotion for Clients

Some of our counselees have never been encouraged to set aside a time for devotion. They may be unchurched or unfamiliar with the practice. A devotion time can amplify our clients' understanding of how the spiritual practices can be interwoven with their therapeutic skill-building. It is also a time of ritual building, a new habit that furthers the work clients are doing in the counseling or therapeutic space—outside of that time, in their daily lives. It might be helpful to encourage them to pair devotion time with an enjoyable ritual such as pouring themselves a cup of coffee or tea, giving them a positive experience each time.

In addition, when you work with your clients out of a particular framework (CBT, family systems, existential, person centered, solution focused, etc.), you can integrate a daily time of devotion to support their growth and learning by focusing on prayers that open up their head spaces or heart spaces or that reinforce certain outlooks or ways of thinking. Using the script later in this chapter, you can incorporate into their daily devotion some reframing exercises such as godly affirmations.

The Benefits of Devotion for Practitioners

As counselors, therapists, social workers, psychologists, and other healing professionals, our own time spent in devotion through the reading of Scripture and prayer keeps us focused and grounded and relieves us of the stresses and burdens we carry. In that time spent with God one on one, we find rest and replenishment so we can engage in our work with empathy and compassion, and promote wise, just, and equitable counsel. Without time in devotion, we may find ourselves fighting countertransference, bias, complacency, or worse yet, indifference in the face of our clients' suffering. We can burn out more easily when we do not engage in self-care that involves soul care.

Devotion with Christian mindfulness practices is a time for us as mental health providers to show up each day and to prepare for and reflect on what God has in store for us. Times of devotion help us find strength and peace so we can fully focus on our clients' needs. Whether our devotion is at the beginning of the day or at the end, the time we spend with God listening, learning, and gleaning is a daily respite and a safe haven.

Porges (2017) discusses feeling safe through neural processes—specifically, the vagus nerve, which helps us evaluate risk. Our feeling safe depends on cues in our environments and relationships. Christian mindfulness practice produces a safety cue through a neurological effect that is processed through our bodies. In a study I (Regina) conducted, Centering Prayer and *Lectio Divina* were used as part of a treatment for social workers. After a six-week Christian-mindfulness intervention, heart-rate variability (a measure for feelings of safety) improved (Trammel et al., 2021). This six-week intervention was a devotion time for social workers during which they engaged their breathing, quieted their minds, and provided their bodies space to decompress.

As we listen to God through Centering Prayer, or as we meditate on Scripture through *Lectio Divina*, we not only grasp Scripture's meaning but let it sink deeper, affecting our psyches and souls. The effectiveness of our work as healing practitioners is parallel to our ability to be a safe, warm place for our clients. Therefore, when we can operate out of a safe space in our own bodies, minds, and souls, our clients pick up on this feeling from us. There is more to say neurologically about this mirroring effect, but we will focus on how we can offer this same daily devotion to promote feelings of safety, which Porges (2017) indicates is underemphasized in modern psychotherapy and counseling.

A Mindful Devotion Script for Healing

In chapter 4, we used *Lectio Divina* to help our clients contemplate a portion of the Lord's Prayer to build their Christian mindfulness skills. Focusing on Scripture readings in a meditative way allows our clients to find the safety of the Word. Devotional time spent in Centering Prayer and *Lectio Divina* builds a daily safe space in God's presence. The following script incorporates both practices so that you can include them in your counseling and therapeutic work. It's important to integrate the theoretical framework you are working out of so that your clients can be with God and get ready for their day with their healing in mind.

Drawing from Keating's (2012) description of the value of Centering Prayer (p. 1), this Mindful Devotion Script for Healing is a way to "consent to God's presence and action within." We consent to God's action and surrender our healing to him. He is the Great Physician, and we must acknowledge that sometimes we get in his way. This script will help your clients find a daily rhythm to meet with God so that he can do his work. As they listen, they can hear his truth and feel his presence through Scripture.

> In this time, I want to encourage you to build a devotion time that helps you start or end your day focused on the steps you are taking in therapy or counseling. We will work through an example that you can shorten as needed. This devotion is something you can do every day, and I hope it will help shape your mindset as well as further the work we are doing when we meet to work on specifics. It is a general devotion meant to promote healing. It is a time of surrender and a reminder that we as humans are limited in our efforts, but God can multiply our work.
>
> So we start first with a time of silence and prayer to center our thoughts and allow God space to give us a fresh outlook.
>
> First, let's work on finding our breath in order to transition our bodies and minds to focus on healing. Let this breath be a healing breath. Take a few deep, cleansing breaths. On your last inhalation, you can say, "Lord, I ask today for your healing touch." On your exhalation, you can say, "God, I receive your healing touch."
>
> I'll have you start in Centering Prayer. Begin with silence and solitude. In this moment of silence, be aware of your relationship with God. Notice how God is in solidarity with you in your healing. If it's helpful, you can do a *Lectio Divina* with Psalm 28:7. Speak the verse out loud or just in your thoughts, and then in your heart. I'll speak it three times:

> The LORD is my strength and my shield;
> my heart trusts in him, and he helps me.

In the silence of your thoughts and your heart, notice what is feeding you in this devotion. Notice the simplicity of the truth of the verse. Note any ways you are drawn to this verse, and any phrases that do not ring true right now.

Now surrender. Move toward unity with Christ, who is your healer. Walk toward him in your mind and in your heart. If you feel so led, talk to God about the strength you need, the shield you need. Surrender and let God know about the state of your heart—whether you trust him, whether you want his help.

Last, pray in the silence, receiving and surrendering, listening and not speaking. Just receive now for a few more silent minutes.

Let's close by asking God to transform your mindset, your outlook, your heart every day. Try this same devotion every day if you can. Sit in the silence, centering your thoughts in stillness in solidarity with God's work of healing. Then contemplate Psalm 28:7 by reading it aloud or in your mind, and close out your time in surrender to God, listening, allowing him to move and work in the silence, fully receiving his healing touch where it is needed: in your mind, emotions, heart, soul.

The benefit of a devotional practice rooted in Christian mindfulness is that there is no ritual to be performed. Your clients can practice it anywhere and anytime. Psalm 28:7 anchors their devotion because no matter how traumatic their histories have been with the church or religious leaders, it acknowledges the protection and safety of their healer. As this practice becomes a habit over time, our clients, who are working so hard in their counseling and therapy work, may find that it is the way they prefer to start or end their day.

As you debrief this script, integrate the points of learning you hope your client grasps. Observe how they react to asking God for help in healing, surrendering to him, and setting their mind on his strength and shielding. Many of these aspects are akin to mindfulness-based-therapy skills of radical acceptance, observation of one's mind, and even some ego-based or attachment concepts, depending on the depth of safety your client feels in their relationship with God. All of these aspects can be explored, and we believe you will notice that, as your client spends time in devotion, these aspects will change, depending on your client's experiences. Add new points of learning after each session with your client to build in and deepen their devotional time between sessions. It could be an affirmation about feeling safe in God's presence or an encouragement to spend a set amount of time in Centering Prayer, listening for God's voice every day.

The Power of a Daily Dose of God's Presence

A simple devotional practice provides rich spiritual and emotional fuel. In the study I (Regina) conducted of Christian social workers, counselors, and psychologists, I asked them about how they integrated mindfulness from a Christian perspective. One of the participants spoke about a client's daily devotion time producing insight into a particularly vexing relationship (Trammel, 2018). The insight came not in therapy but between sessions—likely because this therapist understood that nothing is wasted in times spent in devotion.

We must not underestimate God's healing presence. We do not work in a spiritual vacuum. When our clients carve out time for devotion, they begin to understand the power of their relationship with God. As they spend time daily with him, their mindsets are transformed. As our clients spend time feasting in God's protection, their sense of safety improves because they are engaging their minds daily. Their bodies, including their neurologies, are being shaped too. The daily devotion becomes a cocoon wrapping our clients in the goodness of God, who helps them alongside, if not in front of, us. Our clients experience a devotion to God that acknowledges help from the outside every day. They can turn to Christ daily and find safety in him.

In daily devotion, our clients do not need to find the words to speak to God. The role of silence, the prayer that centers them, and the reading of Psalm 28:7 offers a focus on the strength of surrender in healing. Our clients can experience a devotion every day with almost no effort, which is a relief when so much is demanded of them. The habit can chill the heat of their firing thoughts and provide a safe haven where they meet God in the comfort and safety of his strength and shield. Each day, little by little, as they simply revel in their Christ, they find their healer. They can receive a healing touch from God with no effort, no demand placed on them, because God is the one who helps them. Slowly, almost imperceptibly, their hearts begin to trust God. Now, in God's strength and shield, our clients have a safe haven, a strong tower in our Lord to continue the work we are calling them to do in our sessions and meetings. And step by step, the path they walk in the work of therapy is reinforced by this daily devotional practice of seeking God's strength so they can walk one step farther toward freedom from their afflictions and find who they truly are in Christ in the simple silence.

References for Chapter 20

Devotion. (2016). In Merriam-Webster.com dictionary. Retrieved March 9, 2021, from https://www.merriam-webster.com/dictionary /devotion#:~:text=of%20the%20Day-,devotion,being%20ardently %20dedicated%20and%20loyal

Keating, T. (2012). The seven stages of centering prayer. *Contemplative Outreach News, 23*(2), 1–2. https://www.contemplativeoutreach .org/newsletter/2012-june/

Porges, S. W. (2017). *The pocket guide to the polyvagal theory: The transformative power of feeling safe.* Norton.

Trammel, R. C. (2018). A phenomenological study of Christian practitioners who use mindfulness. *Journal of Spirituality in Mental Health, 20*(3), 199–224. https://doi.org/10.1080/19349637.2017.1408445

Trammel, R. C., Park, G., & Karlsson, I. (2021). Religiously oriented mindfulness for social workers: Effects on mindfulness, heart rate variability, and personal burnout. *Journal of Religion & Spirituality in Social Work: Social Thought, 40*(1), 19–38. https://doi.org/10.1080/15426432.2020.1818358

CHAPTER 21

Christian Mindfulness
and the Blessing

Have you ever been blessed before? What form did the blessing take? Was it during a benediction at a church service? Was it in a written word from a loved one? Maybe you received a blessing from a parent, caregiver, or someone you looked up to. Perhaps it was a speaker, teacher, or professor when you received your degree. But is a blessing really that significant for us or the clients we work with?

What Does It Mean to Receive or Miss the Blessing?

Perhaps you've read in Genesis 27 the story of twins Jacob and Esau. Each longed for their father's blessing. But Jacob (at his mother's urging and with her help) came first and received his brother's blessing for himself. Once given, it was irrevocable. It was now Jacob's, though it was owed to Esau. And then you read that heartbreaking cry when Esau comes in right after his brother and asks for a blessing from his father, and realizes he will *never* receive it from him: "'Do you have only one blessing, my father? Bless me too, my father!' Then Esau wept aloud" (Gen. 27:38).

There is so much to the Blessing that pictures the attachment and love we all long for. And incredible hurt comes from not receiving it. (To go deeper, consider reading *The Blessing* by Trent, Smalley, and Stageberg, 2019.) But let's look at one verse that speaks to us of a choice and a need to bless, and a way to be mindful of choosing blessing in how we do life with our Lord and our loved ones. This verse was spoken to the nation of Israel as they prepared to finally enter the promised land: "This day I call the heavens and the earth as witnesses against you that I have set before you life and death, blessings and curses. Now choose life, so that you and your children may live" (Deut. 30:19).

That's one choice with two parts.

Life or death.

Blessing or curse.

Let's look briefly at this choice set before each of us. First, "life or death." In Hebrew (and in New Testament Greek as well), the word life carries the idea of movement. Things that are alive are things that move. Life is also pictured in Scripture as blood moving through the body.

So set before us is the choice for life. This means, of course, choosing life in God through Christ. But also on a relational level, it means to have God animate or get us moving in newness of life. When we have God's life inside us, we are able to step toward those we love, even as he loves us and steps toward us.

But some of us didn't grow up knowing that God loves us, that he offers us life, that he stepped toward us when he sent his Son, who, "while we were yet sinners, . . . died for us." Instead of growing up knowing about God's life and experiencing people who, in responding to that life inside them, have stepped toward us, we grew up around people who chose death over life.

Many of us in the counseling field and those we counsel have had important people in our lives choose to step away from us. And while God tells us that he will never leave us or forsake us (Heb. 13:5), many of us have experienced incredible hurt when a parent or spouse walked away.

The blessing begins with the choice of life over death.

But right behind that most important choice comes a way to live out life or death.

To bless is pictured first as an attitude—the recognition that the person we're to bless has great value. To bless literally means "to bow the knee." Another picture of what it means to bless in Scripture is to add to someone's life, like adding a coin to a scale. So to bless reflects both our attitude and our actions.

But there's that other choice set before us—to curse. To curse literally is the picture of a muddy stream. Instead of adding lifegiving water to someone, we dam the stream. To curse is a picture of subtracting. Praise God that Jesus, when he met the woman at the well, who had seen so much subtraction in her life, breaks down all the dams set up against her and offers her living water (John 4). And he can bring us life and his blessing, even if we never got the Blessing growing up.

So the Blessing is no minor choice. We are to step toward, not away from, God and our loved ones, to use God's life and love to bless others. With our words and actions, we are to add to our loved ones' lives, not to subtract from them.

Life over death. Blessing over curse.

Giving the Blessing

Many of us in the professional counseling and therapy fields have had opportunities to be blessed. We have been taught that we have value and that our skills and work have value. I (Regina) remember when my parents called me at just the right time while I was away on a retreat to finish my dissertation. I was exhausted, weary of writing, and seeking a renewed hope so I could finish. I expressed my doubts and insecurities to my parents on the phone, and they both reassured me and spoke a blessing over me from their hearts, saying, "We have faith in you." Those five words were like a lighthouse guiding me through the fog that clouded my mind and emotions. My parents' blessing was all that I needed. I meditated on those five words, turned them over, let them sink into my heart and dispel the doubts in my mind. I completed my dissertation soon after that call.

"We have faith in you." I still hear their words today whenever I need them. When life's challenges feel hard, I rely on that simple blessing. It resonates in my heart again and again. Their belief in me, in my value, and in my contributions spoken in those powerful words carries me through.

The Missing Blessing

However, many of us (like me, John) got into counseling because we missed the Blessing. We and many of the clients we see are missing the Blessing. Instead of spoken words that attach high value and build love, acceptance, and attachment, many of our clients have experienced curses—lifegiving words dammed up, leaving a muddy trickle of scorn, criticism, or neglect. They carry the burden of missing the Blessing in their lives. Depression, anxiety, insecurity, trauma, inability to form attachments, relationship problems—the list could go on and on. However, we know from Scripture that God restores them. When they can turn to him, he will prosper them. Part of our being mindful in Christ is listening to our clients and receiving God's blessing as a key point of understanding their worth and identity in Christ.

When our clients engage in a Christian mindfulness practice, not only do they begin to recognize the empty spaces in their thoughts, hearts, and emotions, but also they can begin to speak a word of blessing over themselves and recognize their inherent value as persons born with the image of God. They can put into context the criticisms and curses they feel have been brought on them. As they observe their thoughts and meditate on God's blessings in Scripture, their true nature as Christ followers emerges. Our clients and counselees can begin to let go of the curses or the neglected parts of themselves that have caused them pain. And as they let go, they can see that their sins are forgiven. Like the woman at the well, they can see the source of living water that quenches the deepest thirst.

In Christian mindfulness practice, we have a powerful opportunity to speak over our clients the Blessing that they have needed and may never have received. We have enormous influence over our clients when we speak a blessing over them, and they become equipped to practice the Blessing toward themselves and then toward others.

Keep Deuteronomy 23:5 in mind as we move into a mindful blessing script, particularly for yourself or for those you're working with who have missed the Blessing from someone significant, someone who subtracted from their lives. In Scripture, a sorcerer named Balaam was hired by the enemies of God's people to curse or subtract from them. But there is something even stronger than a curse: God's love. Deuteronomy 23:5 says, "The LORD your God would not listen to Balaam but turned the curse into a blessing for you, because the LORD your God loves you."

A Mindful Blessing Script

To integrate Christian mindfulness with the Blessing, we must mindfully approach the scriptural elements of the Blessing for our clients: meaningful (and ethical) touch, a spoken or written message, attachment of high value, picturing a special future, and an active commitment to the Blessing (Trent, Smalley, & Stageberg, 2019). The following script for a mindful blessing will help your clients find their own blessings in mindful awareness. We also encourage your clients to use appendix 3 to help formulate their blessings to use as therapeutic homework.

This is a blessing exercise to help you form a regular Christian mindfulness practice so you can know your inherent value. No matter what you face, I hope that this blessing will be something you return to again and again.

To begin, work on a breath prayer. With eyes closed, focus just on your breathing. If it's helpful, speak these words in your heart as you inhale: "Lord, speak over me a blessing in my heart." Exhale to the words, "I let go of words of pain spoken in the past." Do this at least three more times.

Next hear some words of blessing spoken by God to his people. As you do so, I ask you to do one of two things with your hands. Place both of your hands either on your heart or on your lap with palms up as a physical sign of receiving this blessing. I will read it slowly, and I would like you to observe your reactions.

Note in your mind which words stand out, which parts of this blessing feel truthful and vibrant. Identify and observe how you hear these words settle in your body, your hands, your heart. Use the space in between the sentences I speak to observe and be curious about your reactions. Remember, there is no wrong way to receive a blessing. Breathe in and receive. Breathe in any tender words of blessing spoken over you, remembering that God is present and available. Receive these words of blessing over you, adapted from Psalm 1:1–3:

> Blessed are you, _____ [say the name of your client], because you do not walk with the wicked or sit in the company of mockers. Blessed are you because you delight in the law of the Lord, and you can meditate on his law day and night. You are like a tree planted by streams of water, which yields its fruit in season and whose leaf does not wither. Whatever you do prospers.

Now picture yourself as that tree yielding fruit by streams of water. Ponder these questions in your heart: What words of love does God speak over you? Receive them into your heart. Picture yourself as a tree rooted beside a nourishing stream. Feel nourishment seeping into places that are parched from years of neglect. How can you reach your roots down to where God's presence quenches your thirst? Place your hands palms down now as a symbolic gesture of rooting these words into your heart and spirit. What words spoken over you today can you reach for again in your mind? What does it mean for you to prosper?

In this moment, with awareness, breathe in that last part of the blessing again: "Whose leaf does not wither. Whatever you do prospers." Ask for God's wisdom in defining what that prospering will be for you. It is a prospering that is defined not by the world but by this image of you as a tree rooted beside God's righteous stream of water. Take another moment to ponder in a listening stance while I am quiet for a couple of minutes. Sit in awareness of your thoughts and emotions as you ponder.

As we end this time, return to your breathing for a few more minutes and soak in and monitor your feelings. Detect any resistance to or easy acceptance of any of these words. How did receiving this blessing feel? What parts of the blessing resonate with you? Why? What parts did not sit as well? Why do you think that is? Is there someone God is calling you to speak a blessing over this week? Be ready to discuss and debrief this exercise with me. Breathe in one last big inhalation, exhale, and then slowly open your eyes.

As you debrief this blessing experience with your client, we encourage you to use appendix 3 to help your client further their work to acknowledge their value and to find tender words of blessing. The benefit of approaching the Blessing in a mindful stance is that there is a space for these words to settle into our clients' minds and hearts. In Christian mindfulness, we can receive and not be distracted by the critics, the harsh words of the past. In relationship with God, and in his presence, our clients sing a new song of blessing over their lives. As they recognize how the Blessing can help them overcome their suffering, we can stay with them in the process of change. In Christian mindfulness, we help our clients make meaning of their suffering in light of where the Blessing was missing at key points in their lives.

A Restoration Blessing Script

The following is another blessing script that you can use when a client feels empty or drained. In a season of drought or when a client is feeling exhausted, you can use this blessing for God's restoration. There is a section in this script where you may want to ask your client's permission to sit nearer and provide an ethical placement of hands over them. You do not have to touch your client, however. You can also simply speak the verses over them. Use your best judgment and ensure that you have done a proper spiritual assessment prior to reading this blessing script over your counselees.

In this exhausting season, you may feel drained, depleted, and in need of restoration. This practice of Christian mindfulness and blessing is intended to help restore your body, mind, and soul. Your only task is simply to receive the blessing and use this time to mentally bathe in it.

I'll have you start by placing your hands on your lap with palms facing up while saying a breath prayer. Inhale: "God, your burden is light." Exhale: "God, please restore me." Breathe and say this prayer three more times.

To engage your body, turn your hands palms down. This is a symbolic way of acknowledging that you let go of the burdens of the past. Let them go in this moment while keeping focused on the scriptural blessing of restoration. As I read God's blessing to you, symbolically and with your permission, I can place my hands palms down over you. I may need to sit a bit closer to you so you can hear clearly the restoration that God can provide. May I have your permission to read this blessing over you in this way? If not, I can simply read it from where I sit now—whichever you prefer. Receive this last blessing from Deuteronomy 30:1–4:

> When all these blessings and curses I have set before you come on you and you take them to heart wherever the LORD your God disperses you among the nations, and when you and your children return to the LORD your God and obey him with all your heart and with all your soul according to everything I command you today, then the LORD your God will restore your fortunes and have compassion on you and gather you again from all the nations where he scattered you. Even if you have been banished to the most distant land under the heavens, from there the LORD your God will gather you and bring you back.

As we end this time, return to your breathing for a few more minutes and soak in and monitor your feelings. Detect any resistance to or easy acceptance of any of these words. How did receiving this blessing feel? What parts of the blessing resonate with you? Why? What parts did not sit as well? Why? Is there someone God is calling you to speak a blessing over this week? Be ready to discuss and debrief this exercise with me. Breathe in one last big inhalation, exhale, and then slowly open your eyes.

The process of counseling and therapy is often a time of renurturing as our clients attach to us temporarily to find a safe haven and an accepting space. When our clients are mindful of the process of therapy, they become aware of the burdens they carry, whether a hurtful past or words spoken over them that were meant to curse and not to bless. Perhaps they come from a position of neglect, like a parched desert, where they needed to hear a blessing over them. Our clients can make space in their hearts when they can observe mindfully how they react to a blessing.

In Christian mindfulness, clients can open up their minds to receive such a blessing, allowing these words to shape their thoughts about themselves, crowding out the lies. In Christian mindfulness, clients can also make room for their hearts. The warmth contained in the blessing forms a blanket over the coldness they may have felt before. When we speak a blessing over our clients, we provide an opening for a renurturing and point them to a permanent attachment figure in Christ—a healthy, stable, unconditional love. As clients sit in mindful, silent moments in God's presence, they ingest the loving and tender words of God. Their bodies register safety, their neurochemistry registers warmth, and their souls register grace and acceptance. We all need tender words spoken over us.

Blessing Moving Outward

In turn, when our clients have received a blessing, they are more able to give a blessing freely to others. The tenderness of the Blessing, over time, shines through. As we nudge our clients toward acceptance of what they are missing by not having been recipients of a blessing, they can work toward relationships that are kindled by the belief in the value of healthy persons. Our clients can commit to being that healthy person and showing up as one for others. No longer reacting, no longer trauma bound, healing or in process, our clients are more than capable of speaking an authentic blessing over others.

Many of our clients have been harsh critics of others. We can provide them with a template for nurturing and acceptance through the Blessing in counseling and therapy. In turn, they can share and put into practice this blessing with those they have loving influence over. Our clients' children, especially, may need the Blessing sooner rather than later. We can help pinpoint words of blessing our clients can bestow on their children, helping to foster a dynamic of care, warmth, and love, healing generational woundedness with persistence over time. God's words of blessing come through when we are not distracted, when we are not hung up on wrongs. When our clients can be mindfully present, they can believe the Blessing, and they can share it more frequently.

Christian mindfulness can assist our clients who are skeptical of passing on the Blessing to others. Many clients who cannot give to others are in need of the gift of the Blessing themselves. In stress, suffering, and hardship, our clients often avoid feelings or latch on to problematic beliefs. In counseling and therapy, we rework the harsh words and latent images our clients carry. As they grow, one sign of healing is that our clients are more able to speak tender words about others. The next step is to form these tender words into a blessing to those around them. Many of our clients find joy and grow in their self-concept and esteem when they are able to speak a blessing over others. The darkness and isolation seem to wane when God's light of love shines within them, helping them carry themselves and others along with them. The cycle of hurt and harsh words permeates families and generations. But the Blessing does not disappoint. It is a beacon amid broken relationships, helping to repair and reattach family and friendship bonds that have been harmed.

Conclusion

What are some words of blessing—even the more difficult ones—that you can genuinely share with your clients? Look back on your notes to identify the strengths you see in your clients. What growth and healing do you see taking place? The clients who stress you out might need your blessing the most. Be sure not to withhold those tender and kind words from them. Work in supervision or consultation with others if you encounter resistance to this nudge. We have both been there and do not make light of the challenging clients you encounter in your work. However, you are the person your client has come to, perhaps by divine intervention. Recall the image of God stamped on each person, the unconditional grace and acceptance he lavishly bestows on us, so we can also lavish them on others.

In Christian mindfulness practice, we let go of the stressors and difficulties of our work, our burdens in God's presence. Remember that he is the third person in that room with you and your clients. Rely on him to give you words for the Blessing. If it's helpful, end each session with a blessing over your clients to guide them and remind them of who they are in Christ.

References for Chapter 21

Trent, J., Smalley, G., & Stageberg, K. T. (2019). *The blessing: Giving the gift of unconditional love and acceptance.* W Publishing Group.

Conclusion

In our sacred work as counselors, therapists, and healing practitioners, we understand that healing, recovery, and growth happen in partnership with the almighty and gracious God. Christian mindfulness is a path toward our relationship with Christ, and it is a practice in which our clients listen to their bodies, notice their thoughts, and search their souls. For ourselves, Christian mindfulness offers the integration of faith with therapeutic and counseling skills that is rarely talked about in our fields and disciplines.

The bifurcation of body and mind is constructed, not inherent to what we know about how God created us. The holistic workings of body and soul, and soul and mind, are also activated in Christian mindfulness integrated into therapy and counseling. We understand that our clients are complex beings created with the full value and benefit of being created by God. Using Christian mindfulness in our work expands the experience of counseling and therapy in an evidence-informed way. We can fully integrate faith with aspects of the soul—that is what makes this practice effective. Our clients can fully participate in the counseling or therapy process with their whole selves, united in their spirits, or at the very least open to hearing about and learning mindfulness practices that are rooted in ancient Christian practice. No matter where the client is, we can start with their breathing. We can foster a quiet space of mindful contemplation. We can support their efforts to battle the symptoms and the suffering.

Our work is a sacred work, and we hope this book gives you confidence and points you toward a more fluid way of integrating mindfulness and faith. We hope this book will serve as a template for creatively weaving into mindfulness practice the wisdom you have garnered throughout your years of training. We hope that you continue on this mindfulness journey yourself for your own self-care. Though you are a giver, allow the ultimate Giver to pour into you.

In the midst of current cultural shifts and societal challenges, we know that Christian mindfulness has been a guiding support to our own psyches and souls. Our sacred work means that we are vulnerable to burnout ourselves, so we hope your Christian mindfulness practice provides the respite and heavenly perspective you need to stay focused on the purpose God gave you to empower, support, and help in your clients' healing process.

Most of all, we want you to be mindful every day of how much God cares for you and for those you serve. Our prayer for you comes from Ephesians 3:17–19:

> And I pray that you, being rooted and established in love, may have power, together with all the Lord's holy people, to grasp how wide and long and high and deep is the love of Christ, and to know this love that surpasses knowledge—that you may be filled to the measure of all the fullness of God.

APPENDIX 1

Progressive Muscle Relaxation with Christian Mindfulness

Using the picture on the left, circle or label any parts of your body where you identify stress or emotion is stored.

Using the picture on the right, circle or label any parts of your body where you have felt a relief of tension or stress.

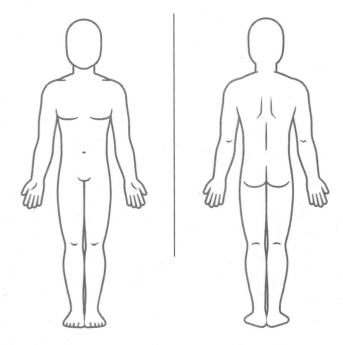

© Sudowoodo/istock

APPENDIX 2

Boundary Keeping Circle

Outside the following circle, label the feelings you experience when you overstep or do not keep boundaries with a person God brings to mind. List the mistaken values you keep when you do not keep boundaries.

Inside the circle, label the feelings you experience when you keep proper boundaries. List the values you uphold when you do so.

The Mindful Blessing

In preparation for the exercise integrating Christian mindfulness with the Blessing, use the following prompts to help you formulate a blessing that you can speak over yourself or even ask a supportive friend or loved one to speak over you.

1. When have you felt a meaningful or ethical touch? Was it in the form of a hug, a touch on the shoulder, or something else? In what form of touch and where can someone touch you ethically that would feel meaningful to you? Write this down:

2. What are some words of blessing you have heard others say about you or someone else? Identify good words that strike a chord in you, that are powerful to you. You can borrow a blessing from the Scriptures or from some other source. Whether you have only a few words or a lot, write them down:

3. Identify qualities or character traits that you observe in yourself or that others have observed in you. These are stable. They make up who you are, no matter the circumstances. Write these down:

4. Picture a near future when you live out this blessing spoken over you. Who (living or passed away) would speak it, and how would it shape you? What are the consequences of living it out? Write it down:

5. Being mindful, aware, and grounded in God's presence, in what ways can you move toward a lifestyle of commitment in your blessing? Write this commitment down:

References

Acker, G. M. (2012). Burnout among mental health care providers. *Journal of Social Work, 12*(5), 475–490. https://doi.org/10.1177/1468017310392418

Albala, K., & Eden, T. (Eds.). (2011). *Food and faith in Christian culture.* Columbia University Press.

Baer, R. A., Carmody, J., & Hunsinger, M. (2012). Weekly change in mindfulness and perceived stress in a mindfulness-based stress reduction program. *Journal of Clinical Psychology, 68*(7), 755–765. https://doi.org/10.1002 /jclp.21865

Bochen, C. M. (Ed.). (2004). *Thomas Merton: Essential writings.* Orbis.

Brinkborg, H., Michanek, J., Hesser, H., & Berglund, G. (2011). Acceptance and commitment therapy for the treatment of stress among social workers: A randomized controlled trial. *Behaviour Research and Therapy, 49*(6–7), 389–398. https://doi.org/10.1016/j.brat.2011.03.009

Brown, L. A., Gaudiano, B. A., & Miller, I. W. (2011). Investigating the similarities and differences between practitioners of second- and third-wave cognitive-behavioral therapies. *Behavior Modification, 35*(2), 187–200. https://doi .org/10.1177/0145445510393730

Charles, V. A., & Wolfer, T. A. (2018). Loneliness and congregational social work. *Social Work & Christianity, 45*(1), 8–23.

Chen, E. Y., Matthews, L., Allen, C., Kuo, J. R., & Linehan, M. M. (2008). Dialectical behavior therapy for clients with binge-eating disorder or bulimia nervosa and borderline personality disorder. *International Journal of Eating Disorders, 41*(6), 505–512. https://doi.org/10.1002/eat.20522

Cloud, H., & Townsend, J. (2017). *Boundaries: When to say yes, how to say no to take control of your life* (2nd ed.). Zondervan.

Crisp, C. D., Hastings-Tolsma, M., & Jonscher, K. R. (2016). Mindfulness-based stress reduction for military women with chronic pelvic pain: A feasibility study. *Military Medicine, 181*(9), 982–989. https://doi.org/10.7205 /MILMED-D-15-00354

Danaan, C. (2015). *Zen and the path of mindful parenting: Meditations on raising children.* Leaping Hare Press.

Devotion. (2016). In Merriam-Webster.com dictionary. Retrieved March 9, 2021, from https://www.merriam-webster.com/dictionary/devotion#:~:text=of%20 the%20Day-,devotion,being%20ardently%20dedicated%20and%20loyal

Ditto, B., Eclache, M., & Goldman, N. (2017). Short-term autonomic and cardiovascular effects of mindfulness body scan meditation. In B. A. Gaudiano (Ed.), *Mindfulness: Vol. IV. Nonclinical applications of mindfulness: Adaptations for school, work, sports, health, and general well-being.* (2017-55495-020; pp. 341–357). Routledge/Taylor & Francis Group.

Ford, K., & Garzon, F. (2017). Research note: A randomized investigation of evangelical Christian accommodative mindfulness. *Spirituality in Clinical Practice, 4*(2), 92–99. https://doi.org/10.1037/scp0000137

Fox, J., Gutierrez, D., Haas, J., & Durnford, S. (2016). Centering prayer's effects on psycho-spiritual outcomes: A pilot outcome study. *Mental Health, Religion & Culture, 19*(4), 379–392. https://doi.org/10.1080/13674676.2016.1203299

Garland, E., Kiken, L. G., Faurot, K., Palsson, O., & Gaylord, S. A. (2017). Upward spirals of mindfulness and reappraisal: Testing the mindfulness-to-meaning theory with autoregressive latent trajectory modeling. *Cognitive Therapy & Research, 41*(3), 381–392. https://doi.org/10.1007/s10608-016-9768-y

Garland, E. L., Farb, N. A., Goldin, P. R., & Fredrickson, B. L. (2015). Mindfulness broadens awareness and builds eudaimonic meaning: A process model of mindful positive emotion regulation. *Psychological Inquiry, 26*(4), 293–314. https://doi.org/10.1080/1047840X.2015.1064294

Gethin, R. (2011). On some definitions of mindfulness. *Contemporary Buddhism, 12*(1), 263–279. https://doi.org/10.1080/14639947.2011.564843

Greeson, J. M., Zarrin, H., Smoski, M. J., Brantley, J. G., Lynch, T. R., Webber, D. M., Hall, M. H., Suarez, E. C., & Wolever, R. Q. (2018). Mindfulness meditation targets transdiagnostic symptoms implicated in stress-related disorders: Understanding relationships between changes in mindfulness, sleep quality, and physical symptoms. *Evidence-Based Complementary & Alternative Medicine (ECAM),* 1–10. https://doi.org/10.1155/2018/4505191

Hadash, Y., Segev, N., Tanay, G., Goldstein, P., & Bernstein, A. (2016). The decoupling model of equanimity: Theory, measurement, and test in a

mindfulness intervention. *Mindfulness, 7*(5), 1214–1226. https://doi.org
°/10.1007/s12671-016-0564-2

Hall, C. (2010). The theological foundations of *lectio divina*. In J. P. Greenman
& G. Kalantzis (Eds.), *Life in the Spirit: Spiritual formation in theological
perspective* (pp. 180–197). InterVarsity Press.

Hamama, L. (2012). Burnout in social workers treating children as related to
demographic characteristics, work environment, and social support. *Social
Work Research, 36*(2), 113–125. https://doi.org/10.1093/swr/svs003

Hanley, A., Garland, E. L., & Black, D. S. (2014). Use of mindful reappraisal
coping among meditation practitioners. *Journal of Clinical Psychology,
70*(3), 294–301. https://doi.org/10.1002/jclp.22023

Harned, M. S., Korslund, K. E., Foa, E. B., & Linehan, M. M. (2012). Treating
PTSD in suicidal and self-injuring women with borderline personality
disorder: Development and preliminary evaluation of a dialectical behavior
therapy prolonged exposure protocol. *Behaviour Research & Therapy,
50*(6), 381–386. https://doi.org/10.1016/j.brat.2012.02.011

Harrison Warren, T. (2016). *Liturgy of the ordinary: Sacred practices in everyday
life*. InterVarsity Press.

Healthwise staff. (n.d.). Stress management: Doing progressive muscle relaxation.
Michigan Medicine. Retrieved September 30, 2020, from https://www
.uofmhealth.org/health-library/uz2225

Hester, J. A. (2017). *Stress and longevity in pastoral ministry: A phenomenological
study* [Unpublished doctoral dissertation]. The Southern Baptist
Theological Seminary.

Howard, E. (2012). Lectio divina in the evangelical tradition. *Journal of
Spiritual Formation & Soul Care, 5*(1), 56–77. https://doi.org/10.1177
/193979091200500104

Hutchison, S. L., Terhorst, L., Murtaugh, S., Gross, S., Kogan, J. N., & Shaffer,
S. L. (2016). Effectiveness of a staff promoted wellness program to improve
health in residents of a mental health long-term care facility. *Issues in Mental
Health Nursing, 37*(4), 257–64. https://doi.org/10.3109/01612840.2015
.1126774

Jones, I. F. (2018). Christian formation of the self strategies. In John C. Thomas
(Ed.), *Counseling techniques: A comprehensive resource for Christian
counselors* (pp. 197–220). Zondervan.

Kabat-Zinn, J. (1994). *Wherever you go, there you are: Mindfulness meditation in everyday life.* Hyperion.

Kabat-Zinn (2009). *Full catastrophe living: Using the wisdom of your body and mind to face stress, pain, and illness.* Delta Trade.

Kabat-Zinn, J. (2011). Some reflections on the origins of MBSR, skillful means, and the trouble with maps. *Contemporary Buddhism, 12*(1), 281–306. https://doi.org/10.1080/14639947.2011.564844

Keating, T. (1992). *Open mind, open heart: The contemplative dimension of the gospel.* Amity House.

Keating, T. (2008). *The heart of the world: An introduction to contemplative Christianity.* Crossroad.

Keating, T. (2012). The seven stages of centering prayer. *Contemplative Outreach News, 23*(2), 1–2. https://www.contemplativeoutreach.org/newsletter/2012-june/

Kettler, S. (2020). Lisa Nowak: Why the astronaut drove 900 miles to attack her ex's girlfriend. *Biography.* https://www.biography.com/news/lisa-nowak-lucy-in-the-sky#:~:text=Subscribe%20to%20Newsletter-,Lisa%20Nowak%3A%20Why%20the%20Astronaut%20Drove%20900%20Miles%20to%20Attack,movie%20'Lucy%20in%20the%20Sky

Kim, S. M., Park, J. M., & Seo, H. J. (2016). Effects of mindfulness-based stress reduction for adults with sleep disturbance: A protocol for an update of a systematic review and meta-analysis. *Systematic Reviews, 5,* 1–6. https://doi.org/10.1186/s13643-016-0228-2

King, A. P., Erickson, T. M., Giardino, N. D., Favorite, T., Rauch, S. A. M., Robinson, E., Kulkarni, M., & Liberzon, I. (2013). A pilot study of group mindfulness-based cognitive therapy (MBCT) for combat veterans with posttraumatic stress disorder (PTSD). *Depression & Anxiety, 30*(7), 638–645. https://doi.org/10.1002/da.22104

Koslowitz, R. (2019). The burnout we can't talk about: Parent burnout. *Psychology Today.* https://www.psychologytoday.com/us/blog/targeted-parenting/201909/the-burnout-we-cant-talk-about-parent-burnout

Lamott, A. (2018). *Almost everything: Notes on hope.* Riverhead.

Lebovits, A. (2007). Cognitive-behavioral approaches to chronic pain. *Primary Psychiatry, 14*(9), 48–54.

Linehan, M. M., & Wilks, C. R. (2015). The course and evolution of dialectical behavior therapy. *American Journal of Psychotherapy, 69*(2), 97–110. https://doi.org/10.1176/appi.psychotherapy.2015.69.2.97

Louth, A. (2003). *Three treatises on the divine images: Apologia against those who deny holy images.* St. Vladimir's Seminary Press.

Markus, H. R., & Kitayama, S. (1991). Culture and the self: Implications for cognition, emotion, and motivation. *Psychological Review, 98*(2), 224–253. https://psycnet.apa.org/doi/10.1037/0033-295X.98.2.224

Mateo, A. (2020).What actually is mindful running and how do you do it? *Runner's World.* Retrieved from https://www.runnersworld.com/training/a22160937/mindfulness-in-running/

McLeod, F. G. (1986). Apophatic or kataphatic prayer. *Spirituality Today, 38,* 41–52. http://www.domcentral.org/library/spir2day/863815mcleod.html

Melnyk, B. M., Jacobson, D., Kelly, S., Belyea, M., Shaibi, G., Small, L., O'Haver, J., & Marsiglia, F. F. (2013). Promoting healthy lifestyles in high school adolescents: A randomized controlled trial. *American Journal of Preventive Medicine, 45*(4), 407–415. https://doi.org/10.1016/j.amepre.2013.05.013

Menahem, S., & Love, M. (2013). Forgiveness in psychotherapy: The key to healing. *Journal of Clinical Psychology, 69*(8), 829–835. https://doi.org/10.1002/jclp.22018

Mindful staff (2017). Jon Kabat-Zinn: Defining mindfulness. What is mindfulness? The founder of Mindfulness-Based Stress Reduction explains. Retrieved from https://www.mindful.org/jon-kabat-zinn-defining-mindfulness/

Moceri, J., & Cox, P. H. (2019). Mindfulness-based practice to reduce blood pressure and stress in priests. *Journal for Nurse Practitioners, 15*(6), e115–e117. https://doi.org/10.1016/j.nurpra.2019.01.001

Moreland, J. P. (2007). *Kingdom triangle: Recover the Christian mind, renovate the soul, restore the Spirit's power.* Zondervan.

Park, G., & Thayer, J. F. (2014). From the heart to the mind: Cardiac vagal tone modulates top-down and bottom-up visual perception and attention to emotional stimuli. *Frontiers in Psychology, 5.* https://doi.org/10.3389/fpsyg.2014.00278

Perel, E. (2017). *The state of affairs: Rethinking infidelity.* Harper Collins.

Porges, S. W. (2017). *The pocket guide to the polyvagal theory: The transformative power of feeling safe.* Norton.

Ramsey, K. J. (2020). *This too shall last: Finding grace when suffering lingers.* Zondervan.

Reeves, G. (2008). *The Lotus Sutra: A contemporary translation of a Buddhist classic.* Wisdom Publishers.

Rohrer, D. (2012). *The sacred wilderness of pastoral ministry: Preparing a people for the presence of the Lord.* InterVarsity Press.

Rosales, A. (2016). Acceptance and commitment therapy (ACT): Empirical evidence and clinical applications from a Christian perspective. *Journal of Psychology and Christianity, 35*(3), 269–275.

Rosenbaum, E. (2017). *The heart of mindfulness-based stress reduction: A MBSR guide for clinicians and clients.* PESI Publishing and Media.

Rousmaniere, T. (2020). Steven Hayes on acceptance and commitment therapy. Psychotherapy.net. https://www.psychotherapy.net/interview/acceptance -commitment-therapy-ACT-steven-hayes-interview#:~:text=Acceptance%20 and%20Commitment%20Therapy%20(ACT)%20founder%20Steven%20 Hayes%20discusses%20the,and%20pain%2Dfilled%20modern%20world

Schneider, J., Malinowski, P., Watson, P. M., & Lattimore, P. (2019). The role of mindfulness in physical activity: A systematic review. *Obesity Reviews, 20*(3), 448–463. https://doi.org/10.1111/obr.12795

Smith, H. (1991). *The world's religions.* Harper One.

Smith, J. B. (2010). *The good and beautiful community: Following the Spirit, extending grace, demonstrating love.* InterVarsity Press.

Sun, J. (2014). Mindfulness in context: A historical discourse analysis. *Contemporary Buddhism, 15*(2), 394–415. https://doi.org/10.1080/14639947 .2014.978088

Trammel, R. (2018). Effectiveness of an MP3 Christian mindfulness intervention on mindfulness and perceived stress. *Mental Health, Religion & Culture, 21*(5), 500–514. https://doi.org/10.1080/13674676.2018.1505837

Trammel, R. C. (2017). Tracing the roots of mindfulness: Transcendence in Buddhism and Christianity. *Journal of Religion & Spirituality in Social Work, 36*(3), 367–383. https://doi.org/10.1080/15426432.2017.1295822

Trammel, R. C. (2018). A phenomenological study of Christian practitioners who use mindfulness. *Journal of Spirituality in Mental Health, 20*(3), 199–224. https://doi.org/10.1080/19349637.2017.1408445

Trammel, R. C., Park, G., & Karlsson, I. (2021). Religiously oriented mindfulness for social workers: Effects on mindfulness, heart rate variability, and personal burnout. *Journal of Religion & Spirituality in Social Work: Social Thought, 40*(1), 19–38. https://doi.org/10.1080/15426432.2020.1818358

Trent, J., Smalley, G., & Stageberg, K. T. (2019). *The blessing: Giving the gift of unconditional love and acceptance.* W Publishing Group.

Twohig, M. P., Hayes, S. C., Plumb, J. C., Pruitt, L. D., Collins, A. B., Hazlett-Stevens, H., & Woidneck, M. R. (2010). A randomized clinical trial of acceptance and commitment therapy versus progressive relaxation training for obsessive-compulsive disorder. *Journal of Consulting & Clinical Psychology, 78*(5), 705–716. https://doi.org/10.1037/a0020508

VICE Asia. (2020, March 9). Meet the superhuman Wim Hof: The iceman. Retrieved from https://www.youtube.com/watch?v=soHwRkIkTHA

Vicinanza, R., Bersani, F. S., D'Ottavio, E., Murphy, M., Bernardini, S., Crisciotti, F., Frizza, A., Mazza, V., Biondi, M., Troisi, G., & Cacciafesta, M. (2020). Adherence to Mediterranean diet moderates the association between multimorbidity and depressive symptoms in older adults. *Archives of Gerontology and Geriatrics, 88.* https://doi.org/10.1016/j.archger.2020.104022

Wang, D. C., & Tan, S.-Y. (2016). Dialectical behavior therapy (DBT): Empirical evidence and clinical applications from a Christian perspective. *Journal of Psychology and Christianity, 35*(1), 68–76.

Warren, R. (2012). *The purpose driven life: What on earth am I here for?* (expanded edition). Zondervan.

Watts, A., & Huang, A. C. (1975). *Tao: The watercourse way.* Pantheon.

Wolever, R. Q., Bobinet, K. J., McCabe, K., Mackenzie, E. R., Fekete, E., Kusnick, C. A., & Baime, M. (2012). Effective and viable mind-body stress reduction in the workplace: A randomized controlled trial. *Journal of Occupational Health Psychology, 17*(2), 246–258. https://doi.org/10.1037/a0027278

Yalom, I. (with Lescz, M.). (2000). *The theory and practice of group psychotherapy* (4th ed.). Basic Books.

Yarhouse, M. A., & Tan, E. S. N. (2014). *Sexuality and sex therapy: A comprehensive Christian appraisal.* InterVarsity Press.